MW00354336

Praise for *Hardiness*

"If there was only one attribute I could give my children, it wouldn't be good looks, athletic ability, or intelligence, it would be hardiness—a powerful constellation of qualities that increases the likelihood that they will engage in the world (v. shy away), be active agents in constructing their lives (v. helpless victims), and ultimately find meaning (v. unreflective boredom) in everything they experience and do. *Hardiness* is the gift that keeps on giving. Steve and Paul have done a masterful job summarizing and integrating almost fifty years of research into one, easy-to-read, simple-to-apply manual on how to construct a life well-lived."

—Scott A. Snook, PhD, MBA Class of 1958, Senior Lecturer of
Business Administration, Harvard Business School

"I'm rushing out to buy a large stash of this book so I can give it away to everyone important to me—my kids, my friends, the business leaders I coach. Steve Stein and Paul Bartone have created a gift to anyone who encounters stress in their life. The authors provide real-world examples from the ranks of rock stars, to POW's, to laypeople, showing how they used these very tools to overcome great difficulties in their lives and encouraging me to do just that same. I appreciate that the book is so well grounded in research, and yet remains so easily readable. Rather than theory, it offers practical advice anyone can put into action for making his/her life more fulfilling."

—Allen Moore, PhD, Global Lead for Executive Coaching,
Korn Ferry

"Highly resilient individuals are a source of competitive advantage. Ensuring that your organisation has sufficient financial capital, sustainable business processes and models, and efficient risk controls and practices to withstand the impact of potentially adverse economic developments is not enough to create a truly sustainable and successful business. This book is essential reading for executives wanting to improve the resilience of their people and themselves. *Hardiness* is full of highly practical tips and techniques on how to do just that! The authors are masters at bringing research and learning to life in a very enjoyable and impactful way through storytelling. My favourite thing about this book is the really thought-provoking questions at the end of each section encouraging us to reflect on our purpose, mindset, habits, attitudes, coping mechanisms, etc. Lots of high-quality reflection and self-discovery!"

—Pedro Angulo, Head of Leadership Development,
AIB Bank (Allied Irish Banks)

"Resiliency has been the topic of considerable research in the military in the years following 9/11. Repeated combat tours in Afghanistan and Iraq took their toll on military members and families separated for long periods of time without end in sight. The need to increase resiliency was quickly understood, and programs were implemented to improve the ability of Soldiers, Sailors, Airmen, and Marines and their families to deal with the long-term challenges of combat and separation. Steven Stein and Paul Bartone have brought the topic into focus and provided insights to help leaders understand and promote a culture of resiliency with the goal of improved productivity, health, and the bottom line. It is a must-read!"

—Major General Randy Manner (US Army, Retired),
Executive Coach

"This brilliant book is a go-to guide for understanding how to bring more hardiness into your life to help make work, health, and relationships *less hard*. The authors are among the world's leading experts in hardiness, applying their insights from research and practice with high-performing, high-demand occupations (e.g., first responders, military) to provide the reader with cutting-edge, understandable explanations of how to use an increased understanding of hardiness to turn stress into life success. They offer fresh, riveting, *easy to relate to,* practical examples that provide striking insights into the hardiness mindset of commitment, control, and challenge. The new, practical strategies on how to develop hardiness in one's life make this book a must-read for mental health practitioners, executives, and anyone who wants a greater sense of hardiness to take on life's challenges."

—Colonel Thomas J. Williams, PhD (US Army, Retired),
Senior Operational Psychologist

"Steven Stein's work on emotional intelligence and this collaboration with Paul Bartone on *Hardiness* is second to none. Building emotionally intelligent leaders who are also hardy and resilient people has been a cornerstone to our work in the development of thousands of leaders from every industry. *Hardiness* is a must-read for anyone looking to enhance their ability to lead more effectively and cope in stressful times."

—Daniel Quinn, Senior Consultant,
Xator's Leadership Foundry

"As a retired US Navy SEAL and now a Team and Leader Development Consultant, *Hardiness: Making Stress Work for You to Achieve Your Life Goals* was an excellent read. It affirmed many thoughts I have had over the years about how people channel stress and why they are successful. Stein and Bartone do an excellent job using data and research to correlate the hardiness components of commitment, control, and challenge to years of experience, education, and assessments. *Hardiness* and its components may be the linchpin development specialists have been looking for to obtain a competitive advantage. I look forward to using *Hardiness* to bring about clarity for my future clients."

—Dr. Chris Auger, LCDR (US Navy SEAL, Retired)

"What a marvelous read! The authors share the essential ingredient to cope successfully with life's stressors. This book truly is a "mental shield"; a must-read for Military Leaders to excel in the midst of stress or change. This book provides data-driven solutions to bring individuals back into their lives and find their purpose. A must-read for all; in my case, the military."

—LCDR Tara M. Smallidge, PhD, MBA, MSC, US Navy, Research Psychologist,
Naval Nuclear Power Training Command (NNPTC) (These views/opinions are her own and
do not necessarily represent the views of the Department of Defense or its Components)

"Stress is an unavoidable part of life, and your health, success, and happiness depend on your ability to manage, not avoid it. With convincing evidence, practical tools, and real-life examples, Dr. Stein and Dr. Bartone show how building a hardier mindset helps overcome the most difficult circumstances and leads to higher performance."

—Michael Katchen, Cofounder and CEO of Wealthsimple,
a leading financial services innovator operating in Canada,
the US, and the UK

"The concepts in *Hardiness* are powerful, practical, and insightful. In my work leading a global coaching and leadership development practice, I have seen thousands of leaders struggle to cope with stress and know it impacts the organization's results. Fusing solid research with practical and relatable stories, this self-help book is a must-read for anyone that wants to live a happier and more productive life."

—Steve Dion, Principal, The DROSTE Group

HARDINESS

Making Stress Work for You
to Achieve Your Life Goals

DR. STEVEN J. STEIN | DR. PAUL T. BARTONE

WILEY

Cover image: © Brian Hagiwara/Stockbyte/Getty Images
Cover design: Wiley

Copyright © 2020 by Multi-Health Systems Inc. and Paul T. Bartone. All rights reserved.

Published by John Wiley & Sons, Inc., Hoboken, New Jersey.
Published simultaneously in Canada.

No part of this publication may be reproduced, stored in a retrieval system, or transmitted in any form or by any means, electronic, mechanical, photocopying, recording, scanning, or otherwise, except as permitted under Section 107 or 108 of the 1976 United States Copyright Act, without either the prior written permission of the Publisher, or authorization through payment of the appropriate per-copy fee to the Copyright Clearance Center, Inc., 222 Rosewood Drive, Danvers, MA 01923, (978) 750-8400, fax (978) 646-8600, or on the Web at www.copyright.com. Requests to the Publisher for permission should be addressed to the Permissions Department, John Wiley & Sons, Inc., 111 River Street, Hoboken, NJ 07030, (201) 748-6011, fax (201) 748-6008, or online at http://www.wiley.com/go/permissions.

Limit of Liability/Disclaimer of Warranty: While the publisher and author have used their best efforts in preparing this book, they make no representations or warranties with respect to the accuracy or completeness of the contents of this book and specifically disclaim any implied warranties of merchantability or fitness for a particular purpose. No warranty may be created or extended by sales representatives or written sales materials. The advice and strategies contained herein may not be suitable for your situation. You should consult with a professional where appropriate. Neither the publisher nor author shall be liable for any loss of profit or any other commercial damages, including but not limited to special, incidental, consequential, or other damages.

For general information on our other products and services or for technical support, please contact our Customer Care Department within the United States at (800) 762-2974, outside the United States at (317) 572-3993 or fax (317) 572-4002.

Wiley publishes in a variety of print and electronic formats and by print-on-demand. Some material included with standard print versions of this book may not be included in e-books or in print-on-demand. If this book refers to media such as a CD or DVD that is not included in the version you purchased, you may download this material at http://booksupport.wiley.com. For more information about Wiley products, visit www.wiley.com.

Library of Congress Cataloging-in-Publication Data:

Names: Stein, Steven (Steven J.), author. | Bartone, Paul T., 1952- author.
  Title: Hardiness : making stress work for you to achieve your life goals /
  Dr. Steven J. Stein, Paul T. Bartone.
Description: Hoboken, New Jersey : John Wiley & Sons, Inc., [2020] |
  Includes bibliographical references and index.
Identifiers: LCCN 2019038396 (print) | LCCN 2019038397 (ebook) | ISBN
  9781119584452 (hardback) | ISBN 9781119584810 (adobe pdf) | ISBN
  9781119584827 (epub)
Subjects: LCSH: Stress (Psychology) | Adjustment (Psychology) |
  Self-actualization (Psychology) | Success.
Classification:L CC BF575.S75 S728 2020 (print) | LCC BF575.S75 (ebook) |
  DDC 155.9/042–dc23
LC record available at https://lccn.loc.gov/2019038396
LC ebook record available at https://lccn.loc.gov/2019038397

Printed in the United States of America

V10015551_111219

To our grandchildren,
Gemma Emery and Micah David (Steven's)
and Hazel Grace (Paul's).
Hoping they grow up in a hardier world.

Contents

Introduction

As the world changes around us with technology becoming more and more integrated into our lives, our need for human interactions only increases. Many of us are old enough to remember the days when personal computers first came onto the scene. We were promised that they would save us so much time we could start planning shorter work weeks, longer vacations, and sabbaticals. With the introduction of the Blackberry (remember that?) and the iPhone, the workday suddenly extended into our evenings, nights, weekends, and vacation time. We now know that technological innovations don't always work out quite the way their creators thought they would. Nor do they have the anticipated effects.

Not only are we living through a technological revolution, we live in a new age of information. For example, we know more about mental health and psychology now than we've ever known in history. The number of scientific papers being published in mental health alone is staggering. There are currently 525 scientific journals publishing thousands of articles just on this topic. If you search Amazon.com you can find over 60,000 books related to mental health. And these numbers are growing all the time.

Yet, with this explosion of knowledge about mental health and the increased availability of technology, we still haven't been able to take control of our problems. In fact, in many ways, things have gotten worse.

For example, we've seen dramatic increases in the negative effects of stress. Research reported by the American Institute of Stress shows that on-the-job stress is far and away the major source of stress for American adults. As well, it has escalated progressively over the past few decades. Increased levels of job stress, as evaluated by the perception of having little control but lots of demands, has been found to be associated with more heart attacks, hypertension, and other disorders.

Some sobering statistics on stress at work were reported by the Centers for Disease Control and Prevention, National Institute for Occupational Safety and Health. In one survey 40% of workers reported their jobs were "very or extremely stressful." Another survey found that 26% of workers reported "often or very often being burned out or stressed by their work." And a third, Yale University survey, reported that 29% of workers felt "quite a bit or extremely stressed at work." With regard to our progress in the information/technology era, 75% of employees believe that workers have more on-the-job stress than a generation ago.

Not only do these numbers translate into huge losses to the economy, but they take an enormous human toll. An estimated one million workers are absent every day in the US due to stress. It's also been reported that absenteeism is estimated to cost large American companies an average of $3.5 million a year. One large corporation found that 60% of employee absences could be traced to psychological problems that were due to job stress.

What are some of the causes of workplace stress? One survey found the following breakdown: 46% due to workload, 28% due to people issues, 20% due to juggling work/personal lives, and 6% due to lack of job security (American Institute of Stress, 2006) as seen in Figure I.1. How manageable are these issues? In this book we explore ways in which you can better manage yourself

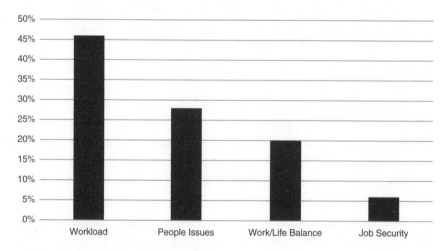

FigURE I.1 Causes of Workplace Stress

and some of these situations. Our hope is that the information and methods that we provide can help you lead a more fulfilling and less stressed out life.

In this book we introduce you to the new (well, 30 years old), little known concept of hardiness. Hardiness is composed of three facets—commitment, control, and challenge. These facets work together to provide a kind of mental shield, helping people to stay healthy and even excel in the midst of stress and change. We'll be discussing these elements throughout the book.

How did we come upon this concept? Paul did his doctoral thesis on this topic over 30 years ago. After learning about how senior executives reacted in a wide variety of ways to the same news about a merger involving their organization—some got extremely stressed out and others were excited about the challenge—he got interested in this phenomenon. For his doctoral dissertation he wanted to see how stress played out with a working-class group of people—city bus drivers. Sure enough, there are wide differences in how bus drivers react to basically the same stressful situations.

As often happens in psychology, in order to study psychological factors, we need to develop measures that can capture them as best we can. Without validated measures we'd just be talking about theories, ideas, and opinions. While these are all useful starting points, we don't really know what's real until we can measure it and validate it. So, we can give you all kinds of theories about stress and how to manage it, but without documented research, it's merely a set of opinions. Paul continued his distinguished career in the military investigating hardiness, eventually reaching the rank of Colonel and teaching at the West Point Military Academy.

As part of this endeavor, Paul developed a tool to help measure hardiness. In order to understand hardiness and its effects on people, it's important to measure it. The tool was originally called the Dispositional Resilience Scale (DRS), which evolved into the DRS15-R after years of research. Now, the instrument has been revised and further improved with large normative samples and greater applicability. The current tool is called the Hardiness

Resilience Gauge (HRG). It is the years of research using this instrument that has helped inform much of what we have learned about hardiness. Many of the studies we talk about in this book have relied on this hardiness measurement tool.

There are many practitioners who have been certified in the use of the HRG around the world. To connect with one of these practitioners, simply contact us at customerservice@mhs.com. To learn how to become a certified user yourself of the HRG, you can contact us at the same email address.

Meanwhile Steven has been involved for over 25 years in establishing and expanding our knowledge in the area of emotional intelligence. Being one of the pioneers in developing and escalating the use of the world's most widely used scientific measures of emotional intelligence (the Emotional Quotient Inventory 2.0 or EQ-i 2.0 and the Mayer-Salovey-Caruso Emotional Intelligence Test or MSCEIT), he has long been interested in factors that lead to emotional health. The hardiness factor, related to the stress tolerance element of emotional intelligence, is a perfect fit to continue this work.

In this book we use many real-life and some fictional examples of people and situations to illustrate our points. For the real-life examples we used people's full names and, when we included their hardiness scores, we obtained their permission. For the fictionalized accounts we tended to use examples of people we've known, but with made-up names and slightly changed details so they wouldn't be recognizable for confidentiality purposes.

We hope that the information, research, case studies, anecdotes, and exercises in this book will help make stress something that works for you (by developing a hardiness mindset) and will help you achieve your life goals.

Steven J. Stein, PhD
Paul T. Bartone, PhD

Chapter 1

Stress: What's All the Fuss?

"The greatest weapon against stress is our ability to choose one thought over another."
—William James (American philosopher and psychologist)

Belinda had been preparing for this day weeks in advance. Her team was counting on her to fly to their head office in New York to present their new plan for the year. It involved a substantial increase in funding and a new direction for their division that would trigger many questions from the senior managers. Belinda could justify the new plan better than anyone, as she was most responsible for putting all the pieces together.

She woke up fresh and alert. She would take her kids to school on her way to the airport. She chose a flight that allowed her some relaxing time in the lounge at the airport. However, after looking out the window, she realized there was an obstacle she hadn't considered. Her driveway was completely covered in snow, and the snow removal guy she hired hadn't arrived yet. She suddenly felt a mild panic. Her heart started beating faster, and her face became a bit flushed.

She counted to five, and then told herself she still had lots of time.

"Be positive," she thought. She could work this out.

She woke her kids and got them to help her start shoveling the snow in the meantime. The snow was heavy and deep, and the clock was ticking. She hoped school would be cancelled, but unfortunately, the school district sent a text notifying parents that all the city schools were open.

By the time they got the driveway half cleared, she started getting anxious again, realizing she was losing valuable time. She then decided she would back out of the driveway by putting her foot to the pedal on her SUV with a force that would get her over the unshoveled snow and onto the road. The car suddenly lurched back and got caught at the end of the driveway, with the rear barely on the road. The snow was too deep. Her rear tires started to spin. She wasn't moving.

She began to shift from reverse to forward, back and forth, stepping on the gas each time. She asked her kids to push the car, but it wouldn't budge. They started shoveling again, then rocking the car. She was completely out of breath from shoveling and the fear of missing her flight. She felt like she might faint.

After 10 minutes of panic, she didn't know what to do. Could she leave her SUV partly on the street, should she call a cab or Uber, what next?

Suddenly she jumped out of the car and looked up and down the street for snow removal trucks. Finally, she saw one turning the corner and breathlessly ran towards it, stopping the driver in the middle of the street.

She asked if he'd help out by clearing the back of her driveway with his plow so she could get her car onto the road. He explained that he had dozens of driveways to clear and was already behind on his schedule. Her breathing, at this point, was so deep, she almost fell to the ground with exhaustion. She begged him, telling him she had to make it to the airport and how it was really important. He finally agreed and cleared the bottom of the driveway.

With her kids pushing her back she was finally able to make it onto the road. By now she had lost almost 40 minutes. She dropped her kids off at school and took off to the airport. The highway was completely jammed as the snow caused massive traffic congestion.

Sitting on the highway, she started sweating profusely. Her heart was racing once again. She had to make this plane. She finally got to the airport and decided to leave her car at the valet parking where she grabbed the ticket from the attendant and ran to the departure gates.

When she got past security and to the gate, she was told the plane was delayed because of the snow. This caused even more anxiety because she knew all the senior team would be there waiting just for her. As she was waiting to board the plane, she got a call from the school telling her that her youngest son was sick and throwing up. By now her hands were sweating even more, and she began shaking. She had to try to reach her mother and ask her if she could pick up her son.

The flight finally took off an hour and a half late. When she arrived, she was able to get a cab and slowly made her way through New York traffic to get to the head office. As she was rehearsing her presentation in her mind and trying to keep calm, she suddenly realized she left behind the handouts that she had prepared for each of the senior team. Now she was in total panic. There was nothing she could do. She never prepared for this many things to go wrong. She now felt completely powerless.

How would you feel after a morning like that? Would you be stressed out, or would it be just another day at the office for you?

Can you remember the last time you were stressed out? Did it involve a major life event—like an illness or death in the family? Was it work or school related—being judged on a presentation, performance review, or exam? Or financial—not having enough money to meet your goals? Or maybe a relationship problem—not being treated fairly by friends who should know better? Perhaps just the everyday demands on your life are enough to stress you out.

How is it that some people are overwhelmed by the slightest disruption or change in their lives, while others seem to make it through catastrophes relatively unscathed? Or that two people, experiencing the exact same event, such as the breakup of a relationship or a serious illness, can react in completely different ways? A colleague of ours, having gone through a similar experience as Belinda's, had a totally different reaction. As Cathy encountered each new obstacle, she saw it as a challenge, something to problem-solve her way through. She wasn't worried about failing, but just kept plowing through each new challenge.

Perhaps getting a better understanding of stress, and how it works, can help us begin to understand these questions. Once we do, we can begin to learn how to better manage the stress in our own lives, and even turn stress into an advantage!

Stress: It's Unavoidable

Stress is a necessary part of life. As the early stress researcher Hans Selye once said, the only stress-free person is a dead one (Selye, 1978). Every day we experience challenges that are more or less stressful, causing our bodies and brains to react in characteristic ways. And although this has been true for as long as humans have walked the earth, modern life only seems to be getting more and more stressful. Novel and changing technologies have shifted the way we live and do business. New systems and approaches are appearing at a fast pace, forcing changes in how many jobs get accomplished (Thack & Woodman, 1994). The internet alone has vastly expanded the information available to us, while at the same time opening the door to misinformation, cybercrime, and loss of personal data (Aiken, 2016).

Jobs and relationships are less stable. Increasing globalization of operations for many organizations means that employees must learn to function and communicate in strange cultures. Changes are coming more often, and futures are harder to predict. At the same time, stress-related diseases and other problems continue to rise, including heart disease, stroke, diabetes, obesity, drug and alcohol abuse, depression, and, yes, suicide. Stress can make you sick, unhappy, and not a very good employee, partner, or parent.

Bad Stress, Good Stress: How Knowing the Difference Can Help You Live Longer

In today's environment, knowing how to cope effectively with stress is more important than ever. Much of the early research on human responses to stress focused on the ill effects of various major life events, such as divorce, a death in the family, or losing your job (Holmes & Rahe, 1967). We hear a lot about the negative effects or the results of "bad stress."

New research, however, is teaching us that not all stress is necessarily bad. One major study, reported in 2012, comes from data collected over a dozen years earlier. Nearly 186 million adults participated in a U.S. National Health Interview in which they were asked dozens of questions about their habits and how they coped with life. These data were later linked to the National Death Index to see if there were any relationships between people's habits and how long they actually lived. While there are many different causes of death, it was thought that by mining such a large database we could at least provide some clues and perhaps connections between people's lifestyles and their longevity.

It may not be that surprising to learn that 55% of the participants reported experiencing moderate to high levels of stress during the year they were interviewed. If we look at many of the people around us, both at work and in our social and family lives, we'd probably come up with a similar finding. Upon further probing, the researchers discovered that 34% described how this stress had negatively affected their health to some extent during that time. So, while over half of the people surveyed were experiencing high levels of stress, only about a third of them felt it was negatively affecting their health in some way.

Later on, the researchers did a follow-up, examining death records and matching them to the people who were interviewed. They made a surprising discovery. Of the people who reported high stress levels, those that said the stress negatively affected their health had a 43% greater chance of premature death. In other words, people who interpret their stress as not having a negative impact on their lives have a better chance of living longer. These researchers went on to find a relationship between people's coping styles with stress and how long they lived, supporting the idea that it's not the stress itself that's bad, but how we manage the stress that's important.

In the words of the study authors, "Stress appraisal plays an important role in determining health outcomes. These findings also suggest that perceived stress and beliefs about the impact of stress on health might work synergistically to increase risk for premature mortality" (Keller, Litzelman, Wisk, Creswell, & Will, 2012).

Many other studies have shown that major stressful events can lead to all kinds of serious illness, from heart disease to cancer. But it's not just the experience of stressful events. Rather, it's how we appraise or think about these events that seems to matter most. For example, a recent study of California women found that those who perceived prior life events as more stressful were at greater risk for breast cancer, as compared to women who experienced the same events but perceived them as less stressful (Fischer, Ziogas, & Anton-Culver, 2018). As the study authors say, "Perception matters."

It's a curious fact that people often respond very differently to the same challenging conditions in life.

People Are Resistant or Resilient to Stress

Our colleague Cathy, whom we referred to earlier, reacted quite differently to a situation quite similar to Belinda's. Cathy, who is very self-confident, likes challenges, yet she still manages to stay in touch with reality. She knows that not all problems are solvable. Perhaps the flight was cancelled, and there was no way to make it for the meeting. While Belinda might blame herself for failing, Cathy would look for alternatives, perhaps a virtual meeting, or try to reschedule.

Cathy also reviewed the experience, looking for lessons she could learn from it to improve on the next time she faced a similar situation. For example, she would check the weather the night before. She might arrange in advance for someone else to take the kids to school. She might even leave a day early to make sure weather or other factors didn't prevent her from getting to the meeting. She realizes that everyone fails sometimes, but it's what you do with the failure, how you process it, that makes the difference.

Your Body's Response to Stress

Bret and Sally were both getting ready to make a presentation at their company town hall meeting. Bret was going to make his first presentation in front of a large group, discussing the financial results of the previous quarter. Sally, also making her first presentation in front of a group, was going to share the company's marketing plans going forward. They expected about 200 of their fellow employees to be there. You'd never know they were both going to the same meeting.

"I am so stressed out," Sally said. "My hands are shaking, I have butterflies in my stomach, and my heart is racing. I could barely sleep last night."

"Wow, and your skin is pretty pale. You'd better get a glass of water," Bret responded.

"What about you, Bret? You must be nervous. Everyone's going to be watching," Sally replied.

"Actually, I'm pretty charged! I've been working with these new graph templates, and I found some really funny graphics to spice up my slides. I can't wait to try them out in front of every-one!" he responded, a bit sheepishly, trying to be sensitive to Sally's unease.

How is it that what is anxiety provoking for one person can be exciting for someone else? We find this same thing happens across many areas of life.

While for some, a job loss may lead to depression and ruin, others see it as an opportunity to branch out into some new area. Some people seem to routinely cope more effectively with the changes and challenges of life. In recent years, this has been labeled "resilience" (Layne, Warren, Watson, & Shalev, 2007). What accounts for these individual differences? What makes some people more resilient than others when confronting stressful situations? We'll present you with some of the latest research and provide you with some ways in which you can practice improving your own abilities in this area.

At some level we all know that stress has a physical component. We've all experienced life's pressures and how we can react to them both mentally and physically. Whether it's just a short-term threat or an ongoing number of issues that weigh on our mind, we often *feel* the stress.

Fight or Flight: Our Immediate Response

What happens to your body when you go into stress mode? Imagine one of your ancestors walking into the jungle and suddenly coming across a lion moving in the opposite direction. The sight of the large beast, and perhaps the slightest eye contact, would most likely send an immediate shock to his system.

When the shock first hits, he experiences an acute stress, which triggers his body's hormones to activate his sympathetic nervous system. Suddenly his adrenal glands release catechol-amines, including adrenaline and noradrenaline. This leads to an increase in his heart rate, blood pressure, and breathing rate. His fast heartbeat and breathing help give his body energy to respond. His skin becomes flushed or pale as the blood flow to the surface of his body is decreased so it can go to his muscles, legs, arms, and his brain. As the blood rushes to his brain, his face starts to alternate between pale and flushed. His blood-clotting ability also increases in case he receives any injury that involves blood loss.

At the same time as all of this, your ancestor's body is pre-paring to be more aware and observant of his surroundings—so he can decide which is the safest way to run. His pupils dilate, allowing more light into his eyes and giving him better vision of his surroundings. His body also immediately starts to tremble or shake, which is the response of his muscles tensing up and being primed for action.

This sudden shock he is experiencing was named the "flight or fight" response by American physiologist Walter Cannon (Cannon, 1915). The idea here is that the shock prepares us physiolog-ically and mentally, as described above, to either flee quickly or stand up to the threat and take immediate action against it—usu-ally physically. Hence, the "fight" or "flight." Alternatively, it was referred to as the first phase of the general adaptation syndrome (GAS) by the previously mentioned physiologist Hans Selye. Once the threat is gone, it may take between 20 and 60 minutes for the body to return to its prearousal levels.

It's this system that has largely allowed us to avoid preda-tors and survive as a species. However, the challenges our ances-tors experienced have significantly changed in today's world. It's only our response to these challenges that has largely remained the same.

STRESS'S LONG-TERM EFFECTS ON HEALTH

Stress, especially when negatively perceived, and chronic, has additional effects on our bodies. The same effects we see in acute stress, such as increased heart rate and blood pressure, over longer periods of time, can produce a chronic wear and tear on the cardiovascular system that can result in disorders such as stroke and heart attacks.

Other effects of being "stressed out" include changes in behavior that have been found to be detrimental to health. These include poor sleep, eating or drinking too much, smoking, drug use, and lack of physical activity (McEwen, 2008). All of these can have direct and indirect effects on your ability to live a long and satisfying life.

POSITIVE WAYS TO HANDLE STRESS

In this book we'll be exploring positive approaches that people have successfully used to handle the stressful situations in their lives. Some of the techniques we present are well documented in scientific research journals. Others have been developed, used, and modified through our collective work across different environments. Our experience includes people from all walks of life and spans military personnel, students, corporate executives, various workplaces (nonprofit, for-profit, government), lawyers, entertainers, athletes (professional, Olympic, and amateur), managers, frontline workers, leaders, homeless people, and homemakers.

Hardiness Can Make a Big Difference in How You Cope with Stress

This is a book about hardiness, something we believe is an essential ingredient that helps people cope effectively with life stressors, and even thrive under stress. While the supporting evidence behind hardiness is based on over 40 years of scientific research, we don't intend to bore you with all the technical details. There is plenty of that to be found in professional books and journals. However, we do include numerous references and an index for the interested reader. Rather, our main aim with this book is to explain hardiness in a way that make sense to the average reader, and to provide tips and strategies to improve your own hardiness and your ability to deal with the stresses of life.

Over 40 years ago, a University of Chicago graduate student wondered about the different reactions within a group of corporate executives who were going through a major organizational restructuring and downsizing. Suzanne Kobasa wanted to know why some of these executives were getting sick and demoralized, while others seemed to be thriving, all while experiencing the same disruptive and stressful conditions. Later, she published her findings in the *Journal of Personality and Social Psychology* (Kobasa, 1979). Her research showed that those executives who developed stress-related health problems were lacking in certain personality features when compared to those who stayed healthy through this stressful reorganization.

Kobasa called this set of attitudes "hardiness." Not long after that, one of the authors of this book (Paul) extended this work by looking at a blue-collar sample of Chicago city bus drivers (Bartone, 1984). It turns out that city bus drivers have a pretty stressful job, dealing with traffic, time pressures, and sometimes angry and even violent passengers. His doctoral research showed that these job stressors often lead to a range of health problems, such as hypertension, heart disease, and stomach problems. But those bus drivers who are high in hardiness are largely protected from these problems, staying healthy despite the job stress.

Since then, hundreds of studies have confirmed the importance of hardiness as a stress resilience resource that protects people from the bad effects that stress can have on health, happiness, and performance.

Introducing the Three Cs

In the high-hardy person, the three facets of commitment, challenge, and control work together in synchrony, creating a mindset or worldview that is highly effective and makes them resilient in coping with stressful conditions. This constellation of qualities, called hardiness, is found in people who stay healthy and continue to perform well in life, despite experiencing a range of stressful conditions (Bartone, 1999; Bartone, Roland, Picano, & Williams, 2008; Maddi & Kobasa, 1984).

HARDINESS AND COMMITMENT

People high in hardiness-commitment see life as overall meaningful and worthwhile, even though it sometimes brings pain and disappointment. Hardiness-commitment also includes a striving for personal competence as first described by the Harvard psychologist Robert White (White, 1959). The sense of competence aids the person in making realistic appraisals of novel and stressful situations, and generates increased self-confidence that one can handle adversity.

To be high in **commitment** means looking at the world as interesting and useful, even when things are difficult. These kinds of people pursue their interests with vigor, are deeply involved with their work, and are socially engaged with other people. They are also reflective about themselves and aware of their own feelings and reactions.

Low commitment people are often bored and don't find much meaning in life. They go to school or work or are unemployed with no real game plan or idea of where they want to be in the future. They tend to be unreflective and disengaged, not much interested in their work, themselves, or other people in general. When presented with a challenge, those low in commitment tend to give up easily. Figure 1.1 gives you some examples of how people with different levels of hardiness relate to commitment.

HARDINESS AND CHALLENGE

People high in hardiness have a strong sense of **challenge**: they enjoy variety and tend to see change and disruptions in life as interesting opportunities to learn and grow. They understand that problems are a part of life, and they set out to solve them, rather than run away from them. For these people, taking on new challenges is an interesting way to learn about themselves and their own capabilities, while also learning about the world.

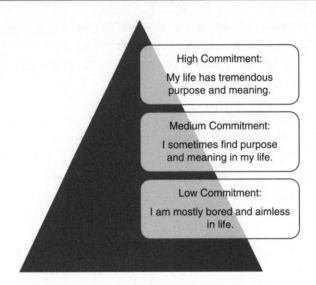

FIGURE **1.1**   Where Do You See Yourself on the Commitment Pyramid?

In contrast, those low in challenge prefer stability and predictability in their lives and tend to avoid new and changing situations. They may be highly reliable, but are not very adaptable when conditions change. Figure 1.2 illustrates how people with different levels of hardiness typically respond to challenges.

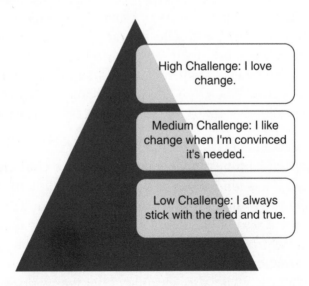

FIGURE **1.2**   Where Do You See Yourself on the Challenge Pyramid?

Hardiness-challenge involves an appreciation for variety and change, and a desire to learn and grow by trying out new things. The main theoretical influences come from work by Fiske and Maddi on the importance of variety in experience (Fiske & Maddi, 1961), and Maddi's ideas on active engagement in the world (Maddi, 1967). Maddi used the term "ideal identity" to describe the person who lives a vigorous and proactive life, with a desire for variety and new experiences. These people are courageous in choosing to look forward and take action, despite the fact that future outcomes are always uncertain. At the other end of the spectrum is the "existential neurotic," who shies away from change and always seeks security and predictability in the old and familiar.

HARDINESS AND CONTROL

Control is simply the belief that your own actions make a real difference in the results that follow, that what you do has effects on outcomes. In contrast, people low in hardiness-control generally feel powerless to control or influence events in their lives (see Figure 1.3).

The control facet of hardiness also derives from existential theory. According to Maddi (1989), the core tendency in existential

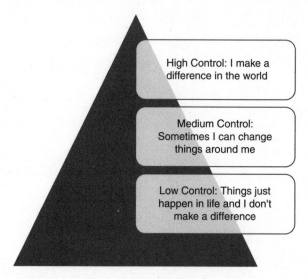

High Control: I make a difference in the world

Medium Control: Sometimes I can change things around me

Low Control: Things just happen in life and I don't make a difference

FIGURE **1.3** Where Do You See Yourself on the Control Pyramid?

personality theory is "striving for authentic being," which involves an honest acceptance of yourself and the world around you, and a willingness to make choices and take responsibility for those choices. The authentic (hardy) person regularly chooses the path of engagement and active involvement in the world, instead of the relative safety of passive withdrawal and inaction.

High-hardy persons are authentic in this sense, seeing themselves as being in charge of their own destinies, even though the future is always somewhat uncertain and frightening. Being in control is well known to lower the effects of stressful conditions. For example, experimental studies have found that when subjects are given control over aversive stimuli such as electric shocks, the stress effects are reduced, as compared to subjects who have no control (Averill, 1973; Seligman, 1975).

In the chapters that follow, we'll cover each of these facets in more detail and show how you can develop your strengths in each of these areas. We'll also give examples on how important these facets have been in both successful and unsuccessful attempts to deal with stress in people's lives. Some of the examples we describe will be of real people you might be familiar with. Other examples will be composites of real-life people and interesting situations that we, the authors, have come across in our work. So let's get started!

Chapter 2

Commitment: Why Pursuing Purpose in Life Matters

"He who has a why to live for, can bear almost any how."
—Friedrich Nietzsche (German philosopher)

Probably one of the most difficult questions we have ever asked is, "Why are we here?" Most people go through life, day by day, just trying to get to tomorrow. It's usually when tragedy strikes around us that we stop and think about what life is all about and whether we are making the most of our own lives. People who are hardy, especially in the factor we've identified as *commitment*, have already thought about their lives and what is meaningful to them.

How do we embrace commitment in our lives? Many of us have set specific goals for ourselves in life. We might want to do a certain type of work, become rich and famous, have a loving family, change the world, have lots of friends, help others, travel, party, or any number of things. These goals become our purpose, the things we wake up and get out of bed for in the morning. Some people are pretty nonchalant about their goals—they just get up and go to work—if they move forward in life today, that's fine, if not, that's okay too. Other people are driven— they may want to stop world poverty, make a million dollars, or become the next Beyoncé. These people work towards their goals relentlessly.

Having goals, or a purpose in life, is like having a destination you want to visit. You may have always wanted to go to Rome, but somehow never quite made it there. However, commitment is your engagement in the process. People who are committed take action and work towards their goals. They also tend to take a more general interest in life and the world around them. They find meaning in their lives.

There's one more aspect of commitment that's important here. Sometimes the commitment, the goal that someone is passionate about, is vocational, a type of work or a life mission. We refer to this as a calling. Some people have a religious calling and enter the clergy. Others have a calling to heal people and become health professionals. We'll explore this in more detail later in the chapter.

What Is the Theory Behind Commitment?

The commitment facet of hardiness is all about being actively involved and engaged in one's activities and the surrounding world. People high in commitment see life as meaningful and worthwhile, even though it is sometimes disappointing and painful.

The theoretical roots behind the hardiness-commitment concept lie in existential psychology, as seen for example in the work of Viktor Frankl (2007) and Ludwig Binswanger (1963). Frankl, an Austrian psychiatrist and concentration camp survivor, argued that finding meaning in life was the most important task humans face. For Frankl, it is the lack of meaning that is behind all sorts of problems, from boredom and apathy to depression and suicide.

Ludwig Binswanger was a Swiss psychiatrist and part of Freud's inner circle. He believed that to fully understand people, you had to take into account how they see and interact with the world on three levels.

The first level is the *Umwelt*, or "around world," which is the physical world and environment around you. This would include, for example, where you live and work, and all your day-to-day activities. Next is the *Mitwelt*, or "with world," which refers to all the people you know and interact with, your social world. Finally, is the *Eigenwelt,* or "self world," or how you see and think about your own self.

Hardiness-commitment encompasses all three of these worlds. People strong in commitment are highly interested in the world and the people around them and see themselves as active participants. This spills over into another hardiness facet, the sense of control, which we discuss in later chapters.

What We Can Learn About Commitment from Prisoners of War

When it comes to surviving adverse situations, few things seem as bad as being held captive as a prisoner of war. What could be worse than being tortured and held in isolation by an enemy? Being a prisoner of war has been described as one of the most brutal of man-made traumas. It includes enduring deliberate, repeated, prolonged, and interpersonal human cruelty (Herman, 1992).

The late John McCain, former US senator and presidential candidate had just such a fate. During the Vietnam War, as a naval aviator, he flew ground bombing missions from an aircraft carrier. During Operation Rolling Thunder over Hanoi in 1967 his plane was shot down. Seriously injured in the crash, he was captured by the North Vietnamese.

McCain was a prisoner of war until 1973. While imprisoned at the notorious Hanoi Hilton, he was beaten, tortured, and suffered from dysentery, severe weight loss, and high fever. He was beaten so badly that his grey hair turned white when he was left to die. How did McCain keep up his morale and survive his imprisonment? By his own account, a key factor that sustained him was his social commitment, beginning with commitment to his fellow prisoners. He didn't want to do anything to let them down. Several times McCain was offered early release by his captors, who knew that his father was an admiral and that this would attract a lot of media attention. Despite being close to death and denied medical care, McCain refused, saying that other POWs should go home first.

He also believed communication with his fellow prisoners was essential for their survival. Though held in isolation for much of his captivity, he communicated by tapping out Morse code messages on the floors and walls. Prisoners were often beaten when caught making these surreptitious contacts. McCain was also deeply committed to his family and didn't want to bring any shame or criticism on them through his actions while a POW. Finally, like most other POWs, he was committed to American ideals and values of freedom, fairness, and democracy. These commitments all helped to sustain him through five and a half years of captivity, torture, and suffering.

This kind of commitment, believing in a higher cause, increases your hardiness by building your strength of conviction and enabling you to withstand greater obstacles. Your hardiness grows, much like the muscles you exercise, through overcoming increasing challenges. Each successful encounter with a difficult situation enables your hardiness factor to grow.

People with a strong sense of commitment also tend to apply it to themselves, engaging in reflection and honest self-examination. They want to be aware of who they are, their strengths and weaknesses. McCain had plenty of time for reflection during his captivity and thought a lot about what was important to him—family, friends, fellow prisoners, service to his country. At one particularly low point he did succumb to the demands of his captors and signed a false confession. He later recounted this failure to resist with some regret, but also with an acceptance of the hard reality that "every man has his breaking point." In this he demonstrates another important aspect of commitment: the recognition of your limitations as a human being and a willingness to accept these limitations with humility (McCain, 2008).

Surviving Post-Traumatic Stress:
Hardiness-Commitment Versus Short-Term Pleasures

In a very unique study, some Israeli researchers looked at the effects of stress (post-traumatic stress disorder) on former prisoners of war over a period of 17 years (Zerach, Karstoft, & Solomon,

2017). At regular intervals the former prisoners were reassessed on a number of measures. The idea was to see if the effects of stress got worse over time, stayed the same, or improved. As well, the researchers looked at whether they could predict these outcomes through exploring certain personality characteristics.

In other words, these researchers, along with many others who study war veterans, were looking to identify risk or resiliency factors. If they could discover factors that prevented soldiers, who experience extremely stressful situations, from suffering the ravages of stress, we could likely use these findings to help others deal with the ups and downs of everyday living.

The Israeli study looked specifically at how two different personality characteristics may have helped determine the long-term effects of severe stress. One factor that researchers thought was important, based on some previous research, was sensation-seeking. This is the degree to which people actively seek out new, exciting, and intense experiences. People who take big risks—whether physical, social, or financial—are high in sensation-seeking. The theory here is that people who seek short-term pleasure, like taking big risks and experiencing new things—sensation seekers—should be less affected by stressful situations. These are people who generally experience lower anxiety in their lives.

If, in fact, sensation-seeking lowers people's stress, then simply teaching people to take more risks or look for short-term pleasures in their lives could help them reduce their stress. This could lead to a whole new set of treatment strategies for people affected negatively by stress.

The other factor examined was hardiness, which included commitment, control, and challenge. Once again, based on previous research with military populations, it was thought that having a hardiness mindset might be a good shield against some of the more destructive elements of these stressful experiences. If hardiness was an important factor here, that could lead to new interventions that could help people to better manage stress.

The results of the Israeli POW study did not work out exactly as the researchers expected. Sensation-seeking did not seem to play a role in differentiating those who suffered more or less over time with post-traumatic stress symptoms. On the other hand, hardiness played a significant role in differentiating those who coped better with their situation from those who continued to suffer over time. Those who were high in hardiness, that is, those who managed stress effectively and directly through commitment, challenge, and control, had significantly fewer post-traumatic stress symptoms over the 17-year time period of the study. While numerous studies have supported the effectiveness of hardiness in managing stress at a single point in time, this was the first study to demonstrate hardiness as a possible buffer against the long-term residues of war captivity.

The authors went on to suggest that screening for hardiness and introducing hardiness training early on—building commitment, control, and challenge—could significantly benefit the military. Imagine, if hardiness can be a protective factor in these extreme situations, how the hardiness skills might benefit you in your day-to-day life.

Hardiness skills or styles can make a difference in the lives of people who have experienced some of the most extreme stress humans can inflict on each other. Adopting some of the components of hardiness may make a difference in your life.

Increasing Commitment in Your Life

Commitment is all about active involvement and engagement in one's activities and the surrounding world, as well as a sense of competence and self-worth. At the opposite pole of commitment is alienation, or meaninglessness.

Mary-Anne was at a crossroads in her life. She had been working at the same job for almost 10 years. As a data entry clerk in customer service at a chemical manufacturing plant, she thought she had nowhere to go career-wise. She felt she was at a dead end. As she thought about her situation, she became angry with herself. Over time she began to experience physical symptoms that included headaches, stomach cramps, and occasional dizziness. She started coming in late to work and missing days when her headaches were too intense. She was in danger of losing her job, with no alternative in sight.

Because her job performance was declining, she was asked to meet with Alicia, the human resource manager at work. It didn't take long for Alicia to discover how unhappy Mary-Anne was at work. With a little exploration, Alicia discovered Mary-Anne had an interest in event planning. She had planned her own wedding as well as her sister's and several of her friends' weddings. Also, her happiest time at work was when she had an opportunity to help the marketing people plan and execute exhibiting at a conference.

Alicia suggested Mary-Anne take some night courses in event planning, an area they established that she had developed an interest in. Over time, Mary-Anne could start applying for any jobs that became available in the marketing department. Suddenly, Mary-Anne felt she had a purpose, something she could strive for. Because this purpose was meaningful for her, and she was motivated to pursue it, her commitment was high. Not only did she feel a new sense of hope and direction, but her headaches and stomach cramps soon disappeared as well.

The ability to overcome these feelings and symptoms increased her hardiness. Hardiness builds on experiences of success in overcoming obstacles. Each time you overcome a challenge in your life, you build more of your hardiness muscle.

What can you learn from Mary-Anne's experience? Take the time to think about what is important, interesting, and meaningful to you…your personal values and goals. Are you getting enough of these things in your current life, whether at work, in your free time, or at all? Think about changing your life to attain more of these goals. Consider how it may build your hardiness factor.

Victor Frankl: Purpose, Commitment, and Meaning

How is it that some people have gone through extremely horrifying situations, yet are still able come out of it and continue to live their lives? Some go on to live relatively ordinary lives while others go on to great accomplishments. One explanation for this phenomenon was offered by Victor Frankl, the noted psychiatrist who survived the labor camp at Theresienstadt and the death camp of Auschwitz during World War II.

Frankl developed a form of therapy called logotherapy which he first conceptualized just before the war. While being held prisoner by the Nazis, he reported that using the principles of this therapy helped him to survive. Even after learning that his mother and brother were murdered at Auschwitz and his wife killed at Bergen-Belsen, he maintained those beliefs. His therapy approach is largely described in his book *Man's Search for Meaning* (Frankl, 1959/2007).

Basically, Frankl had three main ideas. The first he called *freedom of will*. This means that people have the freedom to choose—whether it's internal psychological conditions, or external biological and social conditions. He states that it's within our spirit to make choices in our lives. Even when we are overcome with things like a serious illness over which we have little or no control, there are choices we can make about how to move forward with our lives.

Frankl's second big idea is *will to meaning*. This implies that not only are we free, but we are free to choose to achieve goals and purpose in our lives. This is seen as a primary motivation in most human beings. When people are unable to strive for purpose or meaning in life, they are likely to live lives that feel rather pointless. This, in turn, leads to boredom and increases their risk for aggression, addiction, suicide, depression, and various other mental and physical problems.

Finally, Frankl talked about *meaning in life*. He related this to responsibility. Thus, being free or achieving freedom is a good thing. But it's not all that meaningful unless we use that freedom responsibly and don't just fritter it away on worthless endeavors. So real meaning involves purposeful accomplishments with specific situations and people. This takes it to the next level, beyond wishful thinking into actual accomplishments.

Together, these three factors, *freedom of will*, *will to meaning*, and *meaning in life*, add to our hardiness factor. By knowing we have choices in life, have a purpose, and can execute those choices, we become stronger, more resilient—hardier in our lives. This hardiness gives us added strength when we encounter our next life challenge.

There have been a few criticisms of Frankl's work in more recent years (Langer, 1982; Szasz, 2003). Some of this has to do with the idea that *purpose* is not necessarily limited to serving the good of mankind. Frankl believed his purpose was to survive the death camps so that he could eventually get back to helping people through his therapy, lectures, and writing. However, purpose can also have a dark side. For example, the Nazi soldiers going through their own hardships could also motivate themselves through their (dark) sense of purpose—to eliminate Jews from the world.

Somewhere along the line we should add goodness to purpose—that purposeful acts are for the betterment of people, animals, or the planet. While being hateful may give some people purpose, there are serious personal and public health costs associated with hate (Abuelaish & Arya, 2017). In fact, in some of our own research developing a new measure of hate, we found that one of the factors of hate we identified, intolerance (being unwilling to learn about other groups of people), was negatively related to hardiness. In other words, people who are high in hardiness tend to be more tolerant and willing to learn about others (Abuelaish, Stein, Stermac, & Mann, 2019).

How much time have you spent thinking about your purpose in life? What do you consider the most important things in your life? For some people it's putting food on the table and a roof over their family's head. Are your priorities centered around your family, work, career, money, fixing the environment, eradicating poverty, fame, education, or (fill in the blank) _____?

Think about your values and write down your most important priorities.

The Role of Commitment in Success: Jim Carrey

Jim Carrey is a well-known comedian and actor. He's a two-time Golden Globe winner and was a cast member of the Fox sketch comedy *In Living Color* (1990). He had leading roles in *Ace Ventura: Pet Detective* (1994), *Dumb and Dumber* (1994), and *The Mask* (1994) which established him as a bankable comedy actor.

He gained his biggest success starring in serious roles in *The Truman Show* (1998) and *Man on the Moon* (1999), where he earned his Golden Globe Awards for Best Actor.

But Carrey wasn't always successful. In fact, he had his share of difficulties growing up. His family often struggled to make ends meet. He was born in Newmarket, Ontario, just north of Toronto. He loved performing and performed for anyone who would give him the time when he was young. During his teenage years, his family was hit with serious financial difficulties, and they were forced to move to smaller quarters in Scarborough, a suburb of Toronto.

He and his parents had to take security and janitorial jobs in a factory in order to survive. Jim worked eight-hour shifts after school let out. His grades and morale both suffered. When the family finally deserted the factory, they lived like nomads out of a Volkswagen camper van until they could return to Toronto.

In spite of all this, Carrey saw himself as an entertainer. He kept subjecting himself to open mics and auditions even though he was often ridiculed and told he had no talent. Eventually he was noticed by comedian Rodney Dangerfield and given his first break.

Carrey believed in himself and the fact that he could make it someday, despite all the difficult times he experienced. He also had a great deal of support from his family. Even during their most difficult times his father drove him to perform at unpaid open mics at local comedy clubs.

He had a real purpose to his life. In an interview with Oprah Winfrey on February 17, 1997 (Winfrey, 1997), he revealed that as a struggling actor he would use visualization techniques to get work. He also stated that he visualized a $10,000,000 check given to him for "acting services rendered," placed the check in his pocket, and seven years later received a $10,000,000 check for his role in *Dumb and Dumber* (Winfrey, 2017).

The adversity in Carrey's life seemed to increase his hardiness. It enabled him to persist and follow his dreams despite failures experienced along the way. His hardiness acted as a shield, likely giving him the strength to tell himself, after the next bump in the road, something like, "Okay, this is pretty bad, but I've already gone through worse experiences, so why let this stop me now?"

WHAT YOU CAN LEARN FROM JIM CARREY'S EXPERIENCE

Sometimes we set goals that seem unachievable. Visualization is a process that therapists have used with their clients and sports psychologists have used with elite athletes to overcome obstacles and achieve success. Once you know your purpose, where you want to be in the future, and you are truly motivated to reach it, your hardiness-commitment comes into play.

Visualization involves picturing yourself achieving that goal. It can also involve imaging the steps, and perhaps obstacles, towards the goal. It's a process that helps you maintain or even enhance your commitment. In addition, it can give you added purpose, a reason to keep trying to achieve that goal. Take a minute and think about some of the things you may want in your future. Imagine yourself achieving some of those objectives.

When Commitment Leads to Calling: The Success Factor for Musicians

What does it take to become a successful musician? The music business is extremely competitive with only a small percentage of the people who want to make their living playing music achieving that goal. If we can learn more about success in this field, perhaps that can help us understand success in other, less competitive fields as well.

One of the authors (Steven) contributes time to a nonprofit program aimed at helping early career musicians learn the business, legal, marketing, and psychological aspects of success in the music business. One of the personality characteristics these artists are tested on is their hardiness. We are involved in a long-term study looking at the role hardiness plays in the success (or lack of success) of these young performers.

Fortunately, there has already been a fair bit of research that has been carried out looking at success in the music business. Perhaps one of the most popular beliefs is that musical talent or ability is the best predictor of making it as a musical artist. It seems logical that the artists with the best-selling songs are the most technically competent and talented musicians or performers.

The role of talent (musical ability) and intrinsic motivation—also known as a "calling"—were examined in a creative long-term study that followed 450 amateur high school musicians for 11 years (Riza & Heller, 2015). The subjects were surveyed multiple times, starting from their adolescence up until their early adulthood.

You're probably somewhat familiar with the concept of a calling. Some people report having a calling early in life to help others, and they follow their calling, for example, by eventually entering medical school and becoming doctors. Others may have religious callings at an early age and become priests, ministers, or rabbis. Another way of framing this could be through the well-known statement made by Steve Jobs that "the only way to do great work is to love what you do. If you haven't found it yet, keep looking. Don't settle" (Jobs, 2005).

Riza and Heller gathered ability ratings from the students' music teachers as well as information on any awards they had achieved or competitions they had participated in. They also surveyed the students as to how well they self-rated their own musical ability. Interestingly, the students' actual musical ability, as rated by professionals, did not always match the students' self-perceived ability. In other words, there were students who believed they were much more talented than their teachers thought they were, and others who thought they were less skilled.

Most likely, you would expect the level of objectively rated talent to be the best predictor of success in this group. However, when the researchers looked at who actually became successful musicians, it was not their actual talent or ability that predicted their success. Rather, it was the degree to which they reported having a calling and their own *perceived* rating of their talent (as opposed to objective ratings of their talent) that better predicted their success.

What does it mean to have a calling? For this study, and several others like it, a person's level of calling is determined by the degree to which they agree to a set of specific items, such as these examples:

> My existence would be much less meaningful without my involvement in music.
>
> I am passionate about playing my instrument/singing.
>
> Music is always in my mind in some way.

The stronger the endorsement of the items, the more intense one's sense of calling. If you are committed to your calling, you will fulfill your calling. The uber-talented musicians may be the best musicians on the continent, but if it's not their calling, they're not committed and won't succeed the way those committed to their calling will, even if those musicians aren't as talented.

Consider some of the activities that are meaningful in your life. How often do you think about them? What actions do you take in fulfilling them? Are there additional things you can do to make them more a part of your life?

One of the great things we've learned about the hardiness mindset is that it's changeable. You can actually learn to become more committed to something in your life. In the next chapter we'll explore some specific ways in which you can increase the commitment in your life.

Chapter 3

Building Commitment

"It's not enough to have lived. We should be determined to live for something."
—Winston S. Churchill (British politician and prime minister)

Thinking about commitment may seem a long way off from dealing with all of the stresses—large and small—that you encounter. You may not see any clear connection between what seems like contemplating life and the rigors of your day-to-day activities. Think of it the same way a boxer might approach lifting weights in the gym. The exercise gym is removed from the actual boxing match in time and space, but preparation in advance is a necessary part of being a successful fighter. In the same way, there are exercises you can do to build up your commitment to help protect yourself from some of the negative aspects of stress.

Commitment is all about active involvement and engagement in your activities and the surrounding world, as well as a sense of competence and self-worth. At the opposite pole of commitment is alienation, or meaninglessness. Considering this, let's start looking at some steps to help build up hardiness-commitment.

Take Time to Think About What Is Important and Interesting to You

Most of us have busy lives. We're consumed with our daily activities—and messages on our smartphones. How often do we stop to take a breath and think about our lives? Do we really know what matters to us? Do you know what you're committed to? We all have values at some level that we base many of our decisions in life on. But to most of us, these values are rarely clearly articulated, or even in our general awareness.

Sometimes it's important to stop and take stock of ourselves. How happy are you with your life? We can break our lives down and rate ourselves in each of the following specific areas. How happy are you from 1–10 in each of these domains?

Work/school

Family/marriage

Friends

Health

Fitness

Diet

Leisure time

Hobbies

Self-development

Career

Community

Retirement

Religion/spirituality

Now go through these areas and think about how important each one is in your life. What matters to you most right now? Are you in the early stages of building your career? Do you feel you need more family time? Are you looking for a significant relationship? Is there a hobby or some other activity you really want to pursue? Are you planning to leave your current job and find something new for your next chapter? Do you need some time off to explore? Are you looking to retire from work?

Rank order these areas in the order of importance to where you are in your life right now (Figure 3.1). Look at your happiness

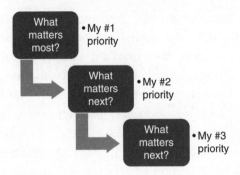

FIGURE 3.1 Setting My Priorities

score for your top three priorities. Think about where it is as compared to where you'd like it to be.

By understanding your priorities in life, you can start to better understand your values. The things that are most meaningful to you are what matter the most. Knowing your values, once you are clearer on what they are, can help you make better decisions. Also, when it comes to hardiness-commitment, people who have a strong sense of themselves, where they stand—why they support the things they do—have a stronger sense of commitment.

Being committed increases your hardiness. By knowing yourself, what you believe in, you become a stronger person. People who fail to take a stand are not sure of themselves, or are wishy-washy, and are less likely to stand up to adversity. The hardier you are, the more you are willing to stand your ground, change directions when you believe it's justified, and withstand needless criticism.

Are You Plagued by the Work/Balance Conundrum?

Joel was a busy mid-level manager in a large multinational organization. He was very conscientious and worked extremely hard. Putting in 60-hour work weeks was common for him. This left him very little time for his family, friends, and hobbies or interests. He wanted to spend more time with his kids, but the early morning and late evening meetings made it difficult.

His work soon began to suffer. Joel was stretched too thin and did not have enough resources to meet his goals. Fortunately, his supervisor recognized the problem and provided Joel with a coach to help him deal with his workload. In the process, the coach began to explore with Joel his life priorities using the categories above as well as the Hardiness Resilience Gauge. It was clear that Joel valued more leisure time with family and friends. Also, he scored low in the areas of commitment and control. At this point in his life Joel felt he had little control over his life and how he spent his time. Together, he and his coach drew up a plan that would pull back some of Joel's work commitments, better prioritize his time at work, give him more focus (and therefore more quality work), and establish more sensible work hours.

Joel's unhappiness in the areas of family, leisure, and friends, as well as their rankings on the priority scale, led to some restructuring in his life. This shift in priorities increased his commitment to what was important to him. By getting a better handle on what mattered, and committing more time to his real needs, he felt renewed in his life.

He also spent some time exploring his purpose and the degree to which he had control over the events in his life. His coach showed him how he could start booking family and leisure time on his calendar, weighing it just as important as business meeting times. Eventually he began to see changes in his life. Not only did his family and leisure time increase, but he became more relaxed. Because of these changes he became hardier. He was much better equipped to take on the challenges that came his way. When he was at work, he was better able to focus on work-related tasks. His supervisor and coworkers all noticed the change in him.

Increase Your Skills and Competence in an Area That Is Important to You

As we saw with Joel, the restructuring of his time was an important element in his improvement. As well, his counseling with a coach opened him up to changing his mindset about work and reevaluating his life. However, there was more needed to enable his transformation.

Joel needed a passion to build on. Having an activity or hobby that you love can help fill a void in your life and give you extra motivation to embrace life more fully. When we're passionate about something, we become much more committed to it. In his coaching sessions Joel recalled that he once had a passion for acting. In his high school years, he had thought about pursuing drama in college but was discouraged by his parents who thought it was not an easy career or financially sustainable.

He got the drama bug after being picked for one of the major roles in his high school play. Acting came easy to him, and he loved the rush of performing in front of an audience. He also got a lot of accolades from other cast members as well as his teachers and the audience. However, once he graduated from high school, he gave up on any further attempts at pursuing drama. He focused on college and then entered the work world with little time to spare.

However, when the idea of acting came up in his coaching sessions, he felt a twinge of excitement just at the thought of it. His coach pointed out that there were several local community theaters always putting on plays. Also, there were acting courses and workshops both at the local college and at one of the professional theaters in town. They put together a plan where Joel would enroll in an evening drama course and further develop his performing skills.

Think back about some of the passions you may have had as a child (Figure 3.2). Did you play a musical instrument? What about

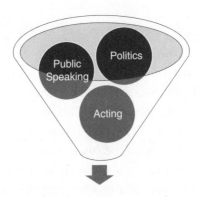

FIGURE **3.2** My Passions When I Was Young

dance, art, photography, gardening, singing, sports, programming, cooking, baking, music, writing, nature, or anything else? How did it make you feel? What did you like about it? Have you ever thought of getting back to it? Are there skills or competencies involved that you could improve?

By perusing these skills, you will find that you can have a more committed, less stressed life. It can also make you feel better about yourself and your contributions to the world. For an example of this, one of the authors (Steven) took up his childhood passion of playing the saxophone after 30 years of not playing. Not only does music and playing music give me pleasure, it allows me to use a different part of my brain from my day-to-day work. As part of my rediscovery of music, I've joined a couple of community concert bands—reliving one of my favorite high school memories, playing in the school band.

But the added benefit to this is that we play concerts in seniors' residences and veterans' hospitals. We bring live entertainment to groups of people who don't have the opportunity to leave their environment, and we provide them with memories of songs they loved from their younger days. I'm often amazed at the power of music, in this case from the big band era, to literally bring tears to people's eyes. On a number of occasions members of our audience have come up after the concert to tell stories of the times they remember dancing to the Benny Goodman or Glenn Miller bands when they came to town.

Take Pride in Your Past Successes and Achievements

Another area that came up for Joel during his coaching sessions was his dismissiveness of past accomplishments, especially at work. Joel worked at a major global organization that was known for hiring only the best people. Their recruitment process was grueling, and much of their talent came from Ivy League schools. He had achieved several awards for his performance while there. His coach asked him to write on a piece of paper a list of his accomplishments since working at the company. He had to think long and hard before he started to come up with some achievements.

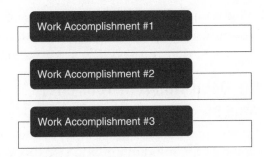

FIGURE **3.3** List of Work Accomplishments

Too often we are so busy with our day-to-day work that we seldom stop to appreciate the things we have already accomplished. Think about some of your own achievements, whether at work or beyond (Figure 3.3). How have you benefited your organization? Have you helped your coworkers in any way? Have you helped your team or organization achieve some of its goals? Do you have specific goals at work or in your personal life? Are there things you would like to accomplish by the end of the quarter, halfway through the year, at year's end, in two years? What about 5 or 10 years from now?

Having goals and stretching ourselves to achieve them helps give us a sense of accomplishment and commitment to our own selves. An important part of achieving our goals is to recognize our past successes. This is not arrogance or hubris, just an honest appreciation for things done well. Feeling good about our success helps motivate us to the next stage.

Often our accomplishments give us a sense of commitment to the greater good. When our deeds benefit others—individuals, groups, teams, organizations, the community, society, or even the world—we feel even more committed and motivated to carry on. This sense of satisfaction and accomplishment in helping others is a powerful motivating force.

Try to list on a piece of paper some of the good things that you achieved over the past year that you are proud of. If you have a significant other, sibling, or close friend, next time you see them have a conversation about some of the things you're most proud of. Tell them you want to talk about some of the things you've done over the past while. You're feeling good about them and just want to share the news.

Remember the Good Things in Your Life, and Count Your Blessings

This leads into our next area, which is to spend a bit of time remembering some of the good things you've experienced in your life. We all have fond memories of our past. However, we don't always appreciate the good things in life that we've encountered. There are many things we can be grateful for—it may be our families, our friends, our community, our country. This helps reinforce the sense that life is valuable and worthwhile—commitment. Most of us have a great deal to be thankful for in our lives. Gratitude has been found to be one of those secret pills that can have a major effect on our lives. In fact, psychologists have discovered that gratitude is a tremendously powerful and healing feeling. But it can be much more than that. It can be an effective antidote to mental health problems.

For example, in a large study that included 2,621 people, a group of psychologists at Virginia Commonwealth University looked at the role that "thankfulness" or gratitude played in protecting people from psychiatric disorders. Their subjects completed a detailed measure of lifetime risk of psychiatric and substance use disorders along with measures of their attitudes and beliefs (Kendler et al., 2003).

The researchers looked at a number of beliefs, in addition to gratitude, which included how religious the participants were, how forgiving, their tendency to be vengeful, their social life, and how much they believed in God. Of all the areas examined, one of those beliefs, the degree to which people believed in thankfulness, was the most important.

Thankfulness was significantly related to nine of the psychiatric disorders assessed. People who were more thankful about their lives had lower risks of major depression, generalized anxiety disorder, phobias, nicotine dependence, alcohol dependence, and drug abuse or dependence. In addition, the researchers found that thankfulness was related to lower rates of bulimia nervosa—a very destructive eating disorder in which people overeat and then force themselves to vomit. This result was especially interesting since it has been found that psychological interventions that increase gratitude also work to improve body image.

How can being grateful increase your resilience, mental health, and commitment to life? Being thankful takes your mind away from your daily concerns and problems. It puts the focus elsewhere and enables you to use positive emotions that can stimulate your brain. It's like putting the brakes on negative emotions, then stepping on the gas pedal of positive emotions. Positive emotions change our outlook on the world; research has found that when you are in a positive mood your view of the world becomes more open. It allows you to see more—widen your vision. And just remembering the things that you're grateful for adds to your sense that life is meaningful and worthwhile—commitment.

Positive emotions, like gratitude, stimulate various regions of the limbic system in the brain. More specifically, this stimulation leads to reduced activity in the amygdala region of the brain, whereas negative emotions are associated with increased activation in the amygdala. In addition, positive feelings have been associated with increased dopamine levels in the brain (Burgdorfa & Panksepp, 2006). So, the more gratitude you show, the more you experience these positive connections. And the more practice you have, the easier the transition from negative or neutral feelings to positive ones, so you don't get as stuck when you have negative feelings.

Experiencing these positive emotions, which enables you to become more open to the world around you, gets you more engaged and committed to your own well-being as well as to the world. Not only does this lead to feeling more confident and having higher self-worth, but it helps you find meaning in life.

So, the next time you experience something good, take some time to be grateful. It not only sends a positive message to the people around you, it's good for your mental health and builds up your hardiness-commitment.

Spend Time with Family, Friends, and People You Care About

Being around people has lots of advantages. Psychologists call it social support. Everybody is "busy" today. But just consider… what are you more likely to say before you leave this world? "I wish I spent more time at work" or "I wish I spent more time with my family and friends"?

Spending time with friends and family, especially those you have a close emotional bond with, is more than just a good thing to do. It can be good for your health. Bert Uchino, a psychologist on faculty at the University of Utah, has summarized dozens of research studies looking at the connection between social support and health. Specific links were reported between positive social support and cardiovascular, neuroendocrine, and immune functions (Uchino, Cacioppo, & Kiecolt-Glaser, 1996).

You may be wondering, how exactly can being more social have an impact on your health in these areas? And how does this enhance your hardiness? Researchers have identified two ways in which social support improves your health and hardiness. The first is that the people around you can support you in living a healthier lifestyle. They can support you in exercising, eating right, not smoking, and sticking to medical regimens when you are sick. They can do this both directly, by providing you with information and encouraging you, and indirectly, by helping you see that life is worth living and doing what it takes to live longer. Being physically healthier improves your stamina, and greater stamina increases your hardiness. You will have more physical and mental energy to deal with life's challenges. Also, by strengthening your desire to live, you are increasing your commitment to life.

The other way social support can affect your health is through a more psychological process. Interacting with family and friends directly alters the way you appraise, feel, or experience emotions. This, in effect, can give you a greater sense of control. These emotions and feelings have been found to be directly related to internal processes that can affect certain medical conditions, including cardiovascular disease and immune system functions. Once again, the positive feelings stimulate the brain, taking the focus away from problems or neutral feelings, and increasing your hardiness. The more you experience positive social relations with people you enjoy, the stronger these neural connections become.

There have been a number of studies that looked at the role of social support in helping manage cardiovascular disease. For example, it has been found that just having people you like around you can help lower your blood pressure. Social support in this case acts as a buffer from the more harmful effects of the disease. Having friends around helps create positive feelings, and these feelings in turn act as a protection against some of the negative effects of stress on your cardiovascular system.

Socializing builds commitment and hardiness: you forget about the problems at work, you play with your kids, you talk through your problems, you participate in activities you enjoy, and you improve your well-being.

So, spending more time with friends and family can be an important way for you to improve your health, increase your hardiness, and manage your stress. The benefits of social activities are often underestimated. This is an intervention that you can implement quickly and easily. And in so doing, you will be further building up your commitment levels. We are social creatures, and other people matter to us. Spending time with the people you care about strengthens your feelings of commitment to the social world and the people around you.

Pay Attention to What's Going On in the World Around You

Part of developing hardiness-commitment is being aware of and engaged in the community and world you live in. How well informed are you about things going on around you? Do you keep up with local, national, or world events? Unfortunately, we live in a time when our news organizations lead with the worst information—otherwise known as "when it bleeds it leads."

In addition, we hear so much about "fake news." With so many sources of information—TV, radio, newspapers, magazines, social media, podcasts, blogs, and other online sources—it's hard to know who or what to believe anymore. What to do?

You can be a skeptical consumer. Read or watch what you can but take most reports with a large grain of salt. Keep in mind that everyone has a point of view; there really is no neutral anymore. So, you can learn more about the events that are going on in the world, but also be less influenced by the opinions the "reporters" give about the events.

For example, you hear about a bomb going off in a crowded marketplace somewhere. Most likely, the nature of the bomb, when it occurred, the number of people injured or killed, and maybe some information about the bomber can be factual. A lot of other information, such as who's behind the bombing (the sponsors), the intended targets, the message sent by the bombing, and the intended purpose of the attack can be speculation. There are facts and opinions. Keeping up with the facts can be helpful. Being aware of the opinions can be informative.

In today's world of information overload there are two useful strategies to follow. The first is critical thinking. This involves asking questions about the story and the events around it. Which parts of the story make sense and which parts don't? Second, try to hear stories from multiple perspectives. Get a sense of what people holding different points of view say and how they interpret the story. This is where it makes sense to get your news and information from multiple outlets and to not rely on just one or two sources.

Social media conveys news almost instantaneously, and that can lead to action (commitment), not just passive receipt of knowledge. Look at the #MeToo movement. The exposé on Harvey Weinstein's behavior with young, attractive women has changed everything. Fifteen years ago, people would have heard about a story of sexual exploitation and might have forgotten about it within a week or two. But this movement is still going on because people are aware of it and have become committed to doing something about it. It has a hash tag, rallies, spokespeople; this one isn't going away soon because of women's (and many men's) commitment to eradicating sexual harassment in the workplace.

In one interesting study, a group of researchers in the Netherlands examined the different ways that watching the news affects us (Boukes & Vliegenthart, 2017). One of the things they looked at concerned some of the specific benefits of following the news. These benefits include arousing our political interest, increasing our knowledge about politics, and motivating political participation. These are basic contributions to our democratic society. Our involvement in the political process leads directly to increasing our commitment to our communities and nations. It gives us a bigger picture of things to care about that go beyond our own personal welfare.

Being a more critical consumer of news can help you be more aware as well as mentally healthier. Whether you tend to lean towards the political left or the right, use your perspective to frame the news you see. There is nothing wrong with having a perspective or point of view, just be open minded and ask questions about the reports you encounter. And by being more informed about what is going on in the world around you, you are also reinforcing your sense of engagement and commitment.

Try Out New Things

New experiences can also help shape our purpose or commitment in life. While trying new things will be discussed more in the challenges section later, we will briefly cover it here. Psychologists often refer to this as risk-taking or change management. Some risks are relatively small, like eating a food you've never tried before, and others can be large, like parachuting out of an airplane.

Another way to look at trying out new things is through your willingness to change or adapt to situations. Adaptability has many advantages in life. People who adapt or are willing to try a new approach to dealing with various situations are likely to be healthier. Changing habits, like quitting smoking or excessive alcohol consumption, are obvious examples.

A group or researchers at the University of Texas at Austin looked at the relationship between adaptability, hardiness-challenge, and symptoms of illness (Soderstrom, Dolbier, Leiferman, & Steinhardt, 2000). They surveyed 111 employees at the 3M Company in Texas who were involved in a wellness program. All these employees completed an earlier version of the Hardiness Resilience Gauge along with measures of their coping styles, perceived stress, and the degrees to which they experienced any illnesses over the previous weeks.

It turned out that their hardiness-commitment scores were significantly related to their coping styles. When it comes to coping with stress, psychologists have identified several different ways people tend to deal or cope with stress, such as trying to avoid the stress altogether. In most cases this does not help the situation.

Getting overly emotional about the stress is also usually not helpful. Or, people may try to deal with the stress head on, by using problem-solving strategies. The problem-solving approach to coping reflects someone's actual willingness to try to view problems in a positive way, come up with action strategies, and then take action. Their problem-solving scores (and likewise, their hardiness levels) were significantly related to lower stress scores and fewer symptoms of illness over the time period.

Coping directly with stress increases our commitment, leading to greater hardiness. By tackling stressful situations head on, we are more invested in getting through the stress—either fixing the situation or managing our reaction towards it better. The more we cope with stress in this way, the stronger our commitment to engaging with the world around us becomes.

As well, problem-solving coping involves coming up with and trying new strategies. People who avoid stress or use emotional coping tend to use the same old approaches over and over. Trying new strategies through problem-solving increases your flexibility and hence your hardiness.

There are many ways in which you can try out new things. Some examples are having a different breakfast, eating a new food you've never tried before, having lunch with someone new, trying a different route to work, listening to a different radio station, starting a conversation with a stranger, trying a new activity, exercise, or sport, and any other example you can come up with.

By trying new experiences, exploring the world, we discover new things in life. Some of these things may not interest us or may feel like we're wasting our time. However, occasionally, you may hit the jackpot. You may discover an experience that's really exciting. It may lead to meeting new people, immersing yourself in a new hobby, advancing your career—you never know! It's this new excitement that increases your commitment. It gives you more reasons to enjoy life and experience more of what life has to offer.

Joanne had broken up with her boyfriend, Matt. She was heartbroken over the breakup and avoided socializing with her friends. She felt sad about losing Matt, but also somewhat embarrassed about the relationship not working out. This kept her from going out with friends and possibly meeting new people.

One of her friends, Susan, got an invitation to an open house office party at an engineering firm from her friend Rob. Susan told Rob about Joanne and asked if she could bring her along. Rob mentioned that one of his colleagues, Mike, had been widowed and had also avoided socializing for some time. Perhaps they could meet.

Susan worked hard to get Joanne to come to the party. She had to beg her to come along, promising they would both leave after an hour if she was bored. Susan agreed to an early departure, if only to get Joanne out of the house. Within 15 minutes of arriving at the party, Joanne was introduced to Mike. The conversation was guarded at first, but when the subject got to favorite restaurants and food, they both became animated. They agreed to meet again and started dating.

It's now 30 years later, and Joanne and Mike are happily married with two grown children and two grandchildren. By agreeing to come to the party, Joanne was opening herself up to a new experience. By immersing herself in that experience she became more committed to the process and then to the relationship that was initiated. Her sense of commitment helped change her circumstances. It not only pulled her out of her slump, but it gave her a whole new lease on life.

In the next chapter we'll look at hardiness-challenge. We'll explore additional approaches to increase your hardiness through the challenge dimension.

Chapter 4

The Role of Hardiness-Challenge

"Variety's the very spice of life, that gives it all its flavor."
—William Cowper (English poet)

Why is it that for some people any type of change is stressful? Whether it's a disruption in their morning routine, reorganizing the items on their desk, unplanned visitors, or upgrading a computer software program. Any type of change that may require accommodation becomes almost unbearable for some. Yet, we know that change is all around us. The rate of change today is unlike ever before. Adapting to the changes in our lives has become a normal part of living. Likewise, there are events that for some people create a lot of anxiety, but for others seem quite exciting and even fun.

As well, there are many people who find life is full of challenges. They like the idea of trying new things, taking risks, or even sensation-seeking. They willingly seek out opportunities and rise to the challenge. Sometimes we are presented with challenging situations that land on our doorstep unexpectedly. How is it that some people successfully confront the challenges they encounter and just keep on moving with life? It's as if they fall down, get right back up, dust themselves off, and continue walking.

When we talk about the challenge mindset in hardiness terms, we mean having the expectation that life is unpredictable and that changes will enhance our personal development. We see demanding situations as exciting and stimulating rather than threatening, enabling us to feel good about life's ups and downs. People high in challenge believe that growth improves their lives through learning rather than by easy comfort and security.

A Tale of Two Accountants

Marlon struggled while preparing for his accounting exam. He always did well in math classes and didn't find any of the concepts hard to understand. He knew that 50% of accounting candidates fail every year. He worried that, through no fault of his own, he might end up in the lower half of the bell curve. After all, there were many people smarter than he was, and there was nothing he could do about it.

He was also stressed out about the process. Just the thought of going into the exam room, the proctor signaling to begin, made him queasy in his stomach. Exams always worried Marlon. He managed to do well in all his courses, but the very idea of sitting in the room, timers activated, made him anxious. He always feared the worst. Of course, there would surely be some tough questions that stumped him, threw him off balance.

Then there was the subject matter itself. Marlon enjoyed math, but accounting principles weren't all that interesting to him. He was mildly interested in business but never got excited about balance sheets and profit/loss statements. In fact, Marlon had a hard time getting excited about most things in life.

His friend Murray, on the other hand, was looking forward to the upcoming exam. He also did well in math, though he had to work harder than Marlon to get the same grade. Murray knew that his performance was directly related to the amount of work he put in. When he worked really hard, his grades went up, and when he slacked off, his marks suffered.

There was something about exams that got Murray excited. He loved the challenge of testing himself and his knowledge. It was like preparing for a boxing match and strategizing on how it would all play out. He imagined himself working through both the easy and the really tough questions. He couldn't wait to see what they would throw at him. Bring it on!

Murray didn't start out liking accounting. In fact, he knew very little about it at first. But the more he delved into it, the more it appealed to him. He kept thinking of questions related to each new concept he read about. His curiosity pushed him on, motivating him to keep learning more.

Both Marlon and Murray ended up passing their accounting exams. But, although they started out in the same place in their careers, their lives went in very different directions. Marlon went on to work as an accountant in a large firm. He worked on tax returns and did pretty much the same work for the next 30 years. Murray, on the other hand, did a brief stint as an accountant but soon got bored and wanted something more.

Murray noticed, while doing the books for a home builder, that they were doing some pretty interesting, and lucrative, work. He soon changed directions and went into home building himself. He eventually went on to develop land and build large condominiums. While Marlon continued filing tax returns for clients at an accounting firm, Murray went on to be a multimillionaire with his own successful development company.

Marlon was afraid of change. He felt more comfortable doing the day-to-day tasks of an accountant and having a steady job. Murray loved change and challenge. When he saw an opportunity, he had no trouble taking the risk and moving on to something new. In fact, Murray scores high on the hardiness-challenge scale while Marlon scores much lower.

How Challenge Prepares You for Change

When Marlon and Murray encountered the exact same situation—their accounting exam—they reacted in different ways. How can we understand the difference between challenge and threat when we encounter what could be a stressful situation? As we mentioned in the first chapter, people high in hardiness have a strong sense of **challenge**: they enjoy variety and tend to see change and disruptions in life as interesting opportunities to learn and grow. They understand that problems are a part of life, and they set out to solve them rather than run away from them. For these people—people like Murray—taking on new challenges is an interesting way to learn about themselves and their own capabilities, while also learning about the world. Murray has a high hardiness-challenge score.

In contrast, those who are low in challenge prefer stability and predictability in their lives and tend to avoid new and changing situations. They may be highly reliable but are not very adaptable when conditions change; Marlon would be low in hardiness-challenge.

Sometimes even small changes in your life can be helpful. Breaking habits and trying new behaviors can actually help you develop new connections in your brain. Here are just a few things you can try to increase your sense of challenge:

- Have a different breakfast from your usual once or twice a week.
- Try taking a new route to work occasionally.
- Try exercising a few times a week, or if you already exercise, change up your routine.
- Try eating foods you've never had before.
- Talk to strangers.
- Learn a new game or sport.
- Have lunch with someone you haven't lunched with before.

Understanding Your Mindset

There's another aspect that differentiates Marlon and Murray. Marlon believed his intelligence was set. Solutions to problems in math always came easily to him. He felt that you either knew the answers or you didn't. Dumber people had to work harder to learn the concepts. His focus was always on whether he got it right or wrong, which of course was a measure of how smart he was.

Murray, on the other hand, was not a natural. He had to work hard at math. He believed if he persisted enough, he would solve the problem. But he learned from his mistakes. If a solution wasn't working, he would eventually move on and try another approach. He didn't measure himself by his achievements the way Marlon did. He enjoyed the process of learning—it was more about the journey, not just the destination. He was inquisitive and asked questions.

Marlon and Murray represent two sides of what Stanford University psychologist Carol Dweck identified as mindsets (Dweck, 2016). Dweck first identified this concept when giving 10-year-old children puzzles, starting with easy ones and working up to much more difficult ones. She was interested in how children coped with challenges beyond their ability. While many of the children were frustrated and gave up, she was surprised to find a few children who were excited by the challenge. In fact, rather than being discouraged, they asked for more challenging puzzles to work on.

This started Dweck on a research journey that led to a redefining of ability. On the one hand, there are people who believe that ability is fixed and that one approaches the world basically confirming their limited aptitude. On the other hand, there are those who believe their abilities are changeable and that they can be continuously developed through learning. It's through these changeable or fixed mindsets that people grow and achieve great things, or basically stay the same, believing there are limits to what they can achieve.

What is your mindset? How do you approach the world? Which of these statements apply to you?

1. I'm either good at something or I'm not.
2. I don't like to be challenged.
3. When I'm frustrated, I usually give up.
4. I can either do something I try, or I can't.
5. I stick to what I know.
6. Failure is an opportunity to grow.
7. I can learn to do anything I want.
8. I like to try new things.
9. My effort and my attitude determine my abilities.
10. Feedback is constructive.

If you agreed with more of the first five statements, you tend towards a fixed mindset. If you agreed with more of the second five statements, you have more of a growth mindset. The growth mindset is closely related to hardiness-challenge.

Our research has found that each of the three Cs of hardiness is related to mindset. The higher one's hardiness, the more one operates from a growth, as opposed to fixed mindset. As we'll explore later in this chapter, of the hardiness three Cs, hardiness-challenge has the strongest relationship with mindset. So, people higher in hardiness-challenge have a stronger growth mindset.

Expanding the Mindset Concept Beyond Abilities

While Dweck's work on mindsets has primarily focused on intelligence, abilities, or aptitudes, there has been some recent work looking at the role of mindsets in how people manage stress. Psychologists at Yale University carried out an innovative set of studies looking at the role of mindsets in people's reactions to stress. They start out by discussing the almost epidemic levels of stress in our society today. They cite studies linking stress to the six leading causes of death—heart disease, accidents, cancer, liver disease, lung ailments, and suicide, as well as the links to absenteeism, medical expenses, loss of productivity, mental illness, aggression, and relationship conflicts. In fact, they make the point that all this focus on stress—the "stress about stress"—may in fact be part of a mindset that itself contributes to its negative impact (Crum, Salovey, & Achor, 2013).

So, what do we mean by a stress mindset? The authors liken it to Dweck's formulation of a fixed mindset and a growth mindset. Somebody who believes that stress can have a positive influence, perhaps by enhancing performance and productivity, health and well-being, and learning and growth, has a "stress-is-enhancing" mindset. On the other hand, someone who believes stress is incapacitating has a "stress-is-debilitating" mindset.

The idea here is that these different "mindsets," which are deep convictions or beliefs, come into play regardless of the amount or severity of the stress, or even how you may cope with that stress. We already know some of the potential negative effects from stress. However, there are a number of documented effects of the *stress-is-enhancing* mindset. These include the following reactions:

Bodily threats: Physiological arousal is raised, and attention is narrowed, leading the person to focus resources on dealing with the task at hand.

At work: Stress at work leads to initiative-taking, by which employees act to acquire the necessary skills needed to meet pressing demands.

Motivation: Anticipating and planning for all possible situational outcomes leads to proactive problem-solving.

Memory and cognitive tasks: Hormones released in the stress response can boost memory and performance on cognitive tasks.

Physiological thriving: Stimulating the body to produce the hormones and other active ingredients that help your body recover from disease and injury and keep you healthy by immunizing you from unhealthy agents.

Body strength: Stress elicits anabolic hormones that rebuild cells, synthesize proteins, and enhance immunity, leaving the body stronger and healthier than it was prior to the stressful experience.

Stress-related growth: Stress can enhance the development of mental toughness, heightened awareness, new perspectives, a sense of mastery, strengthened priorities, deeper relationships, greater appreciation for life, and an increased sense of meaningfulness.

Think of some of your own reactions to new experiences, especially ones that might be threatening. Can you recall being excited, looking forward to the experience? Or were you more worried, wondering about what might go wrong? If you can recall an experience where you felt more worried than challenged, try to re-create that image in your mind. As you think about the experience, try to change your feeling to one of excitement, wonder, and curiosity. Creating a hardiness-challenge mindset involves learning to look at situations differently—changing both your feelings and thoughts about the event.

The stress-is-enhancing mindset helps reinforce your hardiness. This is where the working out in the gym analogy comes into play. All these responses become stronger, become more habitual the more you experience them. Like building your muscles, you build your body's hormonal responses, your motivation, your ability to calmly come up with solutions or actions, and body strength. In addition, as your experience grows, you learn to deal more with the situation at hand and spend less time worrying about what to do. It's the unpleasantness of the experience (such as the worrying) that makes you want to avoid the situation rather than confront it. By confronting new situations more, building hardiness-challenge, you become more confident and more capable. The stress-is-enhancing mindset enables you to embrace change and not mind when changes arise, like Murray the accounting student.

Psychologists and other practitioners have spent decades working on and evaluating various methods of managing and trying to reduce stress. These techniques have largely focused on developing various coping strategies, relaxation processes, such as meditation and mindfulness, and other avoidance mechanisms. Despite all this effort, one of the premier journals of the American Psychological Association, the *American Psychologist*, in 2000 devoted an entire issue to the lack of progress in this area. They concluded, "The explosion of interest in coping has yielded little, and the field is in crisis" (Somerfield & McCrae, 2000).

Why Traditional Coping Methods Don't Always Work

As mentioned above, there are now a number of coping methods for managing stress that are widely practiced. These include meditation, mindfulness, relaxation therapy, cognitive behavioral approaches, and even avoidance techniques. Alia Crum, Peter

Salovey, and Shawn Achor, research psychologists at Yale, proposed three reasons why traditional coping strategies haven't yielded significant results (Crum, Salovey & Achor, 2013). First, they report that it can be difficult and even counterproductive to try and reduce stress. People may not have the capacity to reduce the stressors in their lives. For example, being told you're losing your job is an event that is often beyond your control. Losing your job can lead directly to financial hardships that compound the effects of the original stressor.

Second, the different coping procedures can be complicated, they often vary, and sometimes they can create even more stress. It may be useful to problem-solve your way out of controllable stressful events, but it may be more harmful when dealing with uncontrollable events or when there is no problem to solve, for example, the loss of a loved one or surviving a natural disaster. There may not be a problem to solve, but there may be a need for a period of mourning or recovery to occur. Even not knowing which stress management technique to use can be a source of stress. Some people are anxious about being anxious and not knowing which of the many potential solutions would be right for them.

Third, most traditional approaches to reducing stress operate from a *stress-is-debilitating* mindset. The mindset you adopt when approaching a stressful situation can affect your reaction to it and your success in dealing with it. This is seen as completely different from the process of appraising a stressful event. When you appraise a particular stressful event, you evaluate whether it is more or less stressful. When you use a stress mindset, you are determining whether the *nature of stress itself* is more or less enhancing or debilitating.

This was illustrated in an interesting study carried out at Harvard University (Jamieson, Nock, & Mendes, 2012). Students were assigned to one of three groups, before being given a stressful task. One group was the *reappraisal* group—they were told that increased arousal, through faster heart rate, butterflies in your stomach, and so on, was actually a good sign before a stressful situation. These experiences signal that you are excited about what's to come and your body is getting you ready for the challenge. Basically, they were given a *positive stress mindset* (or what we refer to as a *hardiness mindset)*—in this case, preparing students to use a positive interpretation of their feelings. The second group was the *ignore physical cues* group—they were told to not think about anything before the event, just stare ahead at an X on the wall. The third group, *no intervention control*, were not given any instructions.

All subjects were then given a test measuring their attention before they were assigned the task of making a five-minute videotaped speech in front of two very critical evaluators. After the speech they were asked to perform a mathematical task. They reported on their feelings, and they were monitored for their physiological responses.

The students who were asked to "rethink" their arousal as a good thing had a lower heart rate during the task and performed better on their tests. Changing your mindset, how you think about your *reactions* to stress, can help you better manage the stressful situation.

Examining the "Work of Worrying" Theory

When one of the authors (Steven) was a graduate student in psychology in the mid-1970s, a new approach to therapy was in its beginning stages. It was called cognitive-behavior therapy. The idea, which was pretty revolutionary back then, was that we could manage the challenges in our lives through changing the way we think about them. It involved understanding the connections between thinking, feelings, and behaviors. Cognitive-behavior therapy is one of the most widely practiced therapies today.

There were two popular theories around coping with stress at the time. One, by Irving Janis, stated that the best way to deal with a stressful situation was to increase your anxiety just before the stressful event. He referred to this as the "work of worrying" and reported that people who worried about an event in advance, such as your upcoming root canal surgery, would cope better and be less worried during the actual event.

Another new theory at the time was from Donald Meichenbaum, one of the founders of cognitive-behavior therapy (Meichenbaum, 1975). He proposed a process called "stress inoculation" training. Thinking of stress like a disease, if you inoculated yourself in advance with a number of helpful thoughts, you would be better able to cope with the actual stressful situation when it came.

So, before my root canal surgery, I would prepare and think about what to say to myself before the surgery, during the surgery, and after the surgery. I would think thoughts such as, "I know this will hurt, but I can handle it," and "I've been through worse than this before."

For my master's thesis I looked at how these theories would play out in a stressful situation. I used a video called "It Didn't Have to Happen" which was a work accident prevention video. In the clip that I used, a man working a circular saw slipped and cut off his finger, with blood spurting out all over the place. It was pretty gruesome, even in black and white. I chose to use female subjects in the study since women were shown to react more strongly to the scary scene than men (Girodo & Stein, 1978; Stein, 1976).

I prepared one group of 10 female subjects for the film they were about to see. They were given a detailed description about what was coming, along with a series of 16 coping self-statements that they practiced before the video. I measured their self-reports of anxiety when they arrived at the lab, after they were told about the film and given the coping strategies, after a 10-minute wait period before the film, and immediately after the film. In addition, I hooked them up to heart rate monitoring equipment and monitored their heart rates from the time the treatment was given, throughout the waiting period, and while they were watching the film. After the film, they completed questionnaires about the content of the film to ensure they had paid attention to it.

Immediately after the film description and self-talk training, their anxiety did not increase. However, their anxiety increased during the waiting period, while preparing for the stressor—their "work of worrying." The heart rate of this group also increased significantly while waiting. During the film itself this group reported no increase in anxiety. In other words, their preparation and worrying before the stressful film kept them calmer during the film.

There were two control groups in this study. One group was given the information that they would be watching a gruesome film but not given any strategies to prepare for it. Their anxiety went up significantly after hearing the film description. Their anxiety then went down during the wait period but spiked up while watching the film. A second control group was given no information about the film in advance. Not knowing what to expect, their anxiety remained low until they watched the film, at which point their anxiety increased significantly, just as you would expect.

At this point the results seemed pretty clear. By giving the first group a set of cognitive strategies to prepare for the stressful film, they increased their anxiety during preparation, then decreased their anxiety while actually confronting the stressor or watching the film. This helped support the blossoming field of cognitive-behavior therapy and influenced my interest in stress management and what we now call hardiness. This finding should have been pretty easy to defend in front of my austere thesis committee.

However, there was a wrinkle. I had a fourth group. They were given the same information about the film they were going to see as the first group, then given a number of what we called "denial" or "intellectualization" strategies. These were statements like "but it's just a movie," and "it's not real, it's fake." This group's heart rate did increase somewhat during the wait period, but they reported little anxiety before or during the film.

How would I explain this group to the thesis committee? They didn't go through the increase in self-reported anxiety that the stress inoculation group went through, yet they sailed through the stressful film. Well, one explanation could be that the increased heart rate represented their "work of worrying" and enabled them to manage their stress during the film.

The good news is that I passed my oral thesis examination and went on to complete my doctorate in clinical psychology. However, perhaps now, almost 45 years later, I may have an alternate explanation for these results.

The "intellectualization" strategy used with the fourth group may have changed their *stress mindset*. While it may not have been *stress-enhancing*, it likely neutralized any stress experienced by approaching the situation with a completely different mindset—different from the first group and both control groups. By having the belief that this film was fake, they were not affected by the blood shooting out of the actor's hand. One subject even joked that it looked more like ketchup. This is what we're now referring to as the *hardiness mindset*.

So, the "work of worrying" seen in the light of what we now know about the *stress mindset* and the *hardiness mindset*, can be much better understood today. It's not the "worrying" itself that's important, it's what you tell yourself about the worrying. If you get worried about the physiological worrying response—"Oh my God, how am I ever going to be able to deal with this!!!"—you will do poorly. If you interpret the worry differently—"Oh, this is so exciting. I can't wait to get started with this!"—you will do much better. This is the hardiness-challenge approach to stressful situations, or part of the *hardiness mindset*.

You can use this as an experiment you might want to try when going to see your next horror film. Just tell yourself it's only a movie. The only downside is that you might not get the excitement of the emotional experience of the film.

Stress Mindset Versus Hardiness–Challenge

The Yale University researchers we previously cited found that their *stress mindset* measure was related to overall hardiness, although it was also seen as somewhat distinct. We looked at the relationship between a short stress mindset measure we developed and the Hardiness Resilience Gauge. The mindset scale included statements such as, "There are benefits to experiencing stress," and "Experiencing stress in a situation can enhance my performance." Participants rated these statements as to how much they agreed with them.

In the study we carried out, we tested 270 working adults with both measures along with questions about their current work performance. There was a significant relationship between stress mindset and hardiness-challenge, with about a 20% overlap.

We asked these people how successful they felt they were at work as well as how engaged they were at work. We found that while 90% of people felt they were successful and engaged, about 10% were unsure or unsuccessful. We combined these two items into a "work performance" score. We know that just saying you are successful at work doesn't guarantee that you are, but we are fairly confident that people who tell you they are not successful are likely being honest about it.

Our measure of stress mindset accounted for about 4% of work performance. In other words, of all the factors that influence work performance, such as the nature of the work, the workplace itself, your coworkers, and so on, your stress mindset can account for about 4% of your performance at work. Our measure of hardiness-challenge accounted for about 10% of work performance. Interestingly, hardiness-commitment related the most, accounting for about 25% of work performance.

This is really important for workplace productivity. If you can change or improve your hardiness—both commitment and challenge, you can improve your work performance by up to 25% or more, which is substantial. In fact, what was really interesting about the Yale study was how they were able to demonstrate that you can change your stress mindset.

How Can We Change Mindsets?

Earlier work by Dweck and her associates demonstrated that after an eight-week course, people were able to change their mindsets from fixed to growth or malleable on the intelligence mindset (Chiu, Hong, & Dweck, 1997; Dweck, 2008). However, the course was long and fairly labor intensive.

This time frame was later shortened and automated. In a study by Joshua Aronson and colleagues at New York University (Aronson, Fried, & Good, 2002), the researchers created a short video that promoted either a fixed or malleable mindset and presented it to participants. It was found that they could change the viewers' mindsets in a relatively short time period—just after viewing the video.

In the Yale study they looked at using short videos to see if they could change the mindsets of working people about stress. The study was carried out at a large financial services organization. Researchers created three short videos for each of the experimental groups. Each of the videos presented images, research, and examples that would demonstrate the desired message.

The first group's videos were designed to show a *stress-is-enhancing* mindset, presenting the positive effects of stress in three domains: health, performance, and learning/growth. The second group's videos focused on the same areas but presented a *stress-is-debilitating* mindset. The three videos were watched by subjects within a one-week period. The first group watched the *stress-is-enhancing* videos, and the second group watched the *stress-is-debilitating* videos. There was a third group, a control group, that didn't watch any of the videos, but had the same pretests and posttests.

Here are some examples of the messages they received:

Stress-is-debilitating	**Stress-is-enhancing**
Even small stress can hinder performance.	Stress can fuel peak performance.
Stress can hijack your rational mind and cause you to think less clearly.	Stress can increase energy and heighten alertness.
Stress can deteriorate your focus.	Stress can enhance your focus.

As expected, subjects in the *stress-is-enhancing* condition developed a more enhanced mindset as was presented in the video clips they watched. Those people exposed to the video clips showing *stress-as-debilitating* developed a more *stress-is-debilitating* mindset. There was no change in mindset of the control group.

Next, the researchers followed up with the subjects at work and monitored their moods and performance. The subjects in the *stress-is-enhancing* condition reported fewer psychological symptoms and better work performance. The subjects in the *stress-is-debilitating* condition and control group showed no changes in symptoms or work performance. The reason given for no detriment in the *stress-is-debilitating* group is that this was most likely the most predominant or pre-existing mindset in this group as it likely is for most people. So, if they started out believing stress was bad, they basically continued thinking along the same lines after the study was over.

Physiological Differences as a Result of Your Mindset

One final part of the research at Yale looked at the relationship between mindset and a physiological measure while under stress. A sample of students at Yale were assessed for their mindset, and on a later date exposed to a stressful situation. They were told that five of them would be randomly selected to give a speech in front of their class. Not only that, but the speech would be videotaped and then evaluated by a group of experts from the business school. And, by the way, they would only have a very brief period of time to prepare their speech.

When we are stressed our physiological stress response involves activation of our fight or flight response. This includes heightened sympathetic nervous system (SNS) activity, a parasympathetic withdrawal, and increased activity of our hypothalamic-pituitary-adrenal (HPA) axis. This fight or flight response, which is initiated through the secretion of cortisol, acts as an adaptive defensive mechanism to life-threatening situations. Cortisol is a hormone that has a number of effects in your body. It can help control sugar levels, regulating your metabolism, acts as an anti-inflammatory, can improve your memory, controls your salt and water balance, and is generally known for being activated when your body responds to stressful situations.

In this study saliva samples were taken from the students over several periods of time to gauge their levels of cortisol. Here's where the results get interesting. The students with a *stress-is-enhancing* mindset showed a positive cortisol profile when they were under the acute stress condition of possibly being selected to give a speech. That is, they had just the right amount of the hormone to ready their body for action. Having too much or too little cortisol can cause your body to react badly in a stressful situation—for example, too much cortisol interferes with your learning and memory and is generally bad for your body.

The researchers reported the following, "For individuals with high cortisol reactivity to stress, having a stress-is-enhancing mindset lowered the cortisol response, whereas for those who had low cortisol reactivity to stress, having a stress-is-enhancing mindset increased the cortisol response." So, it's possible that developing a hardiness-challenge mindset can not only help you deal with stress better but can have physiological benefits for you as well.

You can enhance both your mental and physical health with a hardiness mindset. In the same way that you build up your psychological muscles over time with practice, you can also see that you can change your hormonal response to stress. With a hardiness mindset, over time, you can react better to stressful situations both psychologically and physiologically.

Hardiness–Challenge and Madonna

Hardiness-challenge involves an appreciation for variety and change, and a desire to learn and grow by trying out new things. There are many examples of people who are high in their striving for change. In some industries, the ability to change can be a form of survival. This is not uncommon in the entertainment industry.

Madonna Louise Ciccone, more commonly known as Madonna, has sold more than 300 million records worldwide and is listed as the best-selling female recording artist of all time in the Guinness Book of World Records. According to the Recording Industry Association of America (RIAA), she is the second highest-certified female artist in the US, with 64.5 million album units. *Billboard,* known for its music charts, reports that Madonna is the most successful solo artist in its Hot 100 chart history (Bronson, 2002). She is also the highest-grossing solo touring artist of all time, accumulating US $1.4 billion from her concert tickets (Pietrolungo, 2009).

But life wasn't always rosy for Madonna. Her mother died of breast cancer at the age of 30, when Madonna was only five years old. Later on, when her father remarried, it created a great strain in her relationship with him. Madonna was a straight A student in school. While she was given music lessons at an early age, she gravitated more towards dance.

She experienced another major trauma while working as a backup dancer in New York. One night, on the way home from a dance rehearsal, a pair of men held her at knifepoint and raped her. This incident profoundly affected her, and she felt it showed "a taste of my weakness, it showed me that I still could not save myself in spite of all the strong-girl show. I could never forget it" (O'Brien, 2007).

There have been many opinions on Madonna's career and the factors that have led to her success. There's general agreement among the pundits about some aspects of her career, including that the cause of her success is "certainly not outstanding natural talent. As a vocalist, musician, dancer, songwriter, or actress, Madonna's talents seem modest" (Grant, 2005).

Robert Grant, who tracked her career, goes on to point out that she strayed far from the music industry wisdom of "find a winning formula and stick to it." Rather, her musical career has been a continuous experimentation with new musical ideas and new images and a constant quest for new heights of fame and acclaim. Grant concluded that "having established herself as the queen of popular music, Madonna did not stop there, but continued re-inventing."

By taking up the challenge through change, during both tough times and prosperous times, Madonna has been able to overcome the obstacles and stay relevant. How often have we thought about reinventing ourselves in some way? What about small, piecemeal changes that might lead to some future benefit? Also, what about our ability to take risks? Sometimes we have to get out of our comfort zones to make the best of our lives. Hardiness-challenge is not easy, especially making the right changes at the right time. In the next chapter we'll explore how we can build our hardiness-challenge mindset.

Chapter 5

Building a Challenge Mindset

"Our very survival depends on our ability to stay awake, to adjust to new ideas, to remain vigilant and to face the challenge of change."
—Martin Luther King Jr. (American Baptist minister and civil rights activist)

How you think about stress matters enormously in terms of how you process it. Some people see stress as a threat, while others are able to view it as a challenge. With a challenge response, you get additional energy, your heart rate rises, and your adrenaline goes up, but it differs in a few important ways from fight or flight:

- You feel focused instead of fearful.
- You release a different ratio of stress hormones.
- You are more easily able to access your mental and physical resources.

The result is enhanced concentration, confidence, and peak performance. In fact, people who are able to think about stress more like a challenge and less like a threat report lower depression and anxiety, higher levels of energy, better work performance, and increased life satisfaction. Hardiness-challenge is a positive perspective on change and variety in life. People high in challenge tend to take changes in stride, see variety as part of the richness of life, and are optimistic about the future.

On the opposite pole, people low in challenge are always seeking security, want everything to be simple and predictable, and are fearful of the future. Considering this, this chapter lays out steps you can take to help you build your hardiness-challenge.

Changes Are Always an Opportunity to Learn and Get Better

It's sometimes hard to believe the number of famous people who went through serious hardships before they became successful in our eyes. We all have setbacks growing up, and some of us deal with them better than others. Here are a few success stories that you may not have been aware of.

LEARNING FROM REJECTION

Steven Spielberg, the award-winning director of *Jaws, E.T., Jurassic Park,* and *Schindler's List,* among other films, did not always have it easy in life. He suffered from acts of anti-Semitic prejudice and bullying: "In high school, I got smacked and kicked around. Two bloody noses. It was horrible" (Weinraub, 1993).

In addition, Spielberg was rejected by the University of Southern California (USC) film school twice. However, he made up for it later in life. They awarded him an honorary degree in 1994. Two years later he became a trustee of the university (Fischer, 2000).

For many people rejection feels like the end of the road. You can be rejected along the way to achieving your goals, but it's not necessarily the end of your dreams. People high in hardiness-challenge treat these kinds of rejections as a yield sign on the road. They take an honest look at their situation and chart a new pathway. Using challenge, they are not afraid to push on and try a different direction.

BELIEVING IN YOURSELF

Vincent van Gogh is considered one of the greatest and most influential artists of all time by many art experts. He struggled with mental illness and poverty throughout most of his life. He sold only one painting during his lifetime. With little or no validation of the quality of his work, he still managed to paint more than

900 pieces of art (McQuillan, 1989). He was incredibly persistent in spite of the fact that he had no real external confirmation of his talent.

Many of us feel we need external validation of our worth and abilities. People high in hardiness-challenge believe in themselves and can continue striving towards their goals no matter what others think or say. However, unlike grit—which is the unwavering pursuit of a goal, regardless of the reality of achieving it—people high in hardiness-challenge will objectively evaluate whether the track they are on is worthwhile. For van Gogh he was willing to accept the challenge of constantly creating new pieces of art without regard for how others evaluated his work.

PERSEVERING IN THE FACE OF HARDSHIPS

Franklin Roosevelt, while visiting Campobello Park, in New Brunswick, Canada in 1921 began to feel ill. It's unclear to this day whether he contracted poliomyelitis or Guillain-Barré Syndrome, an autoimmune disease. He eventually became paralyzed from the waist down. In spite of his debilitating illness he chose to continue his political career. He ran for and became governor of the state of New York and then went on to become president of the United States. He managed to be remembered as one of the most respected and memorable US presidents (Goldman & Goldman, 2017; Ward & Burns, 2014).

Even though his physical health was in decline, Roosevelt was determined to carry on in politics and successfully won the country's highest office. It takes a great amount of hardiness-challenge to continue moving forward with your life and career in spite of major physical challenges. Physical hardships can be devastating, but it's really our decision as to whether we can motivate ourselves to continue meeting our life objectives. Politics is full of challenges, and Roosevelt never shied away from meeting them head on. Not even his own physical limitations could stop his challenge mindset.

OVERCOMING NEGATIVE CIRCUMSTANCES

Oprah Winfrey is one of the most successful and richest people in the world today. She is also among the most admired women in

America (possibly in the world). Oprah is a successful entrepreneur and reportedly has a net worth of $2.9 billion (Forbes, 2014). But she didn't grow up privileged. Far from it.

She was born in poverty in rural Mississippi and was raised by a teenaged single mother. She later moved to inner-city Milwaukee, Wisconsin. She reported that she was sexually molested during her childhood and teenage years and became pregnant at 14 years of age. Her son was born prematurely and died during infancy.

Fortunately, Oprah had strong inner resources. She excelled as an honors student in high school. She won an oratory contest which landed her a scholarship to college (Mowbray, 2003; Morgan, 1986). And clearly, she had a strong sense of hardiness-challenge that enabled her to overcome many of the obstacles in her life.

■ ■ ■

We encounter many people who come from difficult backgrounds and who have lived through terrible experiences. Some of these people choose to stay within their life circumstances, giving up any hope of bettering themselves or their situation. Sometimes it's easier to remain a victim of circumstances. Other people we know were determined to break out and change their lives for the better. These people are the heroes, and by no means is that an easy task.

Think of it as one of those old-fashioned vinyl records that are coming back into fashion. Imagine yourself as the needle playing in the grooves. It's as though you get stuck in one of those grooves and continue to play the same musical phrase repeatedly. Perhaps, eventually, the needle decides to move forward, by jumping over the grooves to play a new song. It's not easy to jump out of the groove, but for some people it's even harder to play the same old song over and over again.

You are not a victim of your circumstances. You have the power to change the direction of your life. Having a high challenge mindset enables you to see beyond your current circumstances and is a step towards finding a better life.

ACCEPTING HELP FROM OTHERS

Stephen King is a very successful novelist. As authors, we can only dream of selling a fraction of the number of books that he has. His books have reportedly sold over 350 million copies. He has written bestsellers such as *Carrie, Misery, Dreamcatcher,* and *The Shining.* King has won dozens of awards for his writing. Many of his books have become award-winning movies, such as *The Shining, Stand By Me, The Shawshank Redemption, It,* and *The Mist.*

As I'm sure you can guess by now, it didn't all come easily to Stephen King. His first novel, *Carrie,* was rejected 30 times. It appeared that no major publishing houses were interested in his work. He reports that at one point early on he simply gave up and threw the incomplete draft of *Carrie* into the trash can. His wife, Tabitha, fortunately retrieved the manuscript and urged King to complete it, even offering to help him with the female perspective (King, 1991).

Carrying on when the world seems to be against you can be a difficult and lonely feat. Fortunately for King, he had the support of his wife. Hardiness-challenge is not a natural trait for everyone. Social support can be extremely useful in giving us that extra push that we may need to get over a hump or setback. By encouraging Stephen and assisting in forging a new direction, Tabitha was able to help him launch a highly successful career.

Think about your own challenges and the social support you have. Are there people in your life whom you trust and you feel close to who can offer you encouragement?

CHANGING DIRECTIONS

Christina Aguilera is a singer, songwriter, actress, and television personality. She has won five Grammy Awards and sold more than 75 million records worldwide, making her one of the world's best-selling music artists. *Billboard* recognized her as the 20th most successful artist of the 2000s. Life wasn't easy for Christina growing up. She was born in Staten Island, New York, and moved frequently while growing up because her father was in the military. Both Aguilera and her mother have reported that her father was physically and emotionally abusive towards them. Her parents divorced when she was six years old. She left her high school early to be homeschooled because she was being bullied (Bollinger & O'Neill, 2008).

She reported that she used music as a form of escape from her troubles at home and school (Hirschberg, 2011). Sometimes, when we're in a stressful environment and there's no way out, we can shift directions. Instead of ruminating about how bad her world was at the time, Christina was able to change gears and focus her attention on music. Challenge involves looking for new directions and getting out of the rut you're in. Christina's passion allowed her to rise above the reality of her life circumstances and move forward in a completely different direction.

Just Keep Going

What does it take to escape the unpleasant realities of life and keep going in a totally different direction? Another entertainer who experienced a difficult childhood was Stefani Joanne Angelina Germanotta, better known as Lady Gaga. To date she has sold 27 million albums and 146 million singles. She ranks among the best-selling musical artists in history. Her achievements include several Guinness World Records, nine Grammy Awards, an Academy Award, three Brit Awards, and an award from the Songwriters Hall of Fame.

Although her family was well off (her father came from a working-class background and became a successful internet entrepreneur), she did not always fit in at school. She considered herself a misfit and was mocked for "being either too provocative or too eccentric" (Tracy, 2013).

Gaga reported that in 2014 she had been raped at age 19, for which she underwent mental and physical therapy. She says that she has post-traumatic stress disorder which she attributes to the incident. She has publicly stated that the support she received from doctors, family, and friends has helped her (BBC, 2016).

In 2019 she won an Oscar for best original song, "Shallow," which was in the movie "A Star Is Born" in which she starred. During her acceptance speech she said, "This is hard work. I've worked hard for a long time. It's not about winning. But what it's about is not giving up. If you have a dream, fight for it. There's a discipline for passion, and it's not about how many times you get rejected or you fall down, or you're beaten up. It's about how many times you stand up and are brave, and you keep on going."

Lady Gaga illustrates the power of hardiness-challenge. Once again, the ability to stand up to obstacles and continue with your life is a key component.

Do Not Live Every Day by a Rigid Schedule

How do you start your day? How much of your day is planned out? Do you allow for flex time in your schedule?

We all have schedules in our lives, and these are necessary and useful. We have our favorite routines and activities, and places we like to go. This makes sense and gives us a sense of control over things. But over-relying on schedules and routines can lead to a kind of mental rigidity that can be counterproductive. In an environment that changes a lot, we need to be flexible and willing to try new things in order to adapt successfully.

In the early days of NASA, astronauts all came from the military test pilot community. They were mainly engineers, men who had learned how to do things precisely and follow the rules. The original astronauts had their schedules and activities tightly controlled from the ground, with little opportunity for variation. They needed to be technically competent and able to carefully follow instructions from mission control.

Today, NASA approaches astronaut selection and training very differently. Future missions to faraway places like Mars will require astronauts who can function more independently, with the mental flexibility to adapt quickly to novel and surprising situations. These kinds of people prefer variety and have trouble with daily schedules that are too rigid, so NASA is developing procedures to allow astronaut crews greater variety and control over their work schedules and routines (Bartone et al., 2017).

Back on earth, daily schedules that are too fixed can hamper your creativity and adaptability. Build your sense of challenge by allowing yourself the freedom to do things differently from time to time.

Be Willing to Change Your Plans to Meet Changing Conditions

Today's world is all about change. Yet, for some people change is difficult. Some changes are relatively small, like using a different toothpaste. Other changes can be rather large, like changing your career, your job, or even your home. How you handle change may be dependent on the nature of the change, as well as on your personality characteristics or mindset.

Think about some of the most recent changes you have made in your life. How comfortable have you been with those changes? Do you find that some changes seem easier than others?

Margo was a high potential mid-level manager at an international telecom company. She had been at the company for five years and was comfortable with her current position. When her supervisor recommended her for the company's high potential leadership training camp, she was excited to participate. She had all the trappings of a star performer.

She was well-liked by her subordinates and met all her goals on her performance reviews. Several months after participating in the high potential camp she was offered a promotion with a significant pay increase and more responsibilities. The new position involved leading a larger team at a new location, in the same city, for the company. She told her supervisor she'd have to think about it. This came as a bit of a shock to the senior management team.

Margo was fearful of taking up the new position. Even though the money was better, and it would enhance her career, she was able to convince herself it wasn't worth the disruption. She was aware that changes would be coming that would negatively affect her current team. These changes would likely take them away from the more interesting projects, so it was an opportune time for her to move on.

After discussing the opportunity with her husband, who was completely supportive of her taking the new position, she was still hesitant. She feared taking on some of the new responsibilities, doubted her ability to lead the larger group, and just felt she wasn't quite ready for a change. At some level, she also feared she might fail in the new role.

What would you do in Margo's position? Do you agree with her reasoning in this situation? How would you have handled it? What would you advise Margo? Are you familiar with a similar situation in which someone feared taking a risk at work?

Life is full of plans. We make plans every day—from what to have for lunch, to how to spend our leisure time. Sometimes plans change. Some changes are easier than others. Our ability to change, adapt to life's curves or even roadblocks, helps determine our success in life. To a large extent life is about change and our ability to adapt. Stay behind and you miss many of life's opportunities. People high in challenge are looking for the next opportunity and don't hesitate in taking it.

Whenever You Fail at Something, Ask: What Can I Learn from This?

Who can say they never failed at something? The ability to learn from failures is what sets apart the people who succeed from those who struggle. There are many examples of people who started with failure and went on to experience great success.

Bill Gates, who at one point was the richest person in the world, had his share of failures. His first failure was with a company he started called Traf-O-Data. Together with Paul Allen he started this company in the early 1970s. The company read and analyzed data from roadway counters and created reports for traffic engineers. Unfortunately, while the company made innovative advances in using technology, it continued to lose money.

What did they learn from the failure of Traf-O-Data to become profitable? According to Paul Allen, "Despite efforts to sell our wares as far afield as South America, we had virtually no customers. Traf-O-Data was a good idea with a flawed business model. It hadn't occurred to us to do any market research, and we had no idea how hard it would be to get capital commitments from municipalities. Between 1974 and 1980, Traf-O-Data totaled net losses of $3,494. We closed shop shortly thereafter" (Allen, 2011).

One of the learning points for them was that microprocessors would soon run the same programs as larger computers, but at a lower cost. This led to their development of the Altair-BASIC computer language—the first high-level language that ran on a microcomputer. This was a big step in their moving on to create Microsoft.

Bill Gates described his learning from failures this way: "Once you embrace unpleasant news not as a negative but as evidence of a need for change, you aren't defeated by it, you're learning from it. It's all in how you approach failures" (Gates, 1999). Once again, we see how challenge involves our ability to keep moving, in one direction or another, when faced with adversity.

One of the most famous examples of learning from failure was Thomas Edison and the invention of the light bulb. While he also invented the phonograph, carbon telephone transmitter, electric power distribution, fluoroscopy, motion picture kineto-scope, and many other devices, the light bulb comes first to most people's minds.

Nobody really knows how many attempts Edison made in try-ing to invent the light bulb, but the numbers range from between 1,000 and 10,000 attempts. There have been a number of quotes about this attributed to Edison. Three in particular stand out. The first is, "I have not failed. I've just found 10,000 ways that don't work." A second quote of his is "The three great essentials to achieve anything worthwhile are, first, hard work; second, stick-to-itiveness; third, common sense." And finally, "Negative results are just what I want. They're just as valuable to me as positive results. I can never find the thing that does the job best until I find the ones that don't" (Daum, 2016).

In all the messages we see from Edison we're looking at the elements of challenge. We see him continuing to try even when he fails. He learns from his failures. Finally, he uses a hardiness-challenge mindset in redefining failure into looking at things differently—"10,000 ways that don't work."

Try Out New Things, Take Reasonable Risks

When is the last time you tried something new? Have you been to a new restaurant, tried some new type of food, visited a new place, listened to a new type of music, taken on a new task at work, gone somewhere where you knew nobody? We have count-less opportunities in our lives to try new things. Trying something new and getting out of our comfort zone is a great way to build hardiness-challenge.

For most people the natural inclination is to keep things the same, don't rock the boat, and play it safe. Change can create anxiety and discomfort. It also often entails work. It's easier to keep doing what you've always done and avoid taking risks. But sometimes it's the change and discomfort that goes along with it that help us grow and develop new skills.

This was demonstrated in an interesting study carried out by researchers in New Zealand looking at building resilience, closely related to hardiness, in a sample of students (Hayhurst, Hunter, Kafka, & Boyes, 2015). Their study included 146 young people. Seventy-two of them, in smaller groups, took part in an adventure and developmental voyage on a ship, the *Spirit of New Zealand*. The *Spirit of New Zealand* is a 45-meter, three-masted Barquen-tine that sails around New Zealand.

Although an important part of the voyage entails "sail train-ing" (i.e., learning to sail a masted sailing ship), the core purpose of the voyage is to enhance youth development. During the sail-ing period, students were taught a number of skills that included leadership and sailing. The rest of the students served as a control group. The purpose of the study was not only to see if the stu-dents' resilience skills increased over a period of time after the voyage, but to look at how a number of other personal skills were affected as well.

All participants were assessed as to their resilience skills four times: one month before the voyage, the first day of the voyage, the last day of the voyage, and five months following the last day of the voyage. There were no differences in the control group throughout the time period examined. The sailing group, how-ever, significantly increased their resilience scores from the first day on the ship until the last day. They even maintained their increased scores when retested five months later.

The students who went on the adventure voyage also significantly increased their scores in a number of other personal areas. From the first day until the last day of the voyage they increased their self-esteem, self-efficacy (how competent they felt they were), social acceptance, and social support. In order to understand how the different factors contributed to the increase in resilience, they used a statistical formula to look at the relationships.

This is where the findings get even more interesting. By understanding some of the basic factors that led to the changes, beyond just going sailing, we can improve our interventions for building hardiness-challenge. So, while trying new things, in this case sailing, is important, so are some other aspects of the experience.

One of the factors that boosted their resilience was found to be increasing their social effectiveness. In this case none of the students placed on the ship knew any of the other students. They were put into teams of ten. It was important for them to get to know their teammates and work closely with them. There was a great deal of cooperation required in order to successfully complete their sailing tasks. They took turns taking on the leadership role in each team.

The second area that directly related to improved resilience was their increase in self-efficacy. By learning new skills and mastering them, participants became more self-confident. Having specific tasks and completing them successfully helps us feel better about ourselves and our competency.

The third factor that predicted resiliency was unexpected by the researchers. The participants' perceptions of the weather was a strong predictor of resilience. Watching the weather was an important aspect of the team members' responsibility, as it had a big effect on preparations for safety procedures. The worse the student rated the weather during the voyage, the higher their resilience scores. The authors conclude that the link between greater awareness of the weather and resilience demonstrates the effect of the importance of challenge in promoting the resilience processes. Watching the weather, and being prepared for change, especially when storm clouds appeared, kept the students in an adaptable frame of mind. This ability to adapt to conditions is an important part of hardiness-challenge.

So, when it comes to trying new experiences and taking reasonable risks, you can use these findings as a guide. Try for experiences that allow you to develop your social skills, build your self-efficacy, and provide something that will challenge you along the way.

Imagine Future Positive Outcomes

We previously mentioned the technique of visualization in Chapter 2. This is where you close your eyes and imagine a goal you have selected for yourself. A number of variations of visualization have been used by sports psychologists with both Olympic and professional athletes. Some people like to focus just on the goal or outcome. Others like to focus on the journey to the goal. And still others will focus on the obstacles to the outcome and how to overcome them.

An interesting study looked at just the act of setting goals versus visualizing ultimate success (Munezane, 2015). So, you may decide your goal is to get a great job, and you plan your days around what it takes to get that dream job. Or, you might imagine yourself in that dream job. You can see, in your mind's eye, what you will be doing in that job, how you will handle the opportunities you encounter. Imagine yourself at your ideal workplace, interacting with peers, doing tasks you love to do, working in a great physical space.

A Japanese researcher looked at how these effects might work with a group of university students learning to be fluent in English. One of the problems English teachers have with Japanese students is their frequent unwillingness to communicate publicly in English. A number of studies have attempted to find ways of getting these students to use their English in public. There seems to be a fear of expressing themselves in a new language. By increasing their hardiness-challenge, these students should be more willing to take risks—such as speaking English in public.

The study included 373 students who were learning English. They were assigned into one of three groups. One group took an instructional English course only. The 14-week course was based on a curriculum that was widely used with that population. Each student took a test that measured their willingness to give a presentation in English before starting the course and at the end of the course. They each made a presentation to the group on the last day of class.

The second group of students, the visualization only students, were taught through a series of activities to imagine themselves as proficient English speakers using English in a future, global workplace. For example, students watched a five-minute segment from a *Harry Potter* film. In the scene chosen, one of the main characters, Ron, gets very nervous before a game of Quidditch. At the breakfast table, he drinks a beverage and a friend suggests that Harry had put some magical potion into his cup. Believing that he had drunk the magical liquid, Ron became confident, and with his great performance, his team won the game.

The scene demonstrated a quick transition from hesitance into confidence through a magic potion put into a beverage. In addition, there were examples that were provided of the positive effects of visualization (e.g., Olympic athletes).

In the research study, there were also a number of exercises students were led through. In one exercise students were asked to visualize their ideal future selves with their desired proficiency in English. They were then asked to share their visions in groups of four to five. At home, students drew pictures of a scene where they realized success in their career and life in 15 to 20 years, and then wrote a short essay describing the scene.

The third group, given the same visualization exercises, were also trained in setting long-term and short-term goals. They were introduced to goal-setting with an eight-minute video clip from Disney's *Aladdin*. In the scene, Aladdin comes across the lamp in a cave, meets the genie, and makes his wish. In groups of four or five, students imagined that they came across an ancient lamp and thought about what they might want to wish for.

The students were instructed that we all have a genie in our mind that can make our wishes come true. They were told that setting goals early in life and making an effort to achieve these goals with their own strong will were particularly important for later success. Then they brainstormed the big picture of what they wanted to achieve in their lifetime and shared their ideas in groups.

Over the next several weeks they narrowed down their goals from 20 years, to 5 years, to this year, to this semester. They shared their goals with each other. They also discussed how learning English fit into these goals. They identified the English skills and proficiency they would need to meet their goals.

The goals were then converted into SMART goals. That is, they were specific, measurable, achievable, relevant, and time bound. They included speaking goals for each class, and students kept a record of whether or not they achieved their goals. Examples of goals included "I'm going to speak up at least twice during the group discussion," or "I'm going to use gestures when I talk."

The results of the posttest can be seen in Figure 5.1. While there were differences across the groups, the only significant difference was between the visualization plus goal-setting and the other two groups. The difference between visualization only and

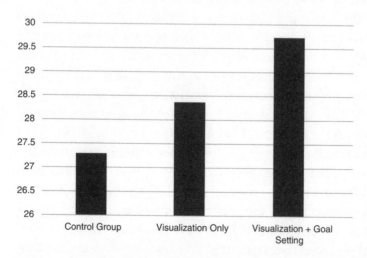

FIGURE 5.1 Group's Willingness to Communicate in English After Intervention

the control group was not significant. It seems the act of goal-setting along with your visualization increases your chances of getting the results you want.

So, what does this mean for you? By setting your own personal goals—start 20 years out, then do 10 years, 5 years, and this year—you start to make the changes you want in your life. Remember, make those goals specific, measurable, achievable, relevant, and time bound. Then use visualization and see yourself living out the goals you planned for. This approach helps you build your hardiness-challenge and overcome obstacles to your life goals.

Do Not Dwell on Past Disappointments: Learn, Forgive, and Look Ahead

How often have things not worked out for you and you couldn't get it out of your mind? You would ruminate about it, ask "what if?" again and again. Reliving the past does not change the past. At some point you will need to move on with life. People high in hardiness-challenge learn from disappointments and move on. Part of the hardiness mindset is to look at the past as a learning experience. Changing the way we look at events can lead to major changes both psychological and physical.

One of the more difficult things for many people is forgiveness. It takes a lot of energy to be angry at people for transgressions of one sort or another. We don't stop and think of the costs of our own holding on to anger or resentment. Researchers from Korea and Wisconsin have taken the time to carefully review all of the published research studies looking at the effects of forgiveness of others on our physical health (Lee & Enright, 2019).

The researchers reviewed 128 published studies that included 58,531 subjects. The studies they looked at all used biomarkers of some sort. These include elevated blood glucose or cholesterol concentration, myocardial infarction, stroke, bone fracture, recurrence of cancer, or patient feelings of well-being. They focused on physical markers because they report that the connection between forgiveness and mental health issues has already been well established with 14 published reviews that include hundreds of studies.

How do you actually define forgiveness? While academics have come up with several different definitions, one interesting one breaks it into two dimensions. The first is decisional. You can decide to forgive someone without experiencing any emotional forgiveness. The second is emotional/motivational. This involves feeling some actual compassion for the offender.

On the other hand, people who are unforgiving harbor prolonged negative emotions, such as anger, resentment, hostility, fear, bitterness, and hatred towards a wrongdoer, including motivations for revenge or avoidance. These feelings have been linked to hyperarousal problems that include feeling jumpy, finding it hard to concentrate, constant anxiety, and being impulsive. The long-term consequences of these symptoms can lead to a hormonal imbalance in your body.

Also, the brain patterns of unforgiving people are similar to the brain patterns of someone going through stressful situations. Cognitive activity in the prefrontal cortex of the brain (specifically the ventromedial prefrontal cortex) decreases. This is the part of the brain used in planning, expressing your personality, making decisions, and moderating your social behavior. As well, the activity in the temporal lobe (specifically the limbic system) increases—this can cause problems with your emotions, behavior, motivation, and memory.

One of the main findings of this review of all the research in this area was that there was a significant, positive association between forgiveness of others and health. This relationship was strong and not affected by age, gender, race, education, employment type, type of positive health factors, or the nature of any of the samples studied.

Of course, it's also important that you be able to forgive yourself. One of the great near-wins in golf history came in the 2009 British Open Tournament, when 59-year-old Tom Watson almost became the oldest man, and the first ever with a hip replacement, to win this golf classic. Watson was one shot away from a historic victory when his final putt came up short and he tied for first place. He went on to lose in the playoff, dashing the hopes of millions of golf fans.

When asked about his loss, Watson said: "When you lose on the golf course, you look at your failures, and you work on what you did wrong. Of course, it was disappointing not to win. The disappointment was great. But I've always been able to take defeat or disappointment and make lemonade out of it. Like Bobby Jones (another great golfer) said, you never learn in victory, you only learn in defeat" (Verdi, 2009).

Our advice is that you should look to the future, and don't dwell on past mistakes or transgressions. Yes you should learn from failures, but take that learning forward. Do not hold grudges. Let go of your past resentments and forgive others. There is no upside to harboring anger. It only hurts you. Besides, letting it go will be good for both your mental and physical health. Hardiness-challenge is about learning from the past, looking forward, taking calculated risks, and making changes. People high in hardiness-challenge learn to take action, evaluate, pivot when necessary, and keep moving.

In the next chapter we will discuss the third C of hardiness—control. You will learn how self-control can have many benefits in turning stress to your advantage.

Chapter 6

Understanding Hardiness–Control

"Ultimately, the only power to which man should aspire
is that which he exercises over himself."
—Elie Wiesel (Writer, professor, Nobel Laureate, Holocaust survivor)

How much do you feel you are in control of events around you? Do you believe the world is getting out of control and there is little anyone can do to change things? Or do you feel there is a piece of the world where you have a good sense of control? Where we see ourselves and our sense of control over the things around us plays an important role in our ability to overcome the challenges that we encounter in life.

The control part of the hardiness model involves a strong belief that you can influence outcomes in your life, and you are willing to make choices and accept responsibility for those choices. It captures how much in control you feel of your destiny, despite the uncertainty that is often associated with the future.

People who have a strong sense of control tend to approach new situations with confidence because they believe that they can influence the results. Researchers have long recognized that people generally want control, and it is to their benefit for an individual to feel like they are in control of situations that are occurring. Feeling in control allows you to think that you can safely and effectively manage your environment and life circumstances, even when stressful situations come your way.

Taking Control When Your Body Can't: Michael J. Fox

Michael J. Fox is a well-known actor, comedian, author, and film producer. He starred in films and TV shows such as *Back to The Future, Spin City, and Family Ties*. His work won him a number of awards including five Primetime Emmy Awards, four Golden Globe Awards, a Grammy Award, and two Screen Actors Guild Awards.

At the age of 29, Fox was diagnosed with Parkinson's disease. He didn't disclose his condition until seven years later. After getting the news from his doctor, Fox started to drink heavily and live recklessly. He was basically in a state of denial about the disease. He eventually got help for his drinking and stopped altogether (Brockes, 2009).

It would have been easy for Fox to simply give up, retreat, and stay at home with his family. He certainly had the money to quit and retire. He could have either kept on denying his disease or simply accepted that things like this just happen "for a reason."

Instead, he admitted his plight and became a huge activist and advocate on behalf of sufferers of Parkinson's disease. He testified before a Senate Appropriations Subcommittee, campaigned for a politician supporting stem cell research, raised funds, and spoke out on numerous platforms. He took control of the direction of his life, in spite of his physical limitations.

At one point, things got even worse for Fox. He started falling. He underwent a medical examination and learned that he had an additional problem with his spinal cord that required surgery. After the operation and some intense physical therapy, he started feeling better, even though he hadn't yet fully recovered. He started taking extra risks and one day he took a misstep, fell, and fractured his arm.

His response about the incident gives us a bit more insight into his use of hardiness-control. He stated, "I try not to get too 'New Age-y.' I don't talk about things being 'for a reason.' But I do think the more unexpected something is, the more there is to learn from it. In my case, what was it that made me skip down the hallway to the kitchen thinking I was fine when I'd been in a wheelchair six months earlier? It's because I had certain optimistic expectations of myself, and I'd had results to bear out those expectations, but I'd had failures too. And I hadn't given the failures equal weight" (Marchese, 2019).

We see that people high in control don't believe they can conquer all the obstacles in their way. They realize they have limitations and learn from their experience. This sets hardiness apart from another popular concept known as "grit" (Duckworth, 2016). People with high grit are more likely to keep forging ahead, persisting even when the goal is unreasonable or unattainable. Hardiness-control, on the other hand, involves understanding your limits and knowing when to push and when to pull back.

Managing Your Internal Drives

There has been a lot of research on self-control and how it impacts us. For example, studies have shown that people higher in self-control do better academically at school, have happier interpersonal relationships, commit less crime, are less involved in drug use, and are less aggressive (DeWall, Finkel, & Denson, 2011; Packer, Best, Day, & Wood, 2009; Tangney, Baumeister, & Boone, 2004).

However, there is a major misunderstanding about what is actually meant by self-control. It's not just a matter of willpower or inner resources to overcome temptations. The research has found that people high in self-control are more likely to develop healthy habits and *avoid* temptations—as opposed to just fighting them. For example, a person with an alcohol problem who has high self-control may just skip that tempting invitation to a tailgate party before the game. On the other hand, the low self-control alcoholic may go along to the party hoping to fight the urge to drink.

In an interesting series of studies, a group of researchers at Texas A&M University looked at self-control in relation to what is termed *visceral states* (Baldwin, Finley, Garrison, Crowell, & Schmeichel, 2018). Visceral states are basically the internal physiological conditions you are in when motivated to act. These include drives such as hunger and thirst. It is when these drives or visceral states are high, such as when you're hungry, that you are motivated to eat, thus breaking your diet. Or when you are sleep deprived you tend to eat more high-calorie foods. Being under stress has been found to reduce people's control, causing them to eat tastier and less healthy items. Having a minor illness, such as a cold, has been associated with fatigue, malaise, and pain in people under stress.

Self-control is associated with the effective use of healthy habits. It is when your visceral states, such as hunger and thirst, get more intense that your ability to control your habits is challenged. The higher your control, the better able you are to resist unhealthy behaviors. For example, by eating more frequently, higher control people are then less tempted to overeat and to choose unhealthier foods. The Texas A&M researchers looked at these habits in 5,598 undergraduate college students who were subjects in their labs. They measured the students' levels of control as well as their visceral states across a number of different conditions and studies over a five-year period.

Their findings showed that people who were higher in self-control experienced less intense and a lower presence of visceral states. In other words, people who scored higher in measures of self-control showed lower levels of hunger and fatigue, lower prevalence of common colds, and less extreme stress. Once again, higher control is related to lower presence and lower intensity of visceral states.

Additional research with this group uncovered more about the relationship between higher self-control and healthier habits, which, of course, leads to healthier lifestyles. The researchers found that people with higher self-control were less hungry when they were tested, partly because they ate more recently. They also had less fatigue at the time they were seen for the study because they reported having slept more the previous night. This research helps us better understand why people higher in control have consistently been found to be healthier.

Planning an Orderly Future

We're also learning that higher control is associated with having an inclination for orderliness, planning, and thinking ahead. Some of these qualities sound very much like the personality trait of conscientiousness. The high self-control person is likely to plan out vacation times carefully, picking the best choice in hotels, knowing which route they will take to get there, making dinner reservations in advance, and pre-purchasing event tickets. The low self-control person is more likely to wing it, possibly getting lost along the way, having to spend time and money finding a decent hotel with a vacancy, searching last minute for things to do, and perhaps discovering that the concert they wanted to see is already sold out.

Research in the field of personality has shown that high conscientiousness is also associated with living more healthily and experiencing less stress. So, where then does conscientiousness come from? There is no simple, complete answer as yet, but we do know the trait is partly inherited and that it is fostered through having meaningful social roles and responsibilities.

Self-control, in addition to influencing orderliness and planning, is also related to intelligence. Some aspects of intelligence, such as rote memory, are more automatic and likely not influenced by control. Other aspects, however, such as logical reasoning and extrapolation (using both reasoning and elaborating on results), have been found to be affected by self-control (Schmeichel, Vohs, & Baumeister, 2003).

Control: Too Much or Too Little

While we've presented some of the benefits of having a strong sense of hardiness-control, there has been some disagreement among psychologists about whether or not you can have too much control. We tend to think of the benefits of high levels of self-control helping us with impulsive behaviors, such as dieting and smoking. It turns out that these are the most difficult kinds of behaviors to control. If they were easy to control, we wouldn't see huge industries developed to try to manage these behaviors. Unfortunately, the research in this area, using follow-up studies, does not find much success in controlling these kinds of behaviors through sheer will power or any amount of consciously trying to manage them.

MANAGING YOUR IMPULSES

There's a lot of evidence that high levels of control or delay of gratification—also referred to as impulse control—are related to higher grades in school. People higher in control are more disciplined and better able to plan and set aside time for doing homework and studying. Procrastination is highly related to low self-control. High procrastinators are easily distracted and side-tracked from tasks. Instead of doing their online research for a school paper or work project, they're more likely to get caught up in gossip, shopping, or travel websites.

You may be familiar with the famous "marshmallow test" carried out by Walter Mischel at Stanford University in the 1960s. Mischel's experiment involved a number of four-year-old children. Each child was seated in a room that contained a chair, a table, and a single marshmallow. The experimenter informed the child that he or she had to run an errand, and made the child an offer. If the child wanted to eat the marshmallow immediately, that would be okay. But if the child waited until the adult returned, the reward would be a second marshmallow.

The kids made their choices. Two-thirds of them managed to hang tough and earn the second marshmallow. The rest did not. Mischel was able to locate them twelve and fourteen years later, when they were about to graduate from high school. At this point, he gained access to their academic records and asked their parents to evaluate how successful they had been in and out of school.

The kids who had gobbled up the first marshmallow, not waiting for the second, were reported as having one or two problems. As a group, they were less adept at making social contacts and more prone to being stubborn and indecisive. They yielded readily to frustration as well as temptation.

Those who had put their gratification on hold—and by doing so, doubled their pleasure with a second marshmallow—were more successful. They showed more social skills, exhibited superior coping mechanisms, and, in general, were ahead of the game. This was reflected in their grades. They were, simply put, better students and had scored remarkably higher on the SAT. It sounds incredible—but the ability, at age four, to wait for a second marshmallow was two times more accurate a predictor of a kid's future SAT score than was his or her IQ (Shoda, Mischel, & Peake, 1990; Mischel, Shoda, & Rodriguez, 1989).

A second area where researchers have found a strong connection with self-control is with impulse control problems such as binge eating and alcohol abuse. There have been a number of different studies linking low control with problem drinking. In addition, people low in control have been found to have more problems in saving money, and a higher incidence of eating disorder problems.

Can Mental Health Problems Be Related to Control Issues?

People low in control have been found to have more adjustment problems. These include a number of mental health disorders. For some disorders this may seem obvious, such as depression and anxiety. These are perceived as problems that involve lack of emotional control. However, other disorders, such as obsessive-compulsive disorder and anorexia nervosa, are seen as problems where there may be too much control or overcontrol.

There is at least one study that shows higher self-control is related to being more mentally healthy in all of the areas that were measured (Tangney et al., 2004). These included somatization (the expression of mental stress through physical symptoms), obsessive-compulsive patterns, depression, anxiety, anger, phobic anxiety, paranoid ideas, and psychoticism.

Rather than thinking of disorders such as obsessive-compulsiveness as "overcontrol," these researchers describe them as problems in self-regulation. In other words, people with these types of problems have difficulty in regulating their emotions. So, having a higher level of control means being able to better control or regulate your emotions and impulses, and being less obsessive-compulsive or less perfectionistic.

We carried out our own research looking at the relationship between hardiness-control (along with the other hardiness factors) and a number of mental health challenges as measured by the validated screening tool, the SA-45 or Symptom Assessment 45. This measure is used by hundreds of medical and mental health centers to screen tens of thousands of patients every year (Maruish, 2004). We surveyed 332 working adults with the Hardiness Resilience Gauge and the SA-45 and looked at the relationships between the presence of mental health symptoms and hardiness.

Our results paralleled the previously cited research in that the higher someone's hardiness and hardiness control, the lower their overall symptom scores. In fact, the higher the control score, the significantly lower the symptom scores, with the strengths of the relationships shown in Figure 6.1.

So, the strongest negative relationship is between hardiness-control and interpersonal sensitivity (being overly sensitive to others). The higher your hardiness control, the lower your interpersonal sensitivity, or the better your ability to get along with people. Also significant, but not quite as strong, is the link between hardiness-control and paranoid thinking.

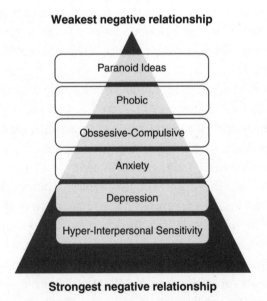

FIGURE **6.1** Hardiness Control and Significantly Related Mental Health Issues

What's really interesting here is the negative relationship between hardiness-control and obsessive-compulsiveness. This has been one of the concerns of researchers in this area as previously mentioned. Can too much control lead to perfectionism or obsessiveness? Our data, just like the previously reported study, doesn't support that. It seems that people high in hardiness-control are better able to control their impulses, whereas people who are overly perfectionistic or obsessive are not able to regulate their emotions and impulses well.

There were three symptom areas where we did not find a significant connection with hardiness control. These were somatization (having physical symptoms, likely due to psychological reasons), hostility, and psychoticism (having unusual thoughts, hearing things, seeing things that others don't experience). So, regardless of a person's hardiness-control score, they can have physical symptoms, be mean to others, or have unusual thinking patterns.

Can Higher Control Have Benefits at Work?

What are some of the positive effects of higher self-control? One study looking at control in the workplace found that supervisors with higher self-control were more trusted by their subordinates. They also received higher ratings of fairness (Cox, 2000).

Max was a manager at a large box manufacturing company. He was referred for coaching by Alice, a vice president of the company. Alice was getting negative feedback about Max from a number of employees who reported to him. They felt that he wasn't treating them fairly. Alice called Max in for a talk. It became pretty clear to Alice after a brief time that Max had no idea how he came across to other people, especially those he supervised. She felt he needed some clarification about his behavior and how he was seen by others.

Max's coach gave him the Hardiness Resilience Gauge. His score in hardiness control was quite low, especially relative to his other scores. He scored higher in commitment and challenge. When asked about his control score, Max talked about his need to be liked and how he hated setting limits on others. He felt that other people were responsible enough to make their own decisions, and he didn't like to interfere in that.

"If things are going to go bad, well, that's just the way it goes," replied Max. "I don't really think my intervention will change anything."

Max's coach pointed out that people like to receive feedback on their work. Giving no feedback implies that either you don't care, or that maybe you don't approve of their work. Leaving people to their own devices to decipher how they are performing at work can be like driving a car without a steering wheel.

Max learned about the importance of giving performance feedback to his staff when they were applying any skill, in order to improve and ensure that they are on the right track. He learned that facial expressions, such as a frown (even if involuntary), can be negatively interpreted and affect someone's performance.

There were a number of areas in Max's life where he didn't take initiative. His coaching led him to learn to be more responsible and responsive to the cues around him. His belief that "things happen" eventually changed to "things happen, and I may have some influence over them." In other words, he learned to increase his hardiness-control by taking more responsibility and taking action to make things happen. Over time his subordinates saw a change in him and felt not only more comfortable, but more fairly treated as he was more consistent in his treatment towards them.

How Control Can Make You More Effective at Work

In a major review of the work on control and its importance in organizations, published in the *Harvard Business Review*, a group of researchers summarized some of the most significant findings to date (Yam, Lian, Ferris, & Brown, 2017).

While repeating some of the results we've already mentioned—that people higher in self-control eat healthier, are less likely to have substance abuse problems, build more quality friendships, and perform better at school—there are also some work-related findings. For example, high self-control leaders demonstrate more effective leadership styles. They are better at inspiring and intel-lectually challenging their followers. They tend to be less abusive of others and micromanage people less.

The researchers report that self-control in the workplace is like physical fitness. You only stay fit as long as you exercise and replenish your strength. For example, they found that when self-control decreases in the workplace, more negative or bad things happen.

One study found that nurses who were lower in control were more rude to their patients. Another study found that tax accoun-tants lower in control were more likely to commit fraud. In gen-eral, it was found that employees lower in control were more likely to lie to their supervisors and steal office supplies from work than fellow employees who scored higher in control on self-assessments.

There were a number of social behaviors at work that were found to be related to control as well. Employees who were lower in control were less likely to speak up when they saw problems at work. And they were less likely to help fellow employees in need. In addition, their social responsibility was lower, as they were less inclined to volunteer for corporate and other events.

Finally, corporate leaders low in control were found to have a number of shortcomings. They engaged in more verbal abuse of their followers and were less likely to use positive motivators. They tended to have poorer relationships with their subordinates and were rated as less charismatic.

How Can You Start to Improve Your Control?

There are also some interesting recommendations that were found to help people increase their control. One factor that made a big dif-ference was the amount of sleep that people got. People who slept well at night—had few interruptions to their sleep—were found to have much better self-control at work and were found to be less abusive toward others. They yelled and cursed less than fel-low employees who had slept poorly. Causing workers to put in extraordinary amounts of time, or even increasing people's stress levels so that it affects their sleep time, can hurt workplace productivity. Some companies, such as Google, have even placed sleep pods at their offices in order to allow employees to nap and re-energize.

Another issue that has been found to affect an employee's sense of control is the "service with a smile" mantra that many companies sponsor. Forcing employees to smile at customers, even while being mistreated, might cause some short-term gain but can create longer-term problems in an employee's health and in the organization.

Training employees in empathy—learning to read other people's emotions—and understanding their perspective can be a healthier approach. It doesn't mean you have to agree or smile with each customer, or even acknowledge whether they might be right. You can let them know you understand how they feel ("I can feel your pain"), and you will do the best you can in the circumstances. It doesn't mean pleasing every customer, but it does let the employees be honest, keep their dignity, and stay healthier.

Studies with physicians have found that doctors who faked empathy reported increased burnout and lower job satisfaction. On the other hand, doctors who could engage in perspective taking—learning to see things through the other person's eyes—and were genuinely empathic, fared much better (Larson & Yao, 2005).

In an organization it's also important to create an ethical culture. Studies have found that in organizations that promote their code of conduct—through signs in the building, in staff meetings, newsletters—there are fewer transgressions associated with lower self-control. These reminders help some people avoid temptations and keep them on the right track. While this approach has mostly been found to be effective in the short term, it can be a cost-effective way of keeping a workplace more civil.

Control is a valuable approach for managing both the expected and unexpected stressors in your life. Developing a better sense of control can help you navigate many of life's challenges. In the next chapter we'll look at some specific strategies you can use to increase control in your life.

Chapter 7

Getting Yourself More in Control

"Control your own destiny or someone else will."
—Jack Welch (American business executive,
former chairman and CEO, General Electric)

Hardiness-control is the belief that you can control or influence what is happening around you as well as what is going to happen. The opposite of control is a sense of powerlessness or helplessness to do anything that will make a difference. With this in mind, this chapter offers some steps you can apply to increase your sense of control.

Focus Your Time and Energy on Things You Can Control or Influence

Jeanine loved her job. She worked in the marketing department of a large agency. It was her dream job. She got to use all her skills and training. The work she did was challenging, and she enjoyed the clients on the accounts she worked on. She even got along well with her boss.

However, there was one troubling aspect at her workplace. That was one of her coworkers. The two of them were very different and didn't see eye to eye on many issues—both at work and outside of work. Jeanine was younger and just hitting her stride professionally. Anne had been at the agency much longer and was somewhat jaded. She wasn't happy at work or with her personal life. It wasn't something she managed to hide. Jeanine found her complaining tiresome and distracting from her work. She tried to avoid Anne, but it was difficult in a small office space.

Jeanine had tried to get further away from Anne, but as her manager pointed out, there was limited space in the office and nowhere else to go. Her troubles with Anne grew from a distraction to an obsession. Jeanine was starting to find it difficult to focus on her work. She worried about what nonsense Anne might bring to the office next—more complaints about the office, their manager, her lazy daughter, problems with her neighbors—it seemed there was no end to the whining. It also seemed that there was no way for Jeanine to change the situation. She was stuck in the same office with Anne.

It finally dawned on Jeanine that she was focusing too much of her time and energy on Anne. It was a situation she couldn't change. She loved her job and didn't want to leave it because of one annoying person in the same office. She had to come up with a strategy. She realized she couldn't control Anne, the physical workspace, or her manager's lack of attention to the situation. What she could control, however, was her own behavior and her own reactions to Anne's irritating ways. Rather than wasting countless hours worrying about Anne's next verbal onslaught, she decided to change her approach.

Jeanine came to understand that she had been too passive about Anne's behavior. She was afraid to speak up or criticize her in any way. It was now time to be assertive. She came up with a number of firm but respectful things she could say to Anne. The goal was not so much to control Anne's behavior or get even with her, but rather to speak up and get out of her system what was really bothering her. The fact that she was allowing Anne to distract her from her work was the most upsetting aspect of the situation.

Some of the statements Jeanine planned on saying included, "Anne, I'm really sorry you are upset with things here, but I'm happy with my work situation and I'd rather not hear any more complaints about work," and "It's unfortunate things aren't going well for you at home right now Anne, but there's really nothing I can do. It's really not a good time to unload these problems on me right now. I've already got a lot on my plate."

With a little rehearsal Jeanine was able to state her case tactfully and unemotionally. She was fully in control of the message and the way it was delivered. She realized she could not control Anne's reaction or any changes in Anne's behaviors.

Jeanine was quite surprised that Anne accepted the message and was able to move on. The unpleasant exchanges stopped after that and Jeanine was better able to pay attention to her work. Whether Anne thought any less of her after that exchange became of no consequence to Jeanine. She wasn't there to win Anne's friendship or support. She was there to do the work she loved doing.

Hardiness-control is about looking at your situation and determining what you can control and what is beyond your control. Knowing how to control the things you have jurisdiction over and taking action is the basis of hardiness-control.

In order to focus your attention in the right direction, you first have to stop and think about what your goals are. It's easy to get distracted in life by things that, in the big picture, are not very important. Once you know what is really meaningful for you in life, it becomes easier to focus on the real prize. Then you can direct your actions and energy towards the things that really matter, as well as the things you really can control, that is, your own thoughts, beliefs, and actions. By taking control of yourself you can gradually better influence others around you. By better managing those around you, you can better influence your community. By having more influence in the community, you are more able to have an effect on the greater environment beyond. This leads to hardiness-control.

Work on Tasks That Are Within Your Capabilities, Moderately Difficult but Not Overwhelming

The psychologist Mihály Csíkszentmihályi, in 1995 identified a state of mind referred to as *flow*. It's sometimes called "being in the zone." A state of flow occurs when the challenge slightly exceeds one's skill level (Csíkszentmihályi, 1990). In other words, when things are not very challenging, you get bored. When they are too challenging, you are likely to get anxious and give up. But, as the Goldilocks rule says, when things are not too hard and not too soft, but just right—your skill is matching or is just below the challenge presented—you can reach the flow state.

The flow state has been found to exist in tasks as varied as athletics, playing a musical instrument, acting, solving complex problems, writing a book, climbing a mountain, religious or spiritual experiences, gaming, or any number of activities. The graph representing flow is seen in Figure 7.1.

Reaching a state of flow requires, of course, knowing your capabilities. Being aware of your level of competence requires you to understand yourself and your level of achievement. Be honest with yourself. Try not to over- or undersell your abilities. Look for objective ways to discover how good you are at something. Get feedback from an objective and trusted person. In some cases, you may be able to get help from automated sources, such as an online assessment. People high in hardiness-control are good at gauging their limits and capabilities.

When one of the authors (Steven) returned to music, playing the saxophone after a 30-year hiatus, it was hard to know what level to start at. Most of what had been learned through high school and college had faded away. Fortunately, I found some great music teaching programs online. One program allowed me to play written passages of music while it recorded and graded my performance. Wrong notes and incorrect timing were objectively

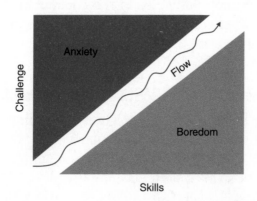

FIGURE 7.1   Flow

graded on screen after playing the passages. I could see (and hear) the percentage of mistakes I made in each category. This feedback prevented me from starting at too difficult a level, after which I would have probably given up after sufficient failures, or at too easy a level, after which I would likely have gotten bored.

One thing we learned from mindset theory, discussed in Chapter 5, is that we can always continue to grow and improve our performance. The flow theory gives us a bit of a roadmap to success. By knowing your capabilities, selecting the right level of challenge, you can successfully navigate your way through challenges without getting overwhelmed. This helps build your hardiness-control.

For Difficult Jobs, Break Them Up into Manageable Pieces So You Can See the Progress

How often have you found yourself procrastinating on a project? Sometimes it seems so easy to find distractions. One of the toughest things about a new project is getting started. Taking that first step can seem overwhelming. How can you be more efficient and get through the bumps?

The first thing you should do is define the project. What is the goal? What are you trying to accomplish? Write a report, analyze a situation, produce a presentation, do a request for proposal, carry out a research project, put together a sales pitch, create a budget, come up with a new idea, or whatever else. Put it down on paper or on your computer screen. This is what I want to do: _____.

One of the best ways to overcome inertia is to simply take a first step at the project. It's important to realize that what you start with is just a draft. Whatever you do can, and likely will be changed. It's basically a mindset that you have to deal with. No matter how bad your first attempt will be, there is a high probability that your next go at it will be better. In fact, there may be no limit on the times you rework something, although you may have time limits on the project itself. So just jump in! Anything, at this point, is better than nothing!

Once you have your description of what you want to do, start breaking it down into pieces or chunks. You should reward yourself every time you complete a chunk. There are a number of ways you can reward yourself do this. You can use a favorite food (if it isn't bad for your health). I'm (Steven) partial to licorice and wine gums (I know, they're not healthy). You can take a short walk, exercise, watch a YouTube video, make a call to someone you want to speak with, or pick your own creative, short-term reward. Hardiness-control improves when you know how to self-motivate.

In an article published in *Harvard Business Review* (HBR) researchers surveyed approximately 20,000 professionals across six continents asking specific questions about their productivity (Pozen & Downey, 2019). They came up with a number of general findings—such as working longer hours did not lead to more productivity, working smarter led to accomplishing more each day, older and senior professionals were more productive than younger and more junior colleagues, and overall, men and women were equally productive (although there were some differences in particular habits).

There were a number of specific approaches that differentiated the highly productive professionals from those who were less productive. Some of them are relevant here. One of the first was that productive people start with a plan. We'll get more into that in the next section. If it's a writing project, start with an outline in a logical order that will help you stay on track.

The most productive people create daily routines to help keep themselves on track. So, just like dressing in the morning, or having breakfast, you should set up a routine than ensures you will do some work on your project each day. It could be reading, writing, researching, or whatever activity. It's important that something gets done each working day. Once again, for hardiness-control to improve it's important to get used to getting something done. Or, as the shoemaker Nike would put it, "Just Do It!"

The HBR survey found that leaving open times in your schedule each day was also a good idea. It wasn't productive to schedule things too heavily throughout the day. There should always be room for emergencies or unplanned events.

One big disruption we all experience today is the constant barrage of incoming emails. Many of us tend to stop what we're doing and jump over to read them upon arrival. Rather than checking them as they come in, it was found to be more productive if you check them once every hour or less. Also, skip over most of your messages by just looking at the sender and the subject line. Only those deemed to be important and needing an immediate response should be tended to in the moment. The rest can wait until you have more time on your hands.

Plan Ahead and Gather Up the Right Tools and Resources for the Task

Pedro never liked to plan before starting a project. He just couldn't wait to jump right in and give it all he had. He knew how to get things started, and he believed once he got going there was no stopping him. That was true up to a point. His enthusiasm and energy took him far, but he seemed to always have trouble completing projects. He would either tire out eventually, run into a roadblock, or run out of ideas for the next phase of the project. At that point he felt dejected, defeated, and lost.

When tasks have multiple components, or stages, we are better off planning them out. Think about the amount of time we might need, whether it can be broken into smaller steps, and what resources are needed. You wouldn't build a house without a set of plans or a blueprint. When it comes to projects, the level of planning can vary. For smaller projects it might just be outlining the steps we need to go through. Larger projects may need more detail in planning.

Writing a book is a good example of a longer-term project. Before we wrote this book, for example, we mapped out the chapters with temporary titles. Then we filled in each chapter heading with a brief paragraph outlining what we planned to cover. Then we put together a page describing the book overall and what we hoped to accomplish with it. This is important for the publisher who might consider publishing it, as well as for us as authors in that it helps us complete the writing process. While mapping out the chapters, we started to think of the content, some of the research we might need to include, how to access it, perhaps some case examples, and so on. Whenever we got stuck or blocked in our writing, we referred back to the detailed outline to get back on track.

Almost any project, proposal, or venture can benefit from a plan. It helps you anticipate the challenges and opportunities that lie ahead. It also helps you prepare for them in advance. Surprises are good for birthdays, but don't always work out well when trying to complete a project. The plan doesn't have to be elaborate, just enough to think through the process. Know where you begin and where you end. By doing more planning you build your hardiness-control as you learn more of which actions are within your control and which may be beyond your reach.

THE BENEFIT OF SETTING GOALS

There's new evidence that setting goals can be good for your mental health as well. A study done by psychologists at the Pennsylvania State University followed over 3,000 adults for over 18 years. The researchers collected data over three time periods from 1995 to 2013. The subjects were asked about their approach to setting goals as well as their ability to master challenges in their lives. At each interval they were also assessed for depression, anxiety, and panic disorders.

It turns out that the people who showed the most goal persistence and optimism during the first assessment in the mid-1990s had less depression, anxiety, and panic disorders over the 18 years. Also, the people who started with the lowest depression, anxiety, and panic disorders showed more perseverance towards their life goals and were better at focusing on the positive sides of negative life events.

In the words of the study authors, "Our findings suggest that people can improve their mental health by raising or maintaining high levels of tenacity, resilience and optimism….Aspiring toward personal and career goals can make people feel like their lives have meaning. On the other hand, disengaging from striving toward those aims or having a cynical attitude can have high mental health costs" (Zainal & Newman, 2019).

Knowing What You Can and Can't Control

Another interesting finding of the study had to do with self-mastery. Here this was the belief that you could do anything you set your mind to. Unlike some previous studies, findings showed that believing you had ultimate control was not related to people's mental health. Also, the amount of control people felt they had over their lives did not change much over the entire time period. This led the authors to suggest that self-control is a trait—or a stable part of personality that does not change.

We don't fully agree with that. We believe your hardiness-control can change. But what the study more likely indicates is that it does not change on its own or naturally. Unless you make a concerted effort to change the way you see yourself controlling your behavior (through coaching, therapy, or experiential learning), it likely won't change. Also, hardiness-control does not mean that you have ultimate control or that you can change anything you set your mind to. People high in hardiness-control feel a strong sense of personal control—and they plan ahead—but they know their limits. They don't have unrealistic expectations of control.

For example, I know I can always change my feelings, thoughts, and behaviors in a situation. But I can't always change the situation. The changes I can make may not be dramatic, but they may lead to reinterpreting the (stressful) situation I am experiencing.

If I'm in the jungle, and I come upon a hungry tiger, I will most certainly be filled with fear. I know I can't "will" the tiger to go away, but I can decide whether to freeze in fear (and get eaten) or run for dear life (and hope I escape). If I interpret the situation as hopeless, I'm more likely to experience the former. If I interpret it as "I have a chance to live," I'll experience the latter. Hardiness-control is about helping you make these kinds of life decisions. By learning how to plan, you get better at visualizing different scenarios and making better decisions.

Ask for Help When You Need It

How do you know when you need help? There's a fine balance between independence and asking for help. Some people are constantly asking others to help them out. Others, even when they don't know what they're doing or where they're going, refuse to listen to anyone else.

Brad was the president of a young, fast-growing technology company one of the authors (Steven) met while giving a presentation at the Young Presidents' Organization (YPO). This is a worldwide organization whose members are all under 45 years of age and presidents of companies worth more than $20,000,000 or with sales of over $10,000,000 per year. A very impressive group.

The topic of the presentation was emotional intelligence and leadership. After the Q&A and discussion, Brad approached me privately. He wanted to tell me how unimportant emotional intelligence was in his success. In fact, he said, he owed all his success to his high IQ. He was the one who created the software that his company sold. He did all the marketing, the sales, managed the accounting, trained users on his product, did technical support, and was in charge of all the hiring and firing decisions. It wasn't clear when he had time to sleep, but he got across the point that he was a very busy person. It was important for him to do all these functions, he reported, because there was no one else as capable as he was in any of these areas.

In fact, he was giving me quite a dressing down, especially around my point of hiring the best people you can find to be responsible for all of these roles in your organization. I had pointed out how successful entrepreneurs such as Bill Gates and Michael Dell had made a point of hiring great talent in their companies and letting them run their departments. As Brad went on about his own special talents, his 2IC (second in command, a young woman named Nancy) stood by patiently listening. When he finished his tirade, he took off to the bar, not even waiting for my response.

"Don't pay attention to a thing he's saying," Nancy piped up after he left. "I have to work with him every day. He's a disaster in each of those areas. The reason he has to run them is because nobody else can work with him. He doesn't listen to anyone and now the company is suffering. We can't keep good people."

"He owes a lot of money to the banks, our sales are down, and I don't know if I'll be there that much longer. Thank you for your talk; you hit the nail on the head. Only, I was hoping he would see it."

Once again, we see the results of over-control or too much self-mastery. Hardiness-control is about knowing your limits and behaving accordingly. If Brad was strong in hardiness-control, rather than taking personal charge of so many functions and spreading himself too thin, he would focus on finding the right people for each position he needed so that he could focus on his strengths.

Leaders high in hardiness-control are confident in knowing they control the company and know they can control who runs each division and how it is run. But it is over-control, and perhaps too much ego, to believe that you can directly control all of these complicated functions by yourself. You don't have to manage everything personally to be in control.

Getting advice from others is not a weakness; it is a strength. Coaching of executives is now one of the fastest growing careers in the corporate world. From once being seen as a bit embarrassing, having an executive coach, like having a personal trainer, is now a badge of honor. Many of the most successful corporate leaders today work with an executive coach and welcome the guidance and advice they receive. Many leaders have told us that not only do they get good advice on management issues, it helps relieve the stress of having few people to talk to at the top. Coaching increases confidence in decisions, which helps build hardiness-control.

Recognize Your Successes

Mariana was the first female vice president at one of the largest financial institutions in the country. She was a role model for women throughout the industry. She had broken through the glass ceiling in an industry that had always been male dominated. She worked her way up from a line position to the executive suite over many years of hard work.

Having spent some of her career in the human resources area, she had an interest in people and what made them tick. As part of exploring that interest, she agreed to undergo a battery of psychological assessments to better understand how it might apply in the workplace. Among those assessments, she took the Emotional

Quotient Inventory 2.0 (EQ-i 2.0), which is the world's first and most widely used measure of emotional intelligence.

Expecting her to score at the highest levels across the board, we were quite surprised with the results. While Mariana had a number of very high scores, including empathy, assertiveness, and interpersonal relationships, she had one particularly low score. That was in self-regard. Self-regard includes knowing yourself, your strengths and challenges, as well as having self-confidence. How could this be? We first thought it might be a scoring error. How could someone who achieved so much in her career express such a low level of self-regard?

When asked about the assessment, Mariana was in full agreement with the results. It was her interpersonal skills and ability to listen and understand others that got her to where she was. However, she believed she was not deserving of any special accolades, as she saw herself as "just doing my job." When we explained that she had accomplished so much, that she was seen as a role model for so many, she downplayed the whole notion. After exploring this for some time, she finally came to see that what she had accomplished was, in fact, unique. And, even more important, by acknowledging her success she could be tremendously helpful to hundreds of other women as an inspirational role model. This put the situation in a totally different light.

We've encountered a number of women high achievers in the corporate world who downplay their success. For many of them it boils down to not recognizing past successes. Part of coaching these women has involved recognizing and acknowledging past successes. It has meant going through their careers, identifying milestones, celebrating those milestones, and connecting them to other successes. What we find is that these successes are not random, and they don't happen by luck.

Hardiness-control includes realizing you have been responsible for certain actions that have gotten you to where you are. One way of reinforcing this is by consciously recognizing successes and celebrating them. This doesn't mean arrogance. It just means honestly seeing your own positive achievements. By acknowledging your contributions to your successes, you become more aware of the connections between actions and results. Solidifying this relationship helps build your hardiness-control.

By increasing Mariana's hardiness-control, we were able to help her connect the dots between her hard work and the successes she achieved. This changed her perception of herself. As a result, she was able to increase her self-regard scores on the EQ-i 2.0. But even more importantly, she became much more active as a role model for other women in her industry. She gave more public talks and became more involved in mentoring other women with high potential in her own financial institution.

When You Just Cannot Solve a Problem, Turn Your Attention to Other Things You Can Control

What should you do when you have a problem and there doesn't seem to be a solution? Sometimes we encounter situations that are beyond our control. We can continue working away at it, hoping something will change, or we can take a more realistic view of the situation and change direction. Being strong in hardiness-control includes realizing what you have the power to change and what lies beyond your control.

The one thing we can always control is our reaction to situations. By managing our thoughts, we can influence our emotions and behaviors. It's what we say to ourselves about situations that determines our feelings and actions. Mario and Claude were both business development reps at a midwestern manufacturing company. The company had been going through some tough times over the past several years. A decision was made from the corporate headquarters to close down the midwestern division. Mario and Claude had very different reactions.

Mario felt the closure was totally unjustified. He immediately petitioned to meet with his boss and the regional vice president to make his views known. He put all his energy into preparing historical sales data, market history, economic predictions, and other pertinent information related to their industry and the local plant. He created an impressive slide deck hoping to convince the VP of sales to help overturn the decision.

Claude took a very different tack. He immediately found his resume and updated it. He enlisted the help of an executive recruiter to refresh the look and feel of it and help him chart a new path. Within a couple of weeks Claude was booking interviews with other manufacturing plants. He worked on his interview skills, researched the companies he was interviewing for, and received a couple of offers in a month's time.

While Mario gave a valiant effort at presenting the virtues of their plant to the regional VP, it was all for naught. The decision was made at corporate headquarters, and there was no turning back. He felt dejected and went into a mild depression. On the other hand, Claude was preparing for a new start and was getting more and more excited about the challenges that lay ahead.

There could not be two more different reactions to the same situation. Both Mario and Claude felt an initial shock upon hearing about the closure. The first night was a sleepless one for both of them. But when morning came, they had channeled their energy into two entirely different directions. Mario convinced himself he could save the company. His job was everything to him. He focused on what he could do to change a major corporate decision. Claude read the situation differently. He saw the writing on the wall. His goal was to move on and find some other option that would be fulfilling, and financially viable, for him.

Hardiness-control includes reading situations, understanding what's controllable, and taking appropriate action. It is not about blindly chasing dreams. Once you have a plan, and it is actionable, high hardiness-control people do what they can to achieve their goals. They know which levers they can pull and which ones are out of reach. When one lever is stuck, they find another one that opens the door.

In the following chapters we will provide you with hardiness-related information on special topics. We suggest you continue working your way through these sections. Even if you're not particularly athletic or you don't perform in front of others, you may find some of the lessons worth exploring. What we learn from high-performance athletes, successful entertainers, or flourishing business leaders can be helpful to you and the people you know.

Chapter 8

How Hardiness Works to Protect Health and Performance

A Look Under the Hood

"Everything outside doesn't matter when I'm on the court; it's just me and nothing else. Family problems, school, what happened to my father, all the stress goes away."
—Kawhi Leonard (Most Valuable Player on Toronto Raptors 2019 NBA Basketball Championship team)

Hardiness emerged on the scene in the late 1970s, at a time when people were just waking up to the fact that stress could make you sick. The odd thing was, when exposed to the same stressful conditions, people responded differently. Why do some people get sick when under prolonged stress, while others stay healthy? It was this question that led researchers at the University of Chicago to discover the hardiness qualities of commitment, control, and challenge. High stress executives who had these qualities managed to stay healthy, while those who lacked them developed various health problems (Kobasa, 1979).

If hardiness helps you stay healthy under stress, can it also help you perform better? One of the first studies to look into this question also came out of the University of Chicago. Researchers there studied a group of high school basketball players and found that hardiness correlated with the players' performance throughout the season (Maddi & Hess, 1992). Since then, many studies have confirmed the link between hardiness and superior performance. Here are just a few examples:

+ In West Point Army cadets studied over a four-year time frame, hardiness predicted higher military and leadership performance as rated by supervisors (Bartone, Snook, & Tremble, 2002).
+ In a rigorous six-week selection course, U.S. Army Special Forces candidates who survived to graduation were significantly higher in hardiness than those who failed the course (Bartone, Roland, Picano, & Williams, 2008).
+ Competitive swimmers who are high in hardiness showed less pre-race worry, more confidence, and a more positive interpretation of their anxiety response (Hanton, Evans, & Neil, 20013).

So how does hardiness work to enhance performance and health under stress? To answer this question, we have to look a little deeper "under the hood" at how the body responds to stress.

The Hardy Stress Response: Appraising the Situation

In Chapter 1, we discussed the normal physiological fight or flight stress response, which involves the heightened activation of the autonomic nervous system and rapid release of stress hormones including cortisol and adrenaline. You will feel this, for example, if you're driving along the highway and a deer suddenly jumps out in front of your car. Before you even realize what's happening, your heartbeat quickens, your muscles tense, and (hopefully!) your foot steps on the brake pedal.

The stress response is useful and adaptive, preparing the body as it does for a quick reaction to a dangerous situation. However, if it goes on too long these same processes can do damage. That's where your parasympathetic nervous system is supposed to kick in, putting the brakes on autonomic arousal, and bringing the body back to a normal state of balance, or homeostasis.

So, the first step in the process, and the first place where hardiness can make a difference, is in how you appraise or size-up the situation you find yourself in. This happens mainly in the very front part of your brain, an area known as the prefrontal cortex. This is the part of the brain responsible for what psychologists call executive functioning, which includes judgments about the situation, threat appraisal, possible response options, and deciding how to react based on the context, your past experiences, and what skills and capabilities you think you have.

It's well established that how a person evaluates a stressful situation will impact the stress response (Lazarus & Folkman, 1984), and hardiness has been shown to affect these appraisals (Kobasa, Maddi, & Kahn, 1982). People who are high in hardiness tend to assess stressful situations more positively, recognizing the danger or challenge, but also judging that they have the skills and capabilities to deal with situations like this effectively. People low in hardiness see stressful situations somewhat differently and are less confident that they can cope effectively with life's challenges. This difference right away can lead to different stress responses.

So, if you're low in hardiness, you'll tend to see more situations as difficult and dangerous, triggering the stress response. If you're high in hardiness, you'll evaluate many situations as not so dangerous or stressful, leading to a subdued stress response. This difference is portrayed notionally in Figure 8.1. Here, the

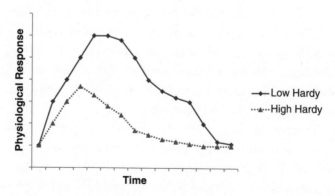

FIGURE **8.1** Physiological Response to a Situation Appraised as Highly Stressful (Low Hardy) Versus Slightly Stressful (High Hardy)

low-hardy response pattern is on top (solid line), and the high-hardy pattern is on the bottom (dotted line).

Faced with a stressor, the low-hardy person goes into a full stress reaction, with a rapid increase in physiological responses such as heart rate, followed by a slow return to baseline. But the hardy person doesn't react as strongly and returns to baseline faster. This reflects the hardy person's more optimistic appraisal of the situation, as well as her sense that she has the skills needed to manage the situation successfully.

For example, consider what happens when Harry, who is low in hardiness, realizes he is going to be late for an important meeting at work because an accident has caused a major traffic jam on his morning commute. His stress levels rise as he thinks about how he is letting down his teammates who were relying on him to present some key data as part of a quarterly report to the division manager. He worries that this may be a black mark on his record, causing the boss to see him as unreliable, maybe even ruining his chances for promotion. He's not sure what to do. After some fruitless attempts to detour around the traffic, he finally calls in to the office to explain the situation. But the meeting is already under way, and he can only leave a voicemail. When he finally gets to the office his coworkers tell him it's no problem. But it takes him most of the morning to calm down.

Now think about Bill, faced with the same problem situation. He also has an initial stress response as he sees that the traffic delay will cause him to be late or even miss the important meeting. But he quickly realizes his coworkers can cover the general points of his report, and he can follow up later with the details. He calls and talks to a team member who agrees to cover his section of the brief. On the remainder of his drive to work, Bill thinks about some final improvements he can make on his report before he emails it to the manager that afternoon.

In this example, Harry and Bill faced the same situation, but appraised it quite differently. Both felt it as stressful, but for Harry the stress was greater and more prolonged. He didn't see a good solution and wasn't confident that he could resolve things in a positive manner. He felt out of control. His physiological stress response was strong and prolonged.

Bill also felt the situation was somewhat stressful, but he was confident he could find a solution, and he started to consider his options. Consequently, his physiological stress response was less severe and relatively brief. He also took control of things, calling the office and making an alternate plan with his coworker. So right from the start, how a problem situation gets appraised can affect the extent and duration of the stress response.

The Hardy Stress Response: Reacting to Stress

After a situation gets appraised as stressful—dangerous or threatening—the prefrontal cortex, which is the executive functioning part of the brain, kicks in to send a signal to the limbic system. These are the deep structures in the brain including the amygdala and hypothalamus that control emotions and regulate a range of bodily functions. The hypothalamus, about the size of a peanut, is like a master switchboard that manages the body's hormones. When the hypothalamus gets the alarm signal from the executive prefrontal cortex, it signals the nearby pituitary gland.

The pituitary in turn sends a message to the adrenals, two little glands about the size of a ravioli that sit on top of your kidneys. The adrenals produce hormones known as glucocorticoids, which serve to mobilize energy resources in the body. At the same time, the sympathetic nervous system stimulates the release of additional hormones from the adrenals known as epinephrine and norepinephrine. These hormones prepare the body for quick action, increasing your heart rate and blood pressure, while boosting the supply of nutrients and oxygen to your brain and muscles.

All this happens in mere seconds, and is good for survival in the short run. But if it goes on too long, it can start to cause damage to other parts of the body. For example, too much of glucocorticoids can interfere with insulin and glucose metabolism, increasing body fat and leading to diabetes and coronary heart disease. So, the stress response needs to be turned off once the danger is past.

This is mainly the job of the parasympathetic nervous system, which puts the brakes on the whole stress reaction process. When the parasympathetic and sympathetic systems are working together in good harmony, we call this autonomic balance. Being high in hardiness means you are better at maintaining and restoring autonomic balance in dealing with stressful situations.

Positively Adapting to Stress

Evidence from several studies indicates that people high in hardiness are able to adapt and recover more quickly following stress exposure. For example, researchers at the Johns Hopkins University conducted an experiment in which a group of soldiers was required to perform multiple tasks under changing and increasingly stressful conditions (Haufler et al., 2018).

Using standard measures of heart rate activity to assess stress response, the researchers found that soldiers higher in hardiness-commitment showed a speedier recovery from the stress condition, indicating a more adaptive and healthy balance between parasympathetic and sympathetic parts of the nervous system. In other words, the high-hardy subjects were better at "putting the brakes" on the stress response once the challenge was past.

Another interesting study of Norwegian police officer trainees showed similar positive effects of hardiness. Here, 84 police academy officers were subjected to a highly realistic simulation in which they had to respond to an active shooter scenario (Sandvik et al., 2019). The officers were required to confront an active shooter in a school situation and react appropriately, without hurting innocent bystanders. The researchers measured stress responses using standard heart rate variability indicators.

Results showed that higher hardiness was linked to faster recovery of parasympathetic control once the stress was over and better bodily adaptation. Interestingly, the study also found that officers high in hardiness showed a somewhat greater initial stress reaction, indicating a higher level of engagement and awareness going into the dangerous situation.

The authors point out this is a good thing for police officers who are dealing with uncertain conditions. Under acute or sharp stress conditions, hardiness is linked to a more vigorous early stress response and also with faster recovery once the situation is resolved. The hardy police officer is more alert and aware, reacts rapidly, and is able to restore bodily calm more quickly once the stress is past.

Another interesting study, this one from the University of Pennsylvania, looked at hardiness, psychological functioning, and baseline levels of stress hormones in healthy college students (Zorrilla, DeRubeis, & Redei, 1995). Their findings showed that somewhat higher baseline levels of the stress hormones cortisol and beta-endorphin are related to higher hardiness, self-esteem, and emotional stability. Thus, high-hardy people begin with a somewhat higher activation level, even before encountering a stressful situation. Being at a higher level of activation serves to heighten their awareness and leave them better prepared to respond quickly to threatening events when they occur.

Figure 8.2 shows what the stress response might look like for high-hardy and low-hardy individuals when confronted with an acutely stressful situation, such as the active shooter scenario in the Norwegian police study.

Here, you can see that the high-hardy person (dotted line) reacts more quickly and also returns to baseline faster once the situation is resolved. The low-hardy person (solid line) also reacts quickly, but takes a longer time to dampen down the stress response after the danger is passed. In addition, notice that those high in hardiness start out at a slightly higher level of activation, even before the stressor is introduced.

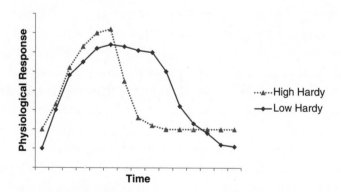

FIGURE 8.2 Physiological Response Pattern to an Acute Stressful Situation

The research evidence to date supports the theoretical stress response patterns displayed in Figures 8.1 and 8.2. To recap, step 1 in the process involves the appraisal or interpretation of the event. The high-hardy person evaluates many events as not so difficult, leading to a reduced stress response, while the low-hardy person sees the same situations as highly stressful, resulting in full-out stress reactions (Figure 8.1). At the same time, the high-hardy person reacts quite vigorously to acutely stressful or dangerous situations like the active shooter. And regardless of the degree of stress, those high in hardiness recover more quickly from stress reactions, returning to a baseline of physiological balance or homeostasis (Figure 8.2).

Stress and the Heart: The Role of Hardiness

Prolonged stress reactions can lead to all kinds of health problems as already mentioned. One of the worst of these is cardiovascular disease. Cardiovascular disease is the leading cause of death in the world, killing nearly 18 million people in 2016 or about 31% of the total population (World Health Organization, 2017). Most of these deaths are from heart attacks and strokes. Many factors increase the risk of cardiovascular disease, including obesity, diet, physical inactivity, health habits, and cholesterol levels in the blood, but stress is a major contributor (Castelli et al., 1986).

To make matters worse, stress is linked to a number of "precursor" physiological and hormonal changes including increased glucose and lowered insulin levels, high blood pressure, and elevated serum lipids, changes that, in turn, can lead to heart disease, diabetes, and stroke to serious diseases states (Manenschijn et al., 2013).

While the link between stress and disease is well recognized, it's also true that individuals vary in how they respond—not everyone gets sick as a result of stress. One factor that appears to increase vulnerability to stress-related disease is the Type A behavior style. A Type A person is marked by impatience, competitiveness, time urgency, and hostility (Friedman & Rosenman, 1974).

Many studies have found the Type A style increases a person's risk for coronary heart disease (CHD) (Houston & Snyder, 1988). However, this effect likewise is not universal, and some people who are high in the Type A pattern show no such ill effects. This suggests that other variables, such as hardiness, are at work to influence how stressors impact a person's cardiovascular status.

A study by researchers at the University of Western Ontario looked at the impact of occupational stress, Type A pattern, and hardiness on cardiovascular health in a group of 278 managers (Howard, Cunningham, & Rechnitzer, 1986). They followed these managers over a two-year period and measured stress in terms of role ambiguity on the job. As expected, the Type A subjects showed substantial stress-related increases in cardiovascular disease risk factors of total cholesterol, triglycerides, and also blood pressure. But they also found an interaction between hardiness and stress among the Type A managers, showing that hardiness was acting as a moderator or buffer of stress for these managers. Managers who were low in hardiness showed the greatest stress-related increases in blood pressure and triglycerides, while those high in hardiness showed less or no increases in these risk factors. Thus, the low-hardy Type A managers were the most vulnerable to work stress, while the high-hardy ones were protected to some degree.

This pattern of results again confirms that persons high in hardiness are less reactive on a physiological and hormonal level to many stressors, compared to their low hardiness counterparts who show more extreme reactions. This is the same pattern we saw earlier in Figure 8.1.

A similar study by Richard Contrada at Rutgers University used an experimental approach to evaluate hardiness and Type A style as potential moderators of cardiovascular responses to stress. Stress in this case was created by having the subjects perform a mirror-tracing task. In this task, you have to trace an image accurately, while only being able to see it through a mirror. Most people find this difficult and fairly stressful (Contrada, 1989). As expected, results showed higher systolic and diastolic blood pressure in the Type A group under stress. And the study also found that hardiness was associated with less blood pressure increase in this group. The lowest blood pressure reactivity of all was seen in the high-hardy, low Type A (Type B) subjects.

Contrada then took the additional step of looking at the hardiness facets of commitment, control, and challenge and found that the challenge facet was mainly responsible for the lower blood pressure reactivity in the high-hardy subjects. These results provide further evidence that hardiness is directly involved in moderating a person's physiological reactivity to stress.

A final relevant study on hardiness and cardiovascular risk was done more recently by one of us (Paul) at the National Defense University (Bartone, Valdes, & Sandvik, 2016). Here, we studied a large sample (338) of middle-age men and women students, looking at hardiness and several measures of cardiovascular health. Results showed that after controlling for age and sex, those high in hardiness had less body fat, lower cholesterol, and higher levels of HDL—high-density lipoprotein, also known as "good" cholesterol because it aids in the removal of fatty deposits from arteries.

One likely pathway for the influence of hardiness on cholesterol levels goes back to the different appraisals made by high- and low-hardy people of stressful events, an activity that takes place mainly in the prefrontal cortex. These executive prefrontal cortex brain areas have lots of nerve connections to the limbic system, including the amygdala and hypothalamus. When faced with novel situations and challenges, appraisals made by high-hardy persons tend to be positive, with an expectation of successful coping and good outcomes. Since the appraisal is positive, the executive center of the brain (prefrontal cortex) doesn't bother to send a wake-up message to the hypothalamus that would trigger a full stress response.

In contrast, the pessimistic threat appraisals made by non-hardy people lead to faster loss of executive control and an all-out stress response. This also means that the stress response goes on for a longer time, with the sympathetic nervous system speeding along without any (parasympathetic) brakes.

This lack of balance between the sympathetic (revving up the engine) and parasympathetic (applying the brakes) nervous systems can lead to all kinds of health problems, including cardiovascular disease (Thayer & Lane, 2007). And while the details of these influence pathways are still being worked out by scientists, recent neuroscience research has confirmed that cholesterol levels in the blood are controlled in part by the brain and hormones associated with the stress response (Perez-Tilve et al., 2010).

Stress and the Immune System

Stress is also known to contribute to various problems with immune system functioning, leading to a wide range of illnesses (Segerstrom & Miller, 2004). Does hardiness make a difference here? Evidence to date suggests the answer is yes. For example, in one study of hardiness and immune system functioning, researchers at the University of Texas-Austin looked at several standard immune system markers in blood samples taken from high- and low-hardy subjects (Dolbier et al., 2001). The researchers exposed the blood to several bacterial and fungal disease agents including staphylococcus, tuberculosis, and candida albicans (a fungus). Then they waited, and later measured the cellular immune response. Results showed a stronger immune response (T and B lymphocyte proliferation) in blood samples taken from the high-hardy group. These are the cells in your blood that track down and kill bacteria and viruses that cause infection.

Hardiness has also been linked to immune system functioning in HIV patients. For example, researchers in Raipur, India, looked at hardiness, social support, and immune functioning in 200 HIV-positive patients (Pandey & Shrivastava, 2017). Their findings showed a substantial effect of hardiness on immune system functioning, as indicated by T lymphocyte counts. Thus, despite being in a diseased condition, HIV patients who are high in hardiness still showed stronger immune systems than those low in hardiness.

One more study in this area is worth mentioning. A group of Norwegian navy cadets were studied while they underwent a highly stressful military field exercise (Sandvik et al., 2013). In addition to hardiness, a number of basic immune system markers were measured including proinflammatory and anti-inflammatory cytokines and neuropeptide-Y. Cytokines are proteins in the blood that help keep the immune system in tune and react to wounds and infections. Neuropeptide-Y is an amino acid in the brain and nervous system that has been linked to stress resilience.

Because the entire group of cadets was high in hardiness, the researchers further broke down the sample into those with a balanced hardiness profile and those with an unbalanced profile. A balanced profile means that hardiness scores are consistent across the three facets of commitment, control, and challenge; that is, you're either high in all three, low in all three, or medium in all three. The unbalanced group in this sample consisted mostly of cadets who were high on hardiness-commitment and control, but low on challenge. With such a profile, a person can still be high in hardiness but is somewhat rigid, lacking the flexibility that hardiness-challenge provides.

As expected, the unbalanced hardiness group showed a less healthy immune system, with lower levels of neuropeptide-Y and proinflammatory cytokines. This study underscores the value of hardiness for maintaining a healthy immune system and points to the importance of all three hardiness facets in the hardiness profile. We'll talk more about hardiness profiles in a later chapter.

Putting Hardiness to Work for You

So, what does this all mean for you? Well, if you're high in hardiness, you are already operating at a somewhat higher level of alertness and engagement than the low-hardy person. When confronted with a new or threatening situation, you're not easily flustered. You size up the situation quickly and are pretty confident that you have the know-how and resources to deal with it. Your body experiences a normal stress reaction, but it's mild and fairly brief.

On the other hand, if you're low in hardiness, it's often hard to tell a really threatening situation from one that you can deal with easily. You don't have much confidence that you can handle a new challenge. Your body goes into a full stress reaction, and it takes a while to realize that the situation is not so bad and you can deal with it.

So, what do you do when disaster strikes? When a real stressor comes along that you have to cope with? This could be anything from a job loss to a storm that destroys your house. Whether you're high or low in hardiness, you're likely to react with a strong stress response. Your stress hormones spike, your heart beats faster, and your blood pressure rises. All thoughts of food leave your mind while you face the new situation.

As time passes and you cope with the problem, your body slowly returns to normal. Unfortunately, if you're low in hardiness, your body's aroused state hangs on longer, sometimes long after the immediate stressor is past. This is where the body's stress response, which is designed to help us adapt to new and dangerous conditions, can start to do damage. When the crisis is over, we need our parasympathetic system to kick in and put the brakes on the stress response.

There are several ways that you can stimulate your parasympathetic nervous system (PNS for short) and help dampen down your stress response. Deep breathing is one of the simplest and a proven technique. By forcing yourself to take long deep breaths, you send a message to your PNS that the stress has passed and it's time to slow the system down (Gerritson & Band, 2018).

Meditation and similar activities like mindfulness, yoga, and T'ai Chi have also been shown to stimulate the PNS and thereby reduce the stress response (Mason et al., 2013). And simply getting a good night's sleep is another useful technique for keeping your PNS in tune and staving off stress-related health problems (Fisher, Young, & Fadel, 2010).

These are some short-term solutions for keeping your body's stress response under control and your nervous system in good balance. For the long term, it's best to increase your hardiness qualities of commitment, control, and challenge. Higher hardiness levels will not only lead you to better performance when dealing with stress but will also help to keep you healthy. We cover some ways to improve your hardiness in the upcoming chapters.

Chapter 9

Hardiness at Work

"The big secret in life is that there is no big secret. Whatever your goal, you can get there if you're willing to work."
—Oprah Winfrey (US talk show host, media executive)

Are you stressed out in your current job? Have you ever thought about how stressful other jobs might be? What would you think are some of the most stressful jobs out there? Does bus driver come up as one of your choices? In this chapter we'll talk about stress in the workplace. By learning how hardiness applies to work, you'll have the tools to better understand how you can improve your work situation. You may want to change your hardiness mindset to better fit your job, or you may want to find a job that's more suited to your current hardiness mindset. This chapter will help you chart your course.

Driving a Bus Is No Walk in the Park

Driving a bus can be a stressful job. In fact, it can be one of the most stressful jobs out there. There are some great rewards for driving a bus—decent pay, good family medical benefits, and a decent pension. But the costs can take their toll. Some of these costs have been documented by Christine Zook, who was president of Amalgamated Transit Union Local 192 in Oakland, California (Boyer & Brunet, 1996; DelVechio, 2019).

Zook, who drove a bus for an urban transit district in Northern California, describes her work as squeezing a 20-ton machine through city streets filled with traffic jams, potholes, road construction, jaywalkers, bike messengers, double-parked trucks, and often careless motorists. Driving a city bus had taken its toll on her. The job's day-to-day stresses on her body and nerves had built up over the years and left her with clenched muscles and crying spells. According to Zook, bus drivers tend to die young. The stress takes a toll on their lives.

There has been over 50 years of research across different countries looking at the effects of driving buses for a living. One of the findings is that urban bus drivers experience higher than average rates of cardiovascular disease, according to a study in the *Journal of Occupational Health Psychology.* "Epidemiological data from samples in several different countries consistently find urban bus drivers among the most unhealthy of occupational groups, particularly with respect to cardiovascular, gastrointestinal and musculoskeletal disorders," the researchers reported. "Further, cardiovascular mortality rates are directly linked to years of service as a driver" (Evans & Johansson, 1998).

This study found that bus drivers are likely to have high blood pressure and increased levels of stress hormones—factors that contribute to sickness and death from heart and blood vessel problems. In addition, these drivers are exposed to whole-body vibration, diesel exhaust, and noise while keeping themselves in a combat-like state of vigilance in order to deal with threatening passengers and crazy motorists. As if this weren't enough, bus drivers must adhere to a brutal schedule of stops or risk being disciplined or fired.

Bus drivers have also been found to be at greater risk of post-traumatic stress disorder than the population at large. This is based on a Montreal study of transit operators (Boyer & Brunet, 1996). Bus operators are always expected to be ready with a smile for the customer, a quick memory for transit information for those who ask, and a helping hand for bicyclists and the disabled.

GETTING OVERWHELMED BY MULTIPLE DEMANDS

City bus drivers also have multiple demands placed on them. They are expected to be on time and follow strict schedules according to their managers. They have no control over traffic and weather conditions. There is little discretion in how they carry out their jobs. They tend to be in a hierarchically structured workplace. As well, they must deal with demands of passengers, regardless of how unreasonable, providing service with a smile.

Studying bus drivers is what led one of us (Paul) into the area of hardiness back in the late 1980's (Bartone, 1989). At the time there was a growing amount of research looking at the stress that people in white-collar jobs were experiencing. The research on people in office jobs began to spread to a variety of different jobs, including air traffic controllers, airline pilots, dentists, engineers, and scientists. No one, however, was looking at blue-collar workers such as bus drivers. Researchers were starting to suggest that a number of blue-collar jobs would, in fact, be more stressful than many white-collar jobs.

For example, there were reports of London bus drivers who worked in the center of the city having more coronary heart disease issues when compared with suburban bus drivers. Other studies looking at bus drivers found that there were high rates of absenteeism, employee turnover, debilitating illness, injuries on duty, and claims for health benefits. There may be many reasons for these effects, but stress was thought to be one of the leading factors. Much of the stress was attributed to things like time pressure, traffic noise and congestion, equipment vibration, air pollution, lack of control over working conditions, and the social isolation of the bus driver from his or her coworkers.

One of the things I (Paul) found interesting at the time was that not all of the bus drivers' responses to stress were negative. As we have seen in many other occupational groups, the relationship between stress and illness is not a simple one. Just like in other occupations, bus drivers showed a range of responses to stress. My interest at the time was, and is to this day, what differentiates people who experience negative effects from stress from the ones who don't have these bad effects. So, the question I wanted to answer is what are the qualities that distinguish bus drivers with high stress who get ill from bus divers with high stress who manage to stay healthy? Understanding this can help us develop effective programs for reducing the negative effects of stress. And this is what I have been studying for the past 30+ years. These lessons can be applied across many different high-stress occupations.

Bus drivers were a logical group for me to study, for I had some personal experience with the job. While a graduate student at the University of Chicago, I worked as a bus driver for the Chicago Transit Authority. So, I'd experienced the job stressors firsthand. I observed many of my fellow bus drivers who seemed anxious and burned out, while others appeared happy and well adjusted. I wanted to find out why, if they're all dealing with the same basic job demands and stressors, are they reacting so differently?

After the Chicago Transit Authority refused to let me survey drivers, I turned to the bus drivers' union, Amalgamated Transit Union Local #241. When I briefed the union president Elcosie Gresham on the study, he was immediately supportive. Mr. Gresham had also been a bus driver and had experienced the stress of the job. He confided in me that during his time as a driver, a pedestrian was killed when she slipped under the wheels of his bus in a snowstorm. Traumatized by this incident, he gave up driving and devoted his life to getting better working conditions for bus drivers.

STRESS IN BUS DRIVERS: WHY SOME STAY HEALTHY AND OTHERS GET SICK

Basically, the research study involved assessing 798 active bus drivers. They were all surveyed about their stress at work, as well as any stressful life events they were experiencing, their methods of coping, their current health status, any psychiatric symptoms, health habits, their social support, as well as their current level of hardiness.

Based on all the information that was collected, we were able to divide these bus drivers into two groups. The first group had high levels of stress and were experiencing a lot of illnesses or negative symptoms. The second group included bus drivers who were also experiencing high levels of stress, but they had few illnesses or unhealthy symptoms. The goal of the study was to find out what factors differentiated these two groups of bus drivers. Several sophisticated statistical analyses were carried out in order to pinpoint these differences.

It turns out there were three factors that made a significant difference:

- *Regressive coping behavior.* The healthy bus drivers were low in regressive coping. This means that rather than avoid stressful situations, they tended to face them head on and look for ways to solve the problem.
- *Constitutional health.* This one should not be too surprising. This refers to people who have a strong medical history of good health and come from families who are healthy. Bus drivers from unhealthy families are at greater risk for stress related illnesses.
- *Hardiness.* Hardiness was the third factor separating the two groups. The most important hardiness facet proved to be commitment. The second most important was control.

A sense of commitment, either to the work, to themselves, or to others, was the main hardiness factor moderating the negative effects of stress. The driver who believes that he or she is doing something important and meaningful has the best protection against the damaging effects of stress. When interviewed, these drivers spoke with great pride about the work they did, which was described as moving passengers safely to their destinations. For the other drivers, those more prone to suffer from stressful situations, they felt that driving the bus was "just a job."

Challenge was not found to be as important as commitment for the health of these bus drivers. However, other occupations which may have less routine to them, such as advertising or sales, might find challenge more valuable. These types of occupations allow for more creative and risky choices in the work. A sense of control may be more important for people who have jobs in which they can define their own schedules, activities, and the nature of the work itself. Certain highly scheduled or routinized jobs may favor people with low levels of internal control. For example, one study found this was the case for offshore oil rig workers. The work is quite repetitive and allows for little deviation from the routine (Cooper & Sutherland, 1987).

A sense of control may also be important in situations where there may not be much opportunity to influence events, and where a sense of meaning or commitment is severely threatened or not able to be fully expressed. In these cases, one can only choose one's mental attitude. Examples of this can be found in more routine jobs like fast food workers, baristas, or house cleaners.

Family support is often cited as an antidote for stress. Interestingly, in our Chicago bus driver study family social support was not a significant protective factor. One reason may be that social support from family members can sometimes be the kind that encourages withdrawal or avoiding the stressful situations at work (Kobasa & Puccetti, 1983). On the other hand, social support from coworkers was found to be a important factor in reducing the negative effects of work stress. Coworkers may be more helpful in fostering active coping strategies, if they can support you in confronting and dealing with stressful situations at work.

Does Hardiness Influence Your Career Choice?

We've collected hardiness data from thousands of people around the world. In this section we'll look at how hardiness differs in some occupational groups that we found interesting. Figure 9.1 shows some of these differences across jobs.

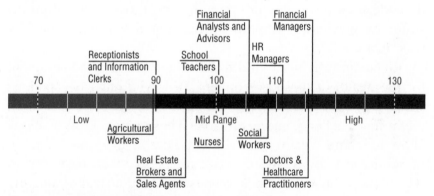

FIGURE 9.1 Hardiness in Different Occupational Groups

(Used with permission from Multi-Health Systems, 2019.)

Agricultural workers' hardiness

Control: Low

Commitment: Low average

Challenge: Low average

One of the job groups that showed the lowest scores in hardiness was agricultural workers. While the type of work these people do may be physically challenging, they are also, to a large degree, at the mercy of the elements. Farmers can't control the weather conditions, and the weather may be a determining factor in their ability to have a successful season. They also have little control over the market price of their crops, often having to accept what the market will choose to pay. Also, much of the work they do is fairly routine and in some cases may be seen as repetitive, with little opportunity for creativity or challenge.

Office receptionists' and clerks' hardiness:

Control: Low

Commitment: Low average

Challenge: Low average

Office receptionists and clerks are often responding to the requests, and sometimes demands, of others. Once again, there may not be much opportunity in these jobs for challenges or innovation. Organizations often don't do enough to instill purpose and commitment in these frontline workers. So they too come out on the lower end of hardiness.

Real estate brokers' and sales agents' hardiness:

Control: Low average

Commitment: Low average

Challenge: Low average

Real estate brokers and sales agents are in the low average range of hardiness. Selling real estate can certainly be very challenging. However, once again you are reliant on others—in this case the whims of buyers and sellers. You must deal with sellers who demand a higher price for their property than you may be able to get from a buyer and, of course, buyers who want to pay less. All the while you have to be careful to keep your cool and not lose patience while going through long hours, and sometimes days, of negotiations with back-and-forth offers and no guarantee of success.

School teachers' hardiness:

Control: Low average

Commitment: High average

Challenge: High average

Nurses' hardiness:

Control: High average

Commitment: High average

Challenge: High average

Teaching and nursing are both occupations with high burnout and attrition rates. They show profiles right in the average range of hardiness scores. In both cases you are dealing with multiple parties with often different, yet demanding needs. Teachers must work with students all day, deal with their parents, and stay within the confines of rules and curricula monitored by principals and school boards. Nurses often deal with difficult patients while juggling the requests of sometimes unpredictable physicians and following structured hospital procedures and medical protocols.

Financial analysts' and advisers' hardiness:

Control: Average

Commitment: Average

Challenge: High

Financial analysts and advisers are average in their overall hardiness. However, they have an interesting profile in that they are average in control and commitment, yet high in challenge. This group operates in an environment where they don't have a lot of control—such as over the market or their client's choice in trades, and they may not have a great sense of purpose in life due to some of the limitations in their work. They tend to be more transactional in nature and live for their next stock trade or new client acquisition. They follow the market closely and focus mainly on short-term, and in some cases, longer term gains. When the stock market goes down, and the average person panics, many analysts see it as a challenge and a time to buy.

Social workers' hardiness:

Control: High average

Commitment: High average

Challenge: High average

Human resource managers' hardiness:

Control: High

Commitment: High average

Challenge: High

Social workers and human resource managers tend to be in the high average range of hardiness. In both cases these professionals deal with people who present with various problems and issues. Social workers often counsel people experiencing challenges in their lives, and human resource professionals deal with people who may have difficulties at work. Both these groups tend to have enough autonomy in their work that they can find challenge and purpose in what they do. They also have a fair amount of control in how they perform their jobs, as they tend to work fairly independently.

Medical doctors' hardiness:

Control: High

Commitment: High

Challenge: High

Financial managers' hardiness:

Control: High

Commitment: High

Challenge: High

Among the highest hardiness occupational groups in our database are medical doctors and financial managers. Both groups, while having a lot of responsibility—whether over peoples' lives or their money—have a high degree of autonomy. They often are in charge of not only their own work, but of others they work with. They have a great deal of control over how they perform their work. Their level of commitment is high, since saving peoples' lives or being in charge of their money are very purposeful types of work. Also, there is a lot of challenge and flexibility in the nature of the work. Both doctors and financial managers have many opportunities to choose how they want to perform their work.

While these occupational profiles are revealing, it's important to remember that we're reporting average hardiness scores here. Within each group, whether farmers or doctors, there is individual variability. Some farmers are high in hardiness, and some doctors are low. No matter what your job is, you can still be high in hardiness and maintain a strong sense of challenge, control, and commitment. However, you might find it a bit stifling if you are high in hardiness and are in a job that doesn't provide you with opportunities to exercise your style.

So, does your hardiness level influence your career choice? Most likely the answer is yes, to some degree. For example, some people decide early on that they want a career in which they believe they will control their own destiny, such as entrepreneurs, doctors, dentists, entertainers, writers, and others. On the other hand, some people are happier applying for a steady, more routine job, such as receptionist, clerk, fast food worker, bank teller, and so on. Hopefully, we select jobs that "fit" our hardiness type. When we end up with a job that doesn't fit our hardiness type— such as a person with high control and commitment taking a routine job that doesn't allow for much control, or something to believe in—we may feel a disconnect. Either you would adjust your mindset or find another, more satisfying job.

Hardiness Scores of Healthcare Professionals

The healthcare profession has long been identified as a stressful line of work. Speculation as to the causes of stress has included the complexity of professional activities, chronic staff shortages, the requirement to provide quality care, emotional overload, role conflicts, and noise, all making work in a hospital more painful and increasingly stressful. Researchers have started to look into why some healthcare professionals exposed to these conditions are still highly effective, while others have professional difficulties.

One interesting study carried out at a large hospital setting in Morocco set out to profile the hardiness levels of their healthcare professionals—150 nurses and 80 doctors (Chtibi, Ahami, Azzaoui, Khadmaoui, & Mammad, 2018). The study used an earlier version of the Hardiness Resilience Gauge (HRG) as one of its measures. They found no difference in hardiness levels of nurses compared to doctors. Length of service, however, was a factor. Healthcare professionals who had worked at the hospital longer scored higher in hardiness than those who started more recently.

Is hardiness related to the health status of these medical professionals? This study addressed this question by looking at certain health indices in the hospital staff. Health conditions included hypertension and cancer. Seventy-eight percent of those who reported hypertension fell in the lowest group of hardiness. In addition, those professionals who had cancer were in the lowest scoring hardiness group.

Overall, most of these healthcare professionals, 81%, scored in the lowest third of hardiness; 16% scored in the middle group; and only 3% were in the high resilience group. Another measure the researchers looked at was the level of engagement of these professionals in their work. There was a significant relationship between how engaged they were in their work and their hardiness levels, with the hardier people being more engaged. The authors report that engagement allows doctors and nurses to get involved in their work and to adapt positively in the professional context. The hardiness-control factor was important in looking at different options for taking action when needed. The hardiness-challenge factor reflects the involvement of healthcare professionals in the process of change.

The authors go on to discuss the importance of these resilience factors in protecting healthcare professionals from work-related stress. Resilient professionals can cope positively with stressful events, while vulnerable people tend to see stressful situations as threatening. Low hardiness professionals tend to reject change and prefer stability.

We can see how these findings may apply to different work groups. Having a high hardiness level in a job that allows for independence, fosters purpose, and offers challenges will make it easier to become more engaged in your work. When you see room for change at work, being high in control helps you make it happen. Your challenge level can make the change happen more smoothly.

What Do We Know About Hardiness and Work Satisfaction?

Most people tend to settle into situations and types of work that will provoke certain kinds of emotional reactions. In an overview of three decades of research on hardiness, Celina Oliver had some interesting conclusions about hardiness and work satisfaction (Oliver, 2009). Because people differ, they generally seek out the kind of work that provides the emotional responses that are best suited for them. For example, people high in hardiness prefer work that provides a lot of independence and more challenging opportunities. Hardy people are more likely to change situations that they see as undesirable. They are more inclined to present a can-do attitude in their work. Also, they are more likely to seek feedback at work, which increases their competency as well as their self-esteem and self-confidence. Hardy people are more likely to set and reach stretch goals.

In the workplace people who are high in hardiness, when they encounter stressful situations, tend to engage in effective problem-focused coping strategies. Or, when there are limited opportunities to change the situation, they will know how to reframe it—that is, look at it from a more positive viewpoint. They are more likely to count their blessings rather than dwell on the unpleasantness of the situation or vent their feelings about the unfairness of it all.

Oliver's review looked at the relationship between hardiness and job satisfaction in a variety of different occupational groups. Hardiness was found to be more strongly related to job satisfaction in jobs such as teaching, healthcare, and human services. In other words, jobs that involved helping or developing people had a stronger relationship between hardiness and job satisfaction. So, people low in hardiness may struggle when they work in jobs that involve a lot of interaction with other people. This may relate to some of the other findings about hardiness at work.

Hardiness-commitment was found to have the strongest relationship with overall work satisfaction. People who have a purpose in life either find the work that is most satisfying to them, or make the most of the jobs they already have. The relationship between control-hardiness and satisfaction was significant, but not as strong. People who are higher in control tend to make the changes they need in order to be more satisfied at work. Either they find ways to make changes in their existing job, or they go out and find a more satisfying job. Challenge-hardiness, while also related to overall job satisfaction, was not as strong as the other two factors. People higher in this area would likely look at their jobs and redefine what they do as interesting, focusing on those parts of their job that they find the most challenging.

Think about your own level of hardiness-commitment. Have you identified the things in life that are most important to you? Is it helping people, improving the environment, creating new things, making the world a better place? Identifying your purpose and finding work that supports that cause will lead you to greater satisfaction both at work and in life.

Challenges Versus Hindrances at Work

What happens when you are asked to do something new at work? Are you likely to treat it as a new challenge, something you're excited about? Or do you see this kind of request as a burden or a hassle that just gets in the way of other work? Some people view any new request at work as a drain on their resources, leading to an increase in work stress. Other people view these requests as new opportunities, or the kind of challenges we have described in previous chapters.

Researchers have built work theories around these perceptions. In one framework, these requests are seen as depleting your resources, adding more stress to your life. In another, some demands are seen as challenges, yet others may be hindrances, or merely interferences with ongoing work. In a study of these two models, researchers have gone one step further, looking at how these kinds of work demands influence workers in two ways—their own sense of self-worth and the perceived meaningfulness of their work (Kim & Beehr, 2019). This then leads to a concept that is described as *flourishing*—an increase in general positive well-being. Flourishing, more specifically, has been defined as having feelings of competence, positive relationships with others, and having purpose in life. People high in the hardiness mindset are more likely to be in a flourishing state.

Researchers have looked especially at the effects of three categories of work demands. The first is workload. This has to do with how hard you have to work. The second is responsibility. This is where there is a lot that depends on decisions that you make. The third is learning demands. This relates to how much you need to learn in order to improve the knowledge and skills you need to do your job.

Most important in these studies is how workers view the demands that are made of them. If someone asks you to do something, and you appraise or judge it as interesting or challenging, that will lead to one set of effects. If, on the other hand, you view the same requests as annoying, or a hindrance, that can affect you in a completely different way. Your entire sense of self-worth and the meaningfulness of your work can be influenced by how you see these demands, either positively or negatively. One of the surprising findings of the research is how these work demands—and your interpretation of them—can spill over into your personal life outside of work.

While we all want to strive for work-life balance (if there is such a thing!) and leave our work issues in the workplace once we go home, this doesn't seem to happen. We carry our feelings from work with us into our personal worlds. If we feel excited and challenged by what we have done at work, we're more likely to be in a good mood and flourish at home. If we are drained and stressed out by our experience at work, we take those bad feelings—along with the health risks they produce—and suffer at home. While we have often heard about the negative effects of work—stress, daily hassles, heavy workloads, interpersonal conflicts—and how they can affect our health, we have rarely, if ever, heard about the positive effects. Higher hardiness, which includes looking at demands as challenges, having commitment to your mission, and having control over your tasks, can lead to increased flourishing in your life overall, including greater feelings of competence, positive relationships with others, and increased purpose in life.

Practicing Hardiness in the Legal Profession

We've covered some of the challenges that blue-collar workers, such as bus drivers, must grapple with and how hardiness can play a role in a healthier life. We also looked at professionals in the healthcare field. One of the professional groups that experiences a lot of stress is lawyers. In fact, it's been reported that not only do lawyers encounter more psychological distress than the general public, but they are in poor mental health with higher incidents of depression, alcoholism, illegal drug use, and divorce than almost any other profession (Beck, Sales, & Benjamin, 1995–96; Allan, 1997; Shellenbarger, 2007).

In one of the earliest studies to look at stress and health in lawyers, Suzanne Kobasa surveyed a group of 157 general practice lawyers who attended a meeting of the Canadian Bar Association (Kobasa, 1982). For these lawyers, stress contributed significantly to symptoms of strain and illness such as heartburn, upset stomach, headaches, and trouble sleeping. More important, the study showed that those lawyers who were high in hardiness-commitment, and low in the use of avoidance coping strategies, were healthier and less likely to experience these stress-related health problems.

Another interesting study carried out at the University of Alabama Law School investigated the relationship between hardiness, stress, and a number of other factors in lawyers and law students (Pierson, Hamilton, Pepper, & Root, 2018). They started out talking about the "lawyer personality." Because of the nature of law school admissions, it's difficult to gain admittance to a law school with an IQ lower than 115. As well, the profession attracts people who are motivated, intelligent, and ambitious. They tend to be more achievement-oriented, aggressive, and competitive than in other professions.

The "lawyer personality" also implies that lawyers are less willing to accept help when they need it. They tend to be self-reliant, ambitious, perfectionistic, and highly motivated to provide good service. In a British study of 1,000 lawyers it was reported that 70% of them said they experienced their workplace as stressful; two-thirds said they would "be concerned about reporting feelings of stress to an employer" (Lyon, 2015). One of the reasons for this is the fear of damaging their reputation and subsequently their client base. Sometimes people high in certain aspects of hardiness, such as hardiness-commitment, will continue pursuing their purpose even though they may be hurting or overstressed. That's where challenge comes in as a balancing factor. A strong sense of challenge increases mental flexibility. People high in challenge can more easily shift directions and take a different approach or path when one isn't working.

The lawyer's lifestyle contributes towards stress as well. The work usually demands long hours. There is a great deal of pressure on attaining enough billable hours. The adversarial nature of the job can also add to the stress. There is a lot of unpredictability in the outcome of cases that can take hundreds of hours to prepare for. Lawyers often have to deal with difficult clients, coworkers, and opponents.

In the Alabama Law School study, Pierson et al. surveyed 530 lawyers and law students about their work, stress, and how they manage it, along with administering some personality tests. The researchers included an earlier version of the Hardiness Resilience Gauge (HRG) measuring challenge, control, and commitment, as well as overall hardiness. Lawyers from throughout Alabama as well as a national group were invited to participate in the study. The goal was to obtain a stress score for each respondent, identify the behavioral patterns of respondents who had lower and higher stress scores, and determine if any of their behavior patterns correlated with stress levels.

The researchers first analyzed the relationships between all responses to individual questions to identify the characteristics of a stress-hardy lawyer. They then cross-tabulated each survey response with all the other survey responses. They looked at relationships that were statistically significant, including demographic variables. A number of the lawyers were interviewed as well.

The results showed highly significant relationships among certain characteristics. For example, the lawyers' sense of control, sense of purpose, cognitive flexibility, and stress hardiness were related. This means that lawyers who had a greater sense of control, sense of purpose, or cognitive flexibility were less stressed, while those who had lower control, sense of purpose, or cognitive flexibility were more stressed. They also found a highly significant relationship between relying on alcohol and drug use to manage stress and stress levels experienced: those lawyers who reported relying on substance use to manage their stress were in turn more stressed.

The lawyers encountered a variety of stressors based on their areas of specialty. Lawyers who represented people in either family or criminal law often found it difficult dealing with people when things didn't go well for them—such as going to jail or losing custody of a child. Lawyers involved in litigation often had trouble dealing with difficult people, especially the lawyers on the opposing side. Managers of law firms were often stressed by dealing with the personnel issues within their firms. Lawyers who worked in government worried about not having the resources they needed to succeed in their work.

The Relationship Between Control and Stress

The Alabama law school study found direct relationships between stress and the hardiness factors of control. For example, as seen in Figure 9.2, lawyers who experienced more stress had a lower sense of control, and those with the least stress had the highest sense of control. This was found to be related to the unpredictability of their work. Unexpected curve balls seem to go along with the practice of law.

One of the interesting things about this study was that they asked the lawyers to describe how they coped with stress. Responses from the hardy lawyers, related to control, were quite interesting. Seven themes emerged as to how lawyers

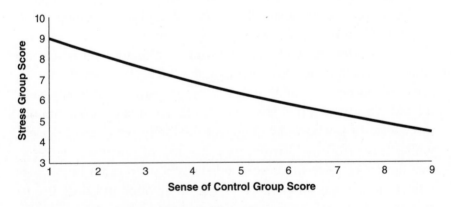

Figure **9.2** Sense of Control Versus Stress in Lawyers

(Copyright 2017. All rights reserved. Used with permission from Pamela Bucy Pierson, University of Alabama School of Law.)

adapt and maintain a sense of control over their professional lives. These are:

♦ Good preparation
♦ Time management
♦ Building a team and asking others for help
♦ Learning how to "turn it off"
♦ Taking charge of their career
♦ Recognizing that law is a business
♦ Setting boundaries with clients.

THE RELATIONSHIP BETWEEN PURPOSE (COMMITMENT) AND STRESS

Hardiness-commitment, which the researchers referred to as sense of purpose, was also found to be directly related to stress in lawyers. This is shown in Figure 9.3.

Purpose was expressed by a number of the lawyers as helping or making a difference in clients' lives. Other examples included unraveling problems, protecting companies, gratitude of clients, helping the legal system render justice, and helping the legal system work better. Overall, the lawyers who reported no sense of purpose had an average stress group score 32% higher than the average stress score of lawyers who had at least some meaningful aspects of practicing law.

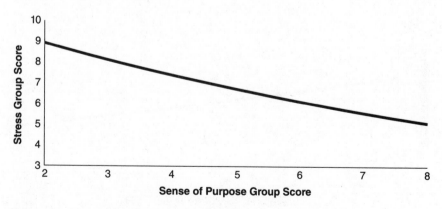

FIGURE 9.3 Sense of Purpose/Commitment Versus Stress in Lawyers

(Copyright 2017. All rights reserved. Used with permission from Pamela Bucy Pierson, University of Alabama School of Law.)

THE RELATIONSHIP BETWEEN COGNITIVE FLEXIBILITY (CHALLENGE) AND STRESS

The study also looked at hardiness-challenge which was referred to as cognitive flexibility. Basically, this was described as a way to make stressful situations make sense. It is described as the ability to pivot, take a different route, or change goals when dealing with a stressful situation. They found that lawyers who had the highest stress were the least cognitively flexible, and those with the least stress were the most flexible. This is shown in Figure 9.4

For example, lawyers who reported that they were "not bothered by interruptions to their daily routine" were more confident about their ability to handle personal problems and better able to control irritations in life. Lawyers who enjoy the challenge of doing more than one thing at a time were more likely to feel on top of things. Flexibility and adaptability were qualities that the lawyers high in challenge endorsed.

Lawyers who excelled in challenge/cognitive flexibility had strategies that fell into eight general categories:

♦ Be prepared to make changes
♦ Learn the market
♦ Develop a niche
♦ Recognize opportunities
♦ Create opportunities

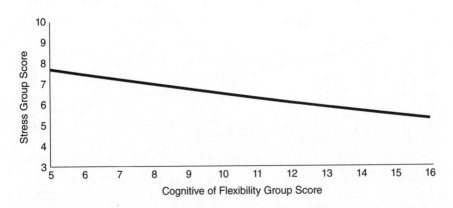

FIGURE 9.4 Cognitive Flexibility/Challenge Versus Stress in Lawyers

(Copyright 2017. All rights reserved. Used with permission from Pamela Bucy Pierson, University of Alabama School of Law.)

- Be "nimble" financially
- Master technology
- Community and professional involvement.

Many of these strategies can be applied beyond the legal profession.

PROFILE OF THE HIGH-HARDINESS LAWYER

Sunny Handa is a senior partner at one of Canada's largest law firms. He heads up the firm's information technology group and the communications group. With a doctoral degree in law he also teaches at the Faculty of Law at McGill University and has written books on computer and intellectual property law. He has been selected among the top lawyers in his field according to several independent lists and rankings of Canada's top lawyers. His clients include some of the world's largest technology companies. Sunny's Hardiness Resilience Gauge scores are shown in Figure 9.5.

As you can see, Sunny's overall hardiness score is in the high range. There's no surprise here. Throughout his law career he's made it through many tough negotiating situations, but he seldom, if ever, gets riled or loses his cool.

His hardiness-challenge score is high as well. When asked about his score, he explained that he feels he is high in confidence because he is comfortable with the unknown. That's a big part of hardiness-challenge. He does not fear whatever unfamiliar situations may be coming down the road, but rather, sees them as interesting problems to be solved.

He also sees himself as a bit lazy, as he has such an academic background. He feels his challenge is influenced by his education and experience. It helps that he teaches new lawyers. New lawyers tend to be scared when presented with tricky situations. He teaches them that if you know the law you can find the answer to frame any problem. All you have to do is break it down into pieces. It's not about the solution, it's about how to get there. When he's confronted with a difficult case, he uses his gut and can usually determine very quickly where the case is likely to go. At his level of practice and clientele, he deals with very smart people. It's the nature of his work.

Sunny Handa
May 27, 2019

TOTAL HARDINESS

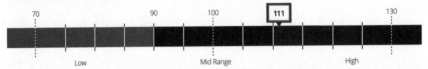

What your score means

- Your result indicates that your total level of hardiness falls in the **High** range.

- You are likely very capable of tackling stressful and unexpected situations that come your way. Your high level of hardiness often protects you from the negative effects of stress and you are able to respond to surprising and stressful situations in a healthy and adaptive manner.

- You likely have the coping skills necessary to help you deal with stressful circumstances. For example, rather than trying to ignore or avoid the stressful situation, you likely try to fix it and work on eliminating the source of your stress.

HARDINESS SUBSCALES

CHALLENGE

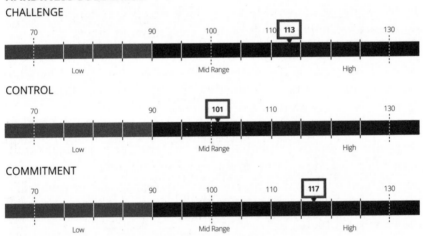

CONTROL

COMMITMENT

On the pages that follow, you will find more information on your Challenge, Control, and Commitment scores. As you move through the report, think about how you might see these hardiness qualities emerge in your day-to-day life. If you choose to implement the recommended developmental strategies highlighted for you, you can ensure that you are setting yourself up for success when faced with stressful and changing situations.

MHS © Copyright of MHS 2019. All rights reserved.

1.1.1

3

FIGURE 9.5 Sunny Handa's Hardiness-Resilience Scores

(Used with permission from Multi-Health Systems, 2019.)

We were surprised that Sunny's hardiness-control score was lower than expected. But when asked about this he said that it made perfect sense to him. He stated that his world is very complex as it involves dealing with a lot of chaos. He has to navigate these situations with the tools and skills that he has. In his world, only 10% of what happens is changeable, making one feel that there is a limited range of control. Going with the flow is often the best option. The parties generally know what they want, and his job is to work within certain parameters. He sees his job as executing and minimizing the risk. As he states it, "I have to decide where we spend our time. I am a libertarian. Many things are out of our control."

Sunny's hardiness-commitment score is his highest. When you talk with Sunny about his work it's understandable. As he puts it, "I believe in the work I do. I am driven by the work I do. I love the work that I do. I feel blessed to be alive. I like people and I love working with people. I also like to spend time alone. If everything I dealt with was rational, I wouldn't have a job. I never feel deflated. My faith in my work is very exciting. Every case is exciting to me. Even if I've done a similar case, I find the next one exciting. There are always twists in these kinds of cases."

When we look at Sunny's emotional intelligence scores we also find a very elevated profile. He scores highest in self-regard. This factor has to do with your self-confidence and your ability to know your strengths and weaknesses. As he states it himself, "I feel confident in myself. I don't mean to overstate it; I don't mean be arrogant."

His next highest score is in empathy. This is the ability to understand people—both their thoughts and feelings—from the other person's point of view. This is especially important for lawyers trying to understand not only their client but their adversaries' perspective. Lawyers also have to know how far they can go in pushing the limits in a courtroom. For example, as Sunny puts it, "I like to hear people out. I think everybody has a valid point of view to express."

The third highest score is in optimism. In emotional intelligence terms, this is the ability to see the positive side of things, even in difficult times. When confronting overly complex and difficult cases, it can be easy to get overwhelmed, especially when the stakes are so high. A certain degree of optimism is needed not only to keep your client happy, but to drive your own belief that you can arrive at a solution. In his own words, "I think things will work out okay. I have a positive view."

When we look at emotional intelligence, we also look at the challenges that people have. In Sunny's case one of the lower scores in his profile was in the area of social responsibility. This has to do with our commitment to helping others in need. It's not that he's low in social responsibility, but rather it is less of a priority than most other areas. He explains his score as, "I am a Libertarian. I feel there's a difference between self-interest and greed. Society won't help me; I need to help myself. I will be socially responsible where I have a personal connection."

A second area of challenge is his flexibility. This is an area that tends to be lower, especially for rule-bound professionals such as lawyers, engineers, and accountants. As Sunny says, "I work within the rules. I tend to support management. I am interested in fairness."

Putting Your Hardiness to Work

As we have seen in this chapter, hardiness-commitment can be a very important part of buffering you from workplace stress. Looking for meaning in your work can not only help you better manage stress but can keep you more engaged in the work you do. It also helps if you build social support among your coworkers. Your coworkers can be a very important sounding board to help you let off steam about frustrating work situations.

The whole idea of the hardiness mindset and how it fits for certain careers is something you can think about. If you have a good idea of where you are in terms of your need for challenge, control, and commitment, you can see how that might apply in various jobs. For example, if you have a high need for control you may want to work in an environment that gives you that latitude. If more meaningful work is important for you, you can look for a job that lets you feel like you are making a contribution to society. If what you look for is challenge, you can find work that offers lots of variety, keeps your mind sharp, and/or keeps your body engaged. Your priority might be jobs with challenging assignments.

Generally, people in jobs that involve helping people in one way or another such as teaching, nursing, social work, medicine, and so on have higher levels of hardiness than people in other, less people-oriented jobs. We don't know for sure whether hardier people choose these kinds of jobs, or time spent in a people-helping job makes you hardier. The answer is most likely some combination of both.

In the healthcare field, length of time in the job was related to greater hardiness. It could be that for many types of work the longer we're there, the more we develop a hardiness mindset. We start feeling more in control, gravitate to more challenging tasks, and find more meaning in our work.

Hardiness is also related to engagement. If we have greater control over our work, we have more choice in how we get things done. This sense of control helps increase our engagement and commitment.

And we also see that hardiness helps protect these healthcare professionals from stress. Rather than having the stress mindset (that change is a threat), the hardiness mindset (change is interesting and challenging) drives these people in their daily activities. To what degree do you operate from a stress mindset versus a hardiness mindset? Do you see changes in your world as threatening or as interesting challenges?

So now you have a few examples of areas of work where hardiness has been found to be important. You can apply much of this to your own work. We'll be exploring hardiness in some other walks of life in the following chapters.

Chapter 10

What We Can Learn from Hardiness in High-Stakes Performance Careers

Musical Artists and Sports

"Mastery is great, but even that is not enough. You have to be able to change course without a bead of sweat, or remorse."
—Tom Peters (American writer on business practices)

There's a certain amount of mental toughness that's required in order to be successful as a high-stakes performer. There's also a certain amount of hardiness. In this chapter we'll focus on hardiness in performers from the sports and entertainment world. Not only do people in these careers have hundreds, or even millions of people watching and judging their performance, but most high-performance athletes and entertainers have had to compete against dozens of other talented people in their fields over the years in order to reach success.

What part do the hardiness factors play in their success or failure? We'll explore the role of the three Cs of hardiness in these groups, looking at case examples and research studies. We'll also examine some of the ways high performers manage their hardiness. There's a lot we can learn about navigating the stresses in our lives from people who compete or perform in high-stakes and high-pressure situations on a regular basis.

Playing Out Hardiness as a Musical Director

Orin Isaacs is a musical director. You've probably never heard of him. But in his field, music production, he has done some amazing and well-recognized work. He has worked with artists that include Mariah Carey, Billy Ray Cyrus, Kid Rock, Paul Anka, Tom Jones, Patti LaBelle, Lionel Ritchie, Anne Murray, Burton Cummings (from the Guess Who), Martina McBride, Roger Hodgson (from Supertramp), Paul Shaffer (from the *Late Night with David Letterman*), Bret Michaels (from Poison), Macy Gray, and many others. He was the bandleader on a popular Canadian late-night talk show called *Open Mike with Mike Bullard.*

He scores and performs the music for dozens of TV shows that include *Big Brother Canada, The Amazing Race Canada, Canada's Got Talent, Canadian Screen Awards,* the *Junos* (Canada's version of the *Grammys*), and many, many others. He's won three Juno Awards himself, as well as one gold and four platinum albums as artist or producer.

Orin grew up in an area of Toronto that was known as Caledonia Village and went to school in Lawrence Heights, an area referred to as "The Jungle" by residents and police alike soon after its completion. Both areas were considered "high risk." One of Canada's national newspapers headlined an article about the area as "Toronto's new murder capital" and gave some insight into the crime in the area: "It's like you're in the jungle. It is like a war," said Linkx, a 20-year-old hip-hop producer from a nearby area who wore Crip gang colors.

The area was heavily Afro-Canadian with many single-parent families. Orin grew up in a single-parent household. While many of his contemporaries completed high school, some ended up on the wrong side of the law. He learned from his music teacher at school that music might be a better use of his time than getting into trouble.

He had a strong mother who always told him to keep his goals in front of him, so in high school he put a sticker on his glasses that said "#1." Fortunately, Orin had a talent for music. His instrument of choice was the bass guitar.

Although his favorite genre was hip-hop urban music, his music teacher taught him to learn all genres of music—classical, rock, folk, electronic, and anything else that would take him out of his comfort zone. He started playing the bass guitar professionally getting $100 a night for weekend gigs. After gigging for many years as a professional musician, he eventually decided he was worth $1,000 per gig. Knowing that it would result in far fewer jobs, it ended up getting him much better playing opportunities.

One time when Orin was with a crew shooting a music video for a hip-hop artist, there was a TV show shooting right next door. The producers came over and asked, "Whose music is that?" They quickly found Orin, and that led to Orin's career in TV. That's where most of his work is today.

In today's TV music production world, he can be contacted in the morning to write 2 minutes and 35 seconds of scary music and 4 minutes and 10 seconds of sexy music and deliver the pieces on the same afternoon. It must all be original so as not to violate copyrights. With the advent of technology, these once impossible requests can now be delivered. Orin says there is nothing more exciting than creating music on Monday and seeing it aired on Tuesday night's TV show.

WHAT'S ORIN'S HARDINESS RESILIENCE GAUGE PROFILE?

Orin agreed to take the Hardiness Resilience Gauge (HRG) assessment for hardiness and the EQ-i 2.0 (Emotional Quotient 2.0) assessment for emotional intelligence to help us get a better understanding of the mindset of someone who came from such humble beginnings to rise to such a high level of success in an extremely difficult and competitive industry. There are literally thousands of talented musicians and composers struggling to support themselves and their families today. Very few successfully make a living at it, let alone become a success story.

You might expect Orin's hardiness score to be generally high, having successfully made it through challenging circumstances. And if so, you would be correct. Orin's hardiness scores are shown in Figure 10.1. His overall hardiness level is in the high range. This indicates his general ability to successfully navigate stressful situations and not avoid them.

Orin Isaacs
April 12, 2019

TOTAL HARDINESS

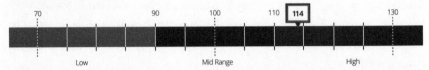

What your score means

- Your result indicates that your total level of hardiness falls in the **High** range.

- You are likely very capable of tackling stressful and unexpected situations that come your way. Your high level of hardiness often protects you from the negative effects of stress and you are able to respond to surprising and stressful situations in a healthy and adaptive manner.

- You likely have the coping skills necessary to help you deal with stressful circumstances. For example, rather than trying to ignore or avoid the stressful situation, you likely try to fix it and work on eliminating the source of your stress.

HARDINESS SUBSCALES

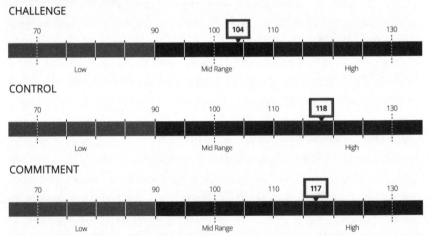

On the pages that follow, you will find more information on your Challenge, Control, and Commitment scores. As you move through the report, think about how you might see these hardiness qualities emerge in your day-to-day life. If you choose to implement the recommended developmental strategies highlighted for you, you can ensure that you are setting yourself up for success when faced with stressful and changing situations.

MHS © Copyright of MHS 2019. All rights reserved.   3

1.1.1

FIGURE **10.1** Orin Isaacs's Hardiness Profile

(Used with permission from Multi-Health Systems, 2019.)

Based on his story, you might expect his ability to take charge, despite the circumstances around him, to be high. It should be clear that Orin doesn't sit around waiting for things to happen. One of the hallmarks of high performers is that they take action—and they tend to act strategically. They don't waste time chasing impossible situations. They know their strengths and weaknesses, what they can do and what may be beyond their ability at the time.

When offered the opportunity to score a TV show, Orin felt that was within his wheelhouse. Taking advantage of that opportunity led to a major career change in the music industry.

How often have you seen opportunities, but hesitated? Have you ever felt that some prospect you were presented with looked and felt good, but you just couldn't convince yourself to take the chance? Did fear of failing or looking bad hold you back? Taking calculated risks, even failing sometimes, can pay off in the longer term. It's sometimes our fears that hold us back from moving forward in our lives.

It may not be surprising then, that Orin's highest score is in hardiness-control. This makes a lot of sense because when you meet him you know he has a strong sense of being able to control his reactions to situations. This is something Orin has shown throughout his career. When faced with obstacles, he continued working hard to meet his goals. While trying to make ends meet as an itinerant musician is tough, one thing Orin could control was what he felt his talent was worth. By increasing his rate from $100 to $1,000 per gig he took more control over his career. This was a big risk. He knew it was limiting in some ways—fewer gigs—but it could be empowering in other ways—working only quality gigs.

How you see yourself is important. It helps determine the direction you might take in life. Orin's ability to see himself and his talent realistically helped him go forward in his career. His hardiness-commitment score was also in the high range. Part of commitment is how you see yourself, or your self-worth. As mentioned, Orin had been taught by his mother to think of himself as #1 since he was a kid, and he has internalized that belief. He certainly behaves, to this day, with confidence. Without any arrogance, Orin exudes self-assurance in his abilities and has proven it time and again.

No musical challenge is too hard for Orin. He's often given the task of working with nonmusical entertainers who have agreed to perform musically on a TV show. He was able to work with William Shatner, the actor who portrayed Captain Kirk in *Star Trek*, and coach him to complete a musical number on TV. Shatner is not a musical performer, so this was quite the challenge. Orin reports that this kind of work takes patience, sensitivity, and creativity.

Commitment also means active engagement in your pursuits. People high in commitment believe they can continue learning and achieving in their lives. Commitment is highly connected to work performance. People high in commitment feel they are excelling in their work. In an interview Orin pointed out how important it is for him to keep up with the new, younger, hot artists in the music scene. To keep his work fresh he must stay current, whether it's with the latest hip-hop artist or the newest blockbuster movie score.

You might also expect that Orin's hardiness-challenge score would be off the charts. This was, however, the lowest of his hardiness scores, and it fell in the middle or average range. How can we explain this? One thing we look at in hardiness scores is the balance among the scales. In this case, the challenge score is lower than the other two. When we look at the relationship between control and challenge, we can see that Orin's motivation to control and influence the outcomes in his life is higher than his motivation to try new things and get new experiences. He may see little value or opportunity in learning situations in which he doesn't have control over the outcome.

We also see his challenge score out of balance with his commitment score. This may reflect his desire to do things that are meaningful that outweigh his motivation to try new things. We all go through stages and shifts in our mindsets. We place different levels of importance on different achievements. At times it may be meaningful work and purpose that is our priority. At other times life may be about going out and trying new experiences. Where do you see yourself at this point in time?

One reason Orin may not be searching as much for new experiences is because he does not fear the future, as he already has a steady supply of work. He has displaced a number of traditional music directors with his ability to create, produce, and deliver original music digitally on time and within budget. Part of being a seasoned performer involves getting into a groove. That is, you have a certain amount of predictability in your life. It may include a bit of healthy skepticism, not knowing where or when your next job will come. The balance between seeking some security with looking for the "next thing" can moderate the challenge score.

BLENDING HARDINESS WITH THE EMOTIONAL INTELLIGENCE (EQ-I 2.0) PROFILE

Orin also took our test of emotional intelligence, the Emotional Quotient Inventory 2.0 or EQ-i 2.0. The 15 emotional intelligence factors measured by the EQ-i 2.0 help us better understand how the hardiness mindset is expressed through more specific emotional skills.

Orin's emotional intelligence scores were high, as expected. But it's the *pattern* of scores that we're most interested in. By understanding the highest or most used skills we get a better picture of how people interact with themselves and the world around them.

In Orin's case, his highest score was in assertiveness—the ability to express your thoughts, feelings, and beliefs in a constructive way. High assertiveness has paid off in several ways for Orin. First, it is what enabled him to increase his gigging fees to 10 times the going rate for itinerant bass players.

Second, in order to be successful in the music production world, Orin quotes the "no asshole rule." People who are obnoxious, don't follow the rules, and showboat their talent don't get hired. While we all know of musicians with reputations for bad behavior, these tend to be exceptions in today's music world. Nowadays producers have little tolerance for irresponsible behavior, when the cost of wasting time is so high. Think about your own level of assertiveness. Do you feel comfortable expressing your thoughts and feelings in a nondestructive way? Do you hold back for fear of offending or being rebuffed? Or have people indicated to you that you are too aggressive, uncaring about other people's feelings?

Orin's second highest score is in stress tolerance. Stress tolerance in the EQ-i 2.0 is strongly related to hardiness on the HRG.

It assesses your ability to directly confront and manage stressful situations, as opposed to hiding and avoiding them or mainly reacting emotionally. People high in stress tolerance tend to view stressful situations honestly and deal with them, often through focusing on the task at hand and problem-solving. Think about your own ability to confront stressful situations.

He also scores very high in self-actualization. High scorers are people who know where they want to be in life and are aligned with their dreams. Orin loves creating and producing music and sharing it with others. Many people in high-performance careers have had to endure numerous challenges in reaching their goals. Being high in self-actualization tendency can reduce the pain of the sacrifices you make along the way. It also implies you know what your goals are and are highly motivated to reach them. When you have clarified your life goals, what really matters to you, and you pursue those goals, you are on your way to being self-actualized. The stressors you encounter turn into challenges that you surmount.

When looking at EQ-i 2.0 scores we also look at areas for improvement, or the scores that are the lowest. They may not be low compared to the general population, but they are lower than an individual's highest scores. One of Orin's lowest scores was in empathy. After exploring this it appears that it's not necessarily a skill that's lacking, but a skill he chooses not to use. People who are extremely high in self-actualization can be very focused. Their attention is consumed by their work and attaining their goals. This can lead to being less concerned about trying to read and understand other people around them. Think about your own use of empathy—your ability to read other people. How relevant is empathy in your day-to-day activities?

Secrets of Long-Term Success as an Entertainer

The entertainment business is exciting and glamorous, but it also has its challenges. The number of musical artists who have succumbed to drugs and alcohol and passed away long before their time is staggering. In fact, the internet's so-called "27 Club" includes artists that have died (mostly through suicide or drugs) at age 27. Included are people like Brian Jones, Jimi Hendrix, Janis Joplin, Jim Morrison, Kurt Cobain, and Amy Winehouse. On the other hand, artists like Mick Jagger, Paul McCartney, Bruce Springsteen, Tony Bennett, Willie Nelson, and others continue to thrive in their senior years and keep on performing.

What differentiates performers who can successfully and healthily maintain a long-term and satisfying career from those who burn out? How do we find the factors that lead to resilience, health, and long life? Typically, as psychologists, we study samples of those who made it and compare them to those who didn't. Obviously, we can't access those who are gone, but we can look for examples of talented, seasoned performers with successful careers and personal lives.

Alan Paul is an incredibly talented vocalist and longtime member of the jazz vocal group The Manhattan Transfer. The Manhattan Transfer has won 10 Grammy Awards since 1980. They made musical history by becoming the first group to win Grammy awards for both popular and jazz categories in the same year—1981. They won best vocal group pop performance for "Boy From New York City" and best jazz vocal performance for "A Nightingale Sang in Berkeley Square."

But Alan was in the entertainment business before he even joined The Manhattan Transfer. He started his career at age 12 in the original cast of the Broadway musical *Oliver.* After college he returned to Broadway as Teen Angel and Johnny Casino in the original cast of *Grease.* He is also a talented writer and arranger, for which he has received four Grammy nominations. Not only has he maintained a successful career, but he's been married to his wife, Angela, for 38 years. Their 33-year-old daughter also has a successful career as a singer/songwriter.

One of the authors (Steven) met Alan after a performance by The Manhattan Transfer. We had a discussion about the entertainment business and maintaining a sense of balance, as well the difficulty of sustaining a long-lasting career in the music business. Alan agreed to be interviewed and take our Hardiness Resilience Gauge and the Emotional Quotient Inventory 2.0. His hardiness profile is in Figure 10.2.

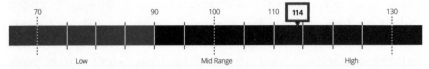

Alan Paul
June 8, 2019

TOTAL HARDINESS

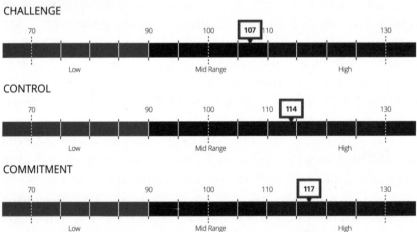

What your score means

- Your result indicates that your total level of hardiness falls in the **High** range.

- You are likely very capable of tackling stressful and unexpected situations that come your way. Your high level of hardiness often protects you from the negative effects of stress and you are able to respond to surprising and stressful situations in a healthy and adaptive manner.

- You likely have the coping skills necessary to help you deal with stressful circumstances. For example, rather than trying to ignore or avoid the stressful situation, you likely try to fix it and work on eliminating the source of your stress.

HARDINESS SUBSCALES

CHALLENGE

CONTROL

COMMITMENT

On the pages that follow, you will find more information on your Challenge, Control, and Commitment scores. As you move through the report, think about how you might see these hardiness qualities emerge in your day-to-day life. If you choose to implement the recommended developmental strategies highlighted for you, you can ensure that you are setting yourself up for success when faced with stressful and changing situations.

MHS © Copyright of MHS 2019. All rights reserved.   3
1.1.1

FIGURE 10.2 Alan Paul's Hardiness Profile

(Used with permission from Multi-Health Systems, 2019.)

Alan's overall hardiness score is in the high range. This high level of hardiness reflects a mindset that is not fearful of stress, but rather sees it as a challenge that one must deal with. In fact, in Alan's words, "Stressful situations are inevitable through one's career. At every stage there will be challenges and goals, decisions that have to be met. I'd say there is more freedom starting out allowing an artist to experiment and take risks."

His highest score is in hardiness-commitment, which reflects one's purpose and goals in life. Successful artists are generally highly driven to succeed, but what is important is aiming for goals that are more than just materialistic. As Alan reflects on his long-term success, "Maintaining a successful career is more stressful because usually there are more people that have to be dealt with, greater time commitments and a greater need for compromise and conflict resolution. There must be a commitment toward a higher goal than personal wants."

We're often asked, how much of success in the industry is due to talent and how much to other factors? While there are different opinions on the importance of various psychological factors and external circumstances, such as luck, good management, and so on, Alan had a very interesting take on this. "Having been gifted with a strong voice and a passion to sing was where I started as a child. Once I decided that I wanted to have a career, it was imperative to set specific goals and to persevere to reach those goals. One must create momentum in order for success to be attained. I don't believe in luck; I believe in grace. I believe we are all connected to a higher power that wants us to succeed. We do our work the best we can and then leave room for grace to unfold."

His hardiness-control score is also quite high, reflecting Alan's ability to take charge of his career and his day-to-day management of stress. When asked about his methods of dealing with stress he responded, "I have been a meditator for many years and practice kriya yoga. Over time this has helped me to maintain a calmness, a state of bliss, and recognize that I am not my thoughts or emotions but rather the higher self, the observer that watches all that unfolds before me." And when asked what he attributes his long-term success as an entertainer to, he identifies "passion, creativity, hard work, flexibility, teamwork, compromise, listening, and above all, grace." Clearly, a worthy, but not easily developed combination.

Alan's emotional intelligence scores were in the extremely high range. His highest factor was in reality testing. This can be so important for people in entertainment. So many young people enter the industry with unreal expectations. They are driven by the emotional and materialistic trappings of success and fail to look at the realistic aspects of the business. While emotions, such as passion, are important, it's also important to keep them in check and pay attention to the cues that are around you. There are important steps to follow for success, and hard work is usually one of them.

Alan's second highest score was in emotional self-awareness. It is clear that he spends a great deal of time becoming aware of his own emotions, which in turn leads to greater emotional management. Through meditation or mindfulness, you can become much more centered and emotionally self-aware. Understanding our emotions is a first big step in regulating them.

His third highest score in emotional intelligence is in empathy. Empathy involves understanding where other people are coming from, both emotionally and cognitively. Working together with three other musical artists and an arranger/conductor requires a great deal of compatibility. Being too self-centered would be a recipe for disaster in a situation like this. Empathy is a building block of teamwork. You must be willing to listen to and understand the people on your team. Knowing where each one is coming from enables you to better navigate differences of opinion or conflicts that may arise.

Finally, we wanted to ask what advice Alan has for aspiring young musical artists in the early stages of their career. Interestingly, much of his advice would apply to almost anyone in the early stages of an entrepreneurial career. Here are his nine tips:

1. Determine who you are as an artist and what you would like to accomplish.
2. Set your goals.
3. Learn how the music business works.
4. Become savvy with social media in order to promote yourself.

5. Be flexible reaching your goals.
6. Ask for help; you can't do this alone.
7. Make room for things to unfold.
8. Don't give up, don't lose faith.
9. Relax and enjoy the journey; in the end that's what it's all about.

These are true words of wisdom and clearly the result of a great deal of experience as a working artist. The ability to set and achieve realistic goals ties in so well with what we've seen as markers of success in so many industries.

Looking at Hardiness in Young Performing Musicians

One of the authors (Steven) volunteers teaching psychological principles (performance issues, emotional/hardiness skills, entrepreneurial mindset, and mental health risks) to emerging young musicians and songwriters through a nonprofit program called Canada's Music Incubator (CMI). In working with young musicians, we know how difficult it can be to get established as a musical artist today. On the one hand, with the advent of new technologies, such as YouTube, SoundCloud, and numerous other social media channels, almost anyone has the opportunity to get their music out there. On the other hand, with vehicles such as iTunes, Spotify, Amazon Music, and Google Play Music, it's not all about getting signed by a record label and having them launch and guide your career.

We have found that hardiness can be an important factor in a successful music career. In our training, in preparing young working musicians for the next level in their careers, we've had the opportunity to test the hardiness and emotional intelligence of many of them. We have also been asked to work with early-career, top-rated, successful country musical artists, as selected by a national radio network and their fans.

In figure 10.3 you can see the hardiness scores of the young working musicians plotted with the nationally selected top performers.

While the top performers scored higher in all the hardiness scales, the biggest difference is in the commitment score. The top performers have a very strong sense of purpose and believe that their work is exciting. They fully immerse themselves in their music career. It is clear these performers work hard and will do what it takes to be successful.

Think about your own commitment to your work. How hard are you willing to work to be at the top of your game? Is work success really important for you?

Hardiness in Sports

Researchers have recently been exploring the role of hardiness in high-performing or elite athletes. They've examined the role of hardiness at various levels of sport—from Olympic athletes, professional players, college and high school teams, and community or Little League teams. Some of the lessons we learn from Olympic-level athletes about coping with stress or high-stakes performance can be distilled and modified to be used by all levels of people who enjoy sports and exercise.

Dr. Colleen Hacker, a professor of kinesiology at Pacific Lutheran University in Tacoma, Washington, is a mental skills coach for the US women's national teams in soccer, ice hockey, and field hockey. Hacker has been part of Team USA through 10

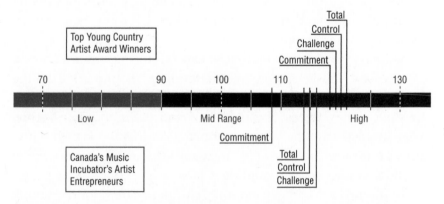

Figure **10.3** Hardiness Scores of Top Performing Young Musicians (Top) and Early-Career Musicians (Bottom)

(Used with permission from Multi-Health Systems, 2019.)

world championships and 6 Olympic Games. As part of her work with high performers she emphasizes the importance of helping them reframe perceived failure experiences into useful, productive, and essential building blocks for success (Hacker, 2013).

She points out that much of the research carried out with Olympic champions has shown that the ability to overcome various obstacles, setbacks, and challenges is essential in pursuit of gold medal performance. Specifically, these athletes share a strong mental resilience that includes a number of key psychological factors, including positive personality characteristics, optimism, confidence, focus, hardiness, and perceived social support. She has been an advocate of hardiness and resilience training for athletes. She also points out the importance of using examples from Olympic and other high-performance athletes as role models for learning hardiness and resilience skills.

What are some of the keys skills for developing hardiness in athletes—many of which apply to any type of performance (Mackenzie, 2018)? Hacker stresses five key skills that can be practiced and improved. The first is to **practice being in the moment.** When you train, you're either "tuned out" (wearing headphones) or "tuned in." It's important for elite athletes to tune in when practicing and performing. That is, you need to learn to be in the moment.

A related part of this skill is learning how to be self-aware. When your mind begins to drift, you need to bring it back to the task at hand. You can let your mind wander, while your body continues to train, but to be truly great you need to pay attention to your body and focus. Being fully aware of your body and your emotions and how they impact your performance can make the difference between a good performance and a great one.

Second, **try not to focus on the environment or the venue**. Some athletes like to wait for the ideal conditions in order to perform at their best. Hacker believes it's about the athlete's ability to adapt to the environment. There have been Super Bowl games played in extremely challenging weather conditions. In 2007 Miami hosted the Super Bowl with the Indianapolis Colts playing against the Chicago Bears. The rain during the game was continuous, with

.92 inches falling over Miami. While there may have been several reasons for the outcome that day, the Colts adapted the best to the weather and ended up beating the Bears 29–17.

Third, **focus is essential**. In order for athletes to compete at their best they need total focus. It's easy to get distracted in competitions by the crowds, performance anxiety, and countless other distractions. A great example of this at the professional level was suggested by Hacker. At the 2018 US tennis open match between Serena Williams and Naomi Osaka, Williams got caught up in an altercation with an official. While they argued back and forth, Osaka removed herself from the fray. She turned away from what was going on and took time to focus on her own game and strategy.

Another competitor might have gotten emotional and injected themselves into the argument, changing the rhythm of the game. Instead, Osaka didn't even look at what was going on. She didn't listen to it; rather, she just focused on herself and what she could control: her own game—an example of hardiness-control.

Fourth, **preparing for mistakes** can be made into a ritual. All athletes make mistakes. It's part of trying to improve your performance. Airline pilots, when training in a simulator, are constantly presented with emergency situations. By preparing for the unexpected you become calmer and better able to react to real mistakes or emergencies when they happen.

When you shoot at the goalie in hockey and miss, take two strikes in baseball, or miss a basket in basketball, elite athletes are taught not to respond with negative emotions that can damage their performance. Instead, they learn mental or physical rituals that set them up for success in the next play. Some examples are squeezing your hands twice quickly, shaking your head to the right, brushing your shoulders (brushing it off), or using self-talk phrases such as, "okay, got it," "let it go," or "move on." These rituals become cues for clearing your mind and starting fresh with renewed energy. For some players these rituals even increase their motivation.

Finally, rather than focusing on winning, **focus on the process**. Did you follow your strategy? Did you speed up when you needed to? Did you make a great pass? Being grateful for even being part of the game is important. Celebrate the small victories as you play. Pay attention moment to moment on what went well. By focusing on the positive, you can put yourself in the right emotional state to keep yourself motivated.

Does Hardiness Differentiate Elite Athletes?

What role does hardiness play in differentiating athletes? We know there are physical strength and skill levels in all sports, but what is the role of the hardiness mindset among athletes? A British study looked at the personality characteristics of 1,566 athletes from 16 different sport classifications. The sample included athletes who compete at international, national, county/provincial, and club/regional levels (Sheard & Golby, 2010).

These athletes were all assessed for their level of hardiness. The researchers found significant differences in hardiness that were related to the level of competition the athlete was involved in. International competitors scored higher in hardiness than all the other groups. This difference held up even when scores were adjusted for age, type of sport, and gender.

Based on hardiness theory, athletes high in the three Cs of hardiness show an active pattern of managing demanding and unpredictable situations by facing them head-on and striving to develop them into growth opportunities. This is especially interesting when looking at the situations that athletes encounter, especially at the highest level. These include worrying about poor performances, injury, constant pressure to perform at a high standard, possibility of being delisted or not selected, coach stress, frequent and long training sessions, interpersonal conflicts, and public, social media, and media scrutiny.

Another study focused on different skill levels of rugby players (Golby & Sheard, 2004). In this study they looked at 115 professional rugby players representing the top three playing levels of the game in Great Britain. These are International, Super League, and Division One. The International players had the highest levels of hardiness, including commitment, control, and challenge. They were significantly higher than Division One players in control and significantly higher than both sub-elite groups in commitment and challenge.

The higher scores in control by the International players may indicate that they felt more able to positively influence the outcome of matches. In addition, this feeling may have allowed them to see highly competitive contests in a less stressful way. With regard to commitment, it may be that International players show higher levels of organization and involvement in the sport. Higher scores in challenge suggest that they can view potentially difficult situations as opportunities for professional growth, as opposed to seeing them as a threat. The study authors conclude that the International players are better able to cope with highly stressful sporting events and keep a high level of competitive performance.

Another interesting finding of this study concerned the greater importance of hardiness over another concept sports psychologists have been looking at called "mental toughness." Mental toughness, while similar to grit, has been defined in several different ways. Generally, the term includes the following seven attributes:

1. Self-confidence—knowing you can perform well and be successful
2. Negative energy control—handling emotions such as fear, anger, and frustration
3. Attention control—being focused
4. Visualization and imagery control—thinking positively in pictures
5. Motivation—willing to persevere
6. Positive energy—having fun and enjoyment
7. Attitude control—unyielding

The three components of hardiness were able to differentiate the player levels, in order of importance, by 46% for commitment, 35% for control, and 19% for challenge. Mental toughness, on the other hand, was only able to account for 9% (negative energy control) and 6% (attention control) of the difference. That means that commitment, how involved you get in the sport, can be of major importance in helping determine how far you can get in that sport. Top-performing athletes are deeply committed to their sport, and design their lives around practicing and performing in competitions. The next most important factor was the amount of control they believed they had over the situation.

Does Hardiness Matter in Younger Elite Athletes?

One of the authors (Steven) had an opportunity to work with 10 young athletes between the ages of 14 to 16 who were nationally ranked at or near the top in their sport. They each represented a different competitive sport and had been identified as highly competitive at the world (or future Olympic) level.

We tested their hardiness with the Hardiness Resilience Gauge and compared their scores, as a group, with 121 randomly selected same-age adolescents as seen in Figure 10.4.

One of the most dramatic differences, as seen in the graph, is in their commitment scores. Elite athletes, even at this young age, dedicate a great deal of time, some as much as five hours per day practicing their sport, in addition to their schoolwork. Some of them leave for school at 8:00 in the morning and don't get home until after 9:00 at night. While this kind of dedication can bring rewards in terms of competition successes, national recognition, corporate sponsorships, and other perks, it can also take its toll on family and social life.

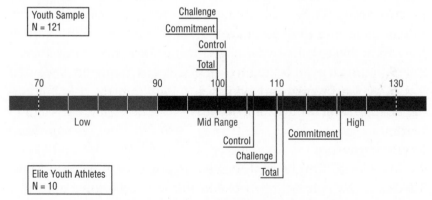

FIGURE **10.4** High-Performance Adolescent Athletes Compared with Sample Group (Used with permission from Multi-Health Systems, 2019.)

UNDERSTANDING HOW HARDINESS AND ANXIETY WORK FOR ATHLETES

Most of us would think that anxiety is a normal part of competing in sports. In fact, dozens of studies have been carried out looking at how athletes can reduce their anxiety. In one series of studies looking at the role of hardiness in athletes in a variety of different sports, it was found that elite and high-performing athletes differed from other athletes. They found that hardiness increased resilience in the elite athletes who had lower levels of somatic or physical anxiety and worry (such as stomach aches, trembling, sweating, and nervousness).

Also, these elite athletes had more positive interpretations of their symptoms with respect to an upcoming performance. In other words, anxiety, which most people view as a negative emotion, was viewed by the elite high-hardy athletes as valuable to their performance. They recognize the anxiety in themselves before an event, understand it as a normal part of their routine, and actually use it to heighten their focus and effort. For them, performance anxiety becomes something like a friend. The finding that these elite athletes saw anxiety, something we usually think of as a negative emotion, as helpful to their performance, suggests that these athletes are coping well when they feel anxious (Hanton, Neil, & Evans, 2013). They are able to channel their anxiety into a positive track, helping them gear up for the event.

The same group of researchers dug even deeper in order to better understand how elite performers' anxiety can turn into a positive force. They looked at athletes who scored high or low in hardiness and then compared them to each other in terms of how they dealt with stress related to performance. They found, once again, that athletes high in hardiness generally reported lower levels of worry and anxiety and higher levels of self-confidence than athletes low in hardiness. Also, those athletes high in hardiness saw stressful situations as less threatening than those low in hardiness.

In order to further explain what is going on, the researchers looked at the connection between the athletes' worry and how they coped with it. They found direct links between hardiness and the types of coping approaches the athletes used. Athletes who were high in hardiness used more planning, active coping, and effort and saw the use of these strategies as more effective in dealing with stressful situations than the lower hardiness athletes did. An important part of this finding was the elite athlete's apparent ability to see anxiety as helpful, and not as getting in the way of performance.

What were the elements of active planning for these athletes? These included making a plan of action, thinking hard about what steps to take to manage the situation, and spending time thinking about the plan. Active coping included trying to do something about their performance, taking one step at a time, taking direct action in dealing with the challenge, and trying different approaches. Effort included actively trying to improve performance, working harder, and taking direct action to improve.

Winning the US Tennis Open

Imagine a 19-year-old female tennis player, playing for the first time in the world's biggest tennis tournament, the United States Open Tennis Championships in New York. Imagine her making it to the finals. Now, think about her facing off against one of the world's greatest tennis players, Serena Williams. And one more thing. The 19-year-old is a Canadian playing against the fan-favorite American about to break a record in winning Grand Slams.

One of the most challenging aspects of competitive sports we have heard from professional athletes has been dealing with the noise of the crowd when they're against you. The noise that Bianca Andreescu had to deal with on Saturday, September 7, 2019, was thunderous. And the crowd was not on the side of the 19-year-old Canadian. The pressure on Bianca, a relative unknown to most American tennis fans, was enormous.

Somehow, Bianca handled it with amazing poise. Her game was aggressive throughout. She won the first set, 6–3, started leading in the second, and then Serena started to come back. This is when most athletes would fold under the pressure. Bianca came back again and won the set 7–5, and the match.

Interestingly, one of us (Steven) had watched her come back from behind just a month earlier at the Canadian Tennis Championship, the Rogers Cup, against Eugenie Bouchard, another Canadian hopeful. Bianca kept her poise and played aggressively and with calculated risk, playing with a mix of heavy, power groundstrokes, deep looped balls, and drop shots.

In postgame interviews Bianca talked about the help she received from her mother. She regularly practiced meditation. As well, she started using visualization when she was 16 years old—seeing herself win the US Open.

Years ago, Bianca Andreescu wrote her name and the prize money for winning the US Open on a mock-up check. "After I won the Orange Bowl back in 2015, a couple of months later I just felt like I could do really big things in this sport," Andreescu told CNN after her US Open victory.

"So, I just grabbed a check and wrote the prize money of that year. But every year I kept increasing it because it kept changing. But I just kept visualizing that moment since that day."

The prize she eventually won was $3.85 million (US). Bianca used visualization and meditation to increase her focus and block out any fear of playing Serena (whom she greatly admired) and the boisterous New York audience cheering on Serena.

Bianca is a great example of hardiness, using the stress she experienced in a positive way, becoming more aggressive, but not losing her cool. This is a delicate balance that few athletes (or people in general), especially at 19 years of age, can achieve.

COACHING A CHAMPION

Championship athletes in any sport go through continual training with their coaches. One of the important roles of the coach is to build resilience, or hardiness, in their athletes. What does it take to build an athlete's hardiness? Can what we learn from elite athletes be applied to our everyday lives?

There have been published research articles focusing on the characteristics of coaches who foster resilience in elite athletes (Kegelaers & Wylleman, 2018). In their study of Olympic coaches, they identified several themes that influenced increased resilience in athletes. These can be broken down into proactive—what can be done to prepare for stress—and reactive—what we do after the experience of stress.

In advance of a stressful event, such as the big competition, strategies include fostering motivation, mental preparation, and promoting life balance. Following a stressful event coaches focus on evaluating setbacks, promoting a positive mindset, and implementing lessons.

One of us (Steven) had the opportunity to interview one of Bianca's coaches to learn more about what it takes to develop a champion. Aref Jallali travelled the world with Bianca Andreescu, training and guiding her through tournaments.

In the case of Bianca, he says that when she was handed to her formation coaches at Tennis Canada, she had a solid foundation including visualizing, which her mother was instrumental in. After the US Open, we asked Aref Jallali, her formation coach from ages 11 to 15 at Tennis Canada, what was the single factor that led him to believe that Bianca would be a champion. Without hesitation Aref answered, "Mental toughness," which in our language most resembled hardiness.

When we spoke with Aref, he reported that he felt he knew, even when she was 12 years old, that Bianca was a Grand Slam winner—worthy of world-level competition. He told that to other elite tennis coaches at that time, to their disbelief. He showed us the congratulatory texts from these same coaches after Bianca won the US Tennis Open.

Another important quality in young athletes, Aref told us, was the ability to learn. When he gives an instruction to an athlete to complete a specific set of moves on the court, some of them tend to get it right away, while others have that somewhat puzzled look on their face. This tells Aref that they clearly don't get it. Bianca was able to follow his instructions perfectly, even at 11 years of age. This falls into hardiness-challenge, the ability to adapt, be curious, learn new things. Also, he told us her mind was strong, and she was determined to win.

Aref explained his use of visualization. He has his players practice it for 15 minutes a day. He has them visualize winning the tournament. Then he has them working backwards, step by step, imagining their way there. Aref tells them, "Think of your body, think about all the situations that are going to happen to you, think about how you are going to overcome the challenges, and think how you're going to beat this guy six love." He teaches his athletes to focus, visualize, and shift, when it counts the most—when they're down.

One of the important aspects of elite coaches is their own hardiness. At this level of competition, elite coaches have to deal not only with the athlete, but family members, tennis organizations, tournament directors, media, tennis clubs, and others. It takes a great deal of strength and interpersonal skill to manage all these relationships.

We thought it would be interesting to test the hardiness of Aref, the coach, as he impressed us so much in his interview. He was extremely knowledgeable about the ins and outs of the tennis world, but also displayed the same hardiness he talked about in his elite athletes. His hardiness profile can be seen in Figure 10.5.

As can be seen, Aref has an extremely high hardiness profile. His highest score is in control. As someone who coaches young players, Aref focuses on all aspects of the athlete's life. He believes they have to be disciplined in life if they want to be successful in their sport. He firmly believes in schedules and regimes, telling us that if the player has a match at 3:00 p.m., he wants them up at 6:00 a.m. to start the routines for that day.

His hardiness-challenge and hardiness-commitment scores are also extremely high. Aref works hard on getting his athletes to overcome adversity through visualization. Likewise, he is committed, as are his athletes, to winning. He told us that he knew when Bianca started losing games to Serena Williams during the second set in the US Open, she would come back. That's what she trained to do since she was 12 years old.

VISUALIZATION: DIGGING DEEPER

Ben Falkenstein, an elite tennis coach who trains elite athletes including many top-level tennis players, also specializes in the

Aref Jallali
September 17, 2019

TOTAL HARDINESS

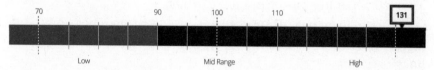

70   90   100   110   **131**

Low   Mid Range   High

What your score means

- Your result indicates that your total level of hardiness falls in the **High** range.

- You are likely very capable of tackling stressful and unexpected situations that come your way. Your high level of hardiness often protects you from the negative effects of stress and you are able to respond to surprising and stressful situations in a healthy and adaptive manner.

- You likely have the coping skills necessary to help you deal with stressful circumstances. For example, rather than trying to ignore or avoid the stressful situation, you likely try to fix it and work on eliminating the source of your stress.

HARDINESS SUBSCALES

CHALLENGE

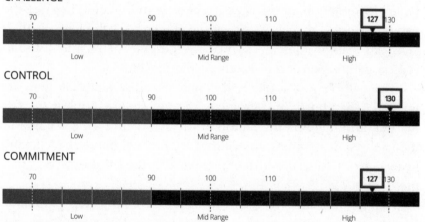

70   90   100   110   **127** 130

Low   Mid Range   High

CONTROL

70   90   100   110   **130**

Low   Mid Range   High

COMMITMENT

70   90   100   110   **127** 130

Low   Mid Range   High

On the pages that follow, you will find more information on your Challenge, Control, and Commitment scores. As you move through the report, think about how you might see these hardiness qualities emerge in your day-to-day life. If you choose to implement the recommended developmental strategies highlighted for you, you can ensure that you are setting yourself up for success when faced with stressful and changing situations.

 MHS © Copyright of MHS 2019. All rights reserved.   3
1.1.2

FIGURE 10.5 Aref Jallali's Hardiness Profile

(Used with permission from Multi-Health Systems, 2019.)

development of preformation athletes (6–12 years old). He told us that young promising athletes are trained early in all aspects of their chosen sport including technical, tactical, physical (age appropriate), rest, sleep, nutrition, how to learn, the mental game, and visualization. He cites mental toughness, the ability to overcome challenges, and visualization, as well as learning, as the factors that separate good from great athletes.

Ben also teaches all his athletes visualization, every day. But, as he describes it, visualization is much more than just using your imagination.

"If they're driving towards a goal, I help them to visualize their goal, and the process of the goal." There's a whole methodology behind the practice of visualization. When done right, it's not just a mind to eye thing. "It's a mind to muscle, and mind to kinesthetic energy. They can feel it in their mind, in their body, and they can feel the stadium."

With young high-potential athletes, aged 11–12, Ben gets them to imagine what it's like winning the big tournaments—US Tennis Open, Wimbledon, and so on. He gets them to feel it, holding the trophy, hearing the cheering crowd, feeling the breeze on their face, the tears in their eyes, rubbing the grass. This initial visualization plants the seed to motivate the player.

They don't just look at the images, they self-dialogue the images. "They imagine standing at the service line, looking across the net, and imagine the shape of the serve, and they say that to themselves, 'It's coming inside and to the backhand and clicking away.'" It's a kinesthetic feeling, backed up by the words and the dialogue.

Ben says he likes to move from the general to the particular. "I'm going to this tournament and this is what the courts look like. I remember full well its play and this is how the ball bounces," and they can see in their mind's eye everything they're experiencing. Then he brings them into the particulars for the match. Let's say they're playing against a lefty and they want to go to the backhand. They're used to playing to a righty's backhand.

"I have them visualizing the lefty standing in front of them, hitting the ball across the court to the backhand, and what that feels like in their body and what the shape of the shot looks like and then the response from the opponent. So, in that moment I am looking for the particular situation. Then in general terms what the stadium's going to feel like." The ability to do this well separates the great athletes from the good athletes.

ATHLETES, HARDINESS, AND FLOW

In a previous chapter we talked about flow. Flow is that positive psychological state you reach when you're in the "zone." It's quite common among high performers, such as elite athletes. Flow is the state of mind you experience when you reach a balance between the challenges associated with a situation and your capabilities to meet those demands.

Several characteristics of flow have been identified by researchers. These include:

- Merging of action and awareness
- Sense of control
- Acute concentration
- Clear goals and feedback
- Loss of self-consciousness
- Transformation of time
- Challenge-skill balance

The flow experience has been referred to as "autotelic" by its creator (Csíkszentmihályi, 1990). This essentially means that the activity giving rise to the flow (swimming, running, rock climbing, etc.) is pursued for its own sake. That is, the reward of just doing the activity is what really matters. It's not about winning, or getting paid, or recognition. For flow to really occur in its purest form you must *love* the activity of running, swimming, playing tennis, basketball, and so on. One of the greatest hockey players of all time, Wayne Gretzky said, "The only way a kid is going to practice is if it's total fun for him... and it was for me."

In a pioneering study, researchers looked at exploring the links between flow and personality characteristics such as hardiness and optimism (Vealey & Perritt, 2015). For example, what aspects of flow are related to hardiness? Because if we can build hardiness then we may be able to increase flow.

These researchers assessed 197 collegiate-level track and field athletes, roughly half female and half male. They included NCAA Division I athletes, NCAA Division II athletes, and NCAA Division III athletes. Along with measures of hardiness and optimism, the athletes were given a test of flow. The first thing they found was that these athletes often experienced many aspects of flow. Specifically, they frequently experienced clear goals, autotelic experience, and unambiguous feedback. They *sometimes* to *frequently* experienced challenge-skill balance, control, concentration, and merging of action/awareness. However, they only sometimes experienced loss of self-consciousness and time transformation.

When it came to hardiness, these athletes reported higher levels of commitment and control as compared to challenge. They scored lower in optimism than Olympic athletes did in a previous study, yet higher than other collegiate-level athletes. Together, hardiness and optimism accounted for almost 30% of the variance of flow. That is, of all the factors that make up flow, these two characteristics can account for roughly one-third of them. That can lead to a substantial increase in flow by improving your hardiness and optimism. Optimism accounted for more of the variance than hardiness, and challenge accounted for the least.

It was surprising that challenge wasn't strongly related to the frequency of flow in this study. This is especially so because the challenge-skill balance is such an important aspect of flow. However, the measure of hardiness used in the study described challenge more as dealing with change or uncertainty as opposed to the link between life's challenges and one's skills.

What You Can Learn from Increasing Hardiness Levels in Competitive Swimmers

One of the things we can learn from research in sports psychology is how to apply techniques that have been shown to work in increasing our hardiness and leading to better performance. There are many studies in sports psychology examining the effectiveness of various positive psychological training approaches and their effectiveness in improving performance. These studies have looked at the use of these techniques by many different types of athletes, including tennis, swimming, rugby, judo, hockey, soccer, basketball, and more.

One particular study looked at using five of the most widely researched techniques by sports psychologists to develop young swimmers. They examined both performance outcomes (swimming speed) and the psychological effects of the training. Results showed that not only did performance improve, but so did most of the psychological factors measured, including hardiness (Sheard & Golby, 2006). Of the hardiness scale scores, only the challenge score did not change with practice in this group.

In this section we'll present these five techniques, along with tips on how you can use them to deal better with stressful events you encounter. The five techniques are goal setting, visualization, relaxation, concentration, and thought stopping.

GOAL SETTING

One technique athletes find particularly useful is goal setting. It's great to think of the big prize—winning the world championship cup—but you also have to consider how you're going to get there. You can start off with small but manageable goals. In sports this involves a combination of outcome, performance, and process goals. It starts with the process. Think about and plan how you are going to deal with an upcoming high-pressure situation. Consider the steps you can take as you confront the situation.

You can practice planning the process several times before you actually encounter the situation. Think about the possible things you can do, along with the possible outcome of each intervention. Practice rehearsing the steps. After doing it several times, then think about the outcome. What would winning look like? How would it feel? How would you celebrate it?

By rehearsing these steps enough times, you will be ready to go over it again just before you confront the situation. Since you have already rehearsed it, it should be easy enough to do. Then, as you are going through the challenge, think about how you are doing and the process you rehearsed. Focus on your thoughts, feelings, and behaviors in relation to your performance. As you rehearse before and during the performance, also think about the benefits of doing well. What will a win look like? Thinking of the benefits will help motivate you through the process.

By setting clear, achievable goals, you will be better prepared to take on challenging situations. Knowing the outcome you want to achieve will help you stay on track. Also, people who have clear goals are more motivated to achieve them. Increasing your motivation can increase your chances of success. Goal setting helps build hardiness commitment by giving you something to strive for.

Visualization

A technique that has been successfully used by sports psychologists with many types of athletes is visualization. While there have been variations of the visualization process, you can benefit from the general use of the technique. In many cases visualization is combined with relaxation exercises.

Using this technique has been found to increase self-confidence and general effectiveness in athletes. With practice, this exercise helps you feel much more secure in your ability to handle stressful events. You simply need to close your eyes and imagine yourself confronting the stress-producing situation. The most successful athletes picture themselves practicing a specific situation under competitive conditions. Imagine yourself at the swim meet with the crowds cheering and your competitors glaring at you. Picture yourself pushing hard in the water, taking the turnarounds as smoothly as possible. You need to learn to focus on the task at hand, not on the distracting crowds or competitors.

You can visualize yourself confronting an upcoming pressure situation. Imagine yourself approaching the situation calmly and confidently. See yourself going through the process, step by step, of dealing with the event. You can even add unexpected obstacles and picture yourself dealing with them. All the while imagine yourself coolly dealing with the obstacles, one by one. You should practice this exercise at various times during the day. You might find imagery works better for you in the morning or at night. Visualization helps build hardiness-control because it helps you see yourself as in charge of the situation.

RELAXATION

Start relaxing right after you read this paragraph by just closing your eyes and imagining a warm, calm beach. Think about the waves slowly rolling onto the shore. Listen to the sounds of the gently swirling water and the birds calling in the background.

You can practice imagining this scene several times, until it becomes effortless for you to put yourself in a more relaxed state. Once you learn to do that, then you can imagine yourself going through the plan you designed in the previous section. As you are in a calm state, see yourself confronting, step by step, your stressful situation. Your ability to combine planning/goal setting and relaxation helps build your hardiness-control because it not only lets you see yourself in charge of the situation, but also shows how you can calmly master something that was once challenging or stressful.

CONCENTRATION

Have you ever watched a major sporting event, such as basketball, and heard the crowd jeering and shouting as loud as can be when an opposing player is taking a penalty shot? How does the player make the shot despite all that noise? If there's one thing we've seen elite athletes excel in, it's their ability to concentrate or focus on the task at hand. They know how to block out distractions of any kind. They can focus on the task and avoid any preoccupying thoughts about negative outcomes.

A technique some elite athletes use is to focus on specific body signals, such as heart rate, breathing, or other kinesthetic bodily signals. Runners who have trained in doing this have significantly improved their running (Masters & Ogles, 1998). So, as you practice confronting your stressful situations, pay attention to your own body. Focus on your breathing. Is it steady? Is it deep? Are you breathing too quickly? Learn your optimum breathing rhythm and try to keep it steady. Increase it when you need more stamina or energy.

THOUGHT STOPPING

Some elite athletes have a tendency to think about the worst of scenarios in a competition. Not only do they think about them, they might find it hard to stop thinking about them. What if I fall skiing down that hill? What if I trip running down the field with the soccer ball? Thinking negative thoughts does not help your performance. There is no benefit to those thoughts. They are basically a distraction from your ability to do your best.

Thought stopping involves catching yourself as soon as you hear those negative voices in your head. Once your negative thoughts start to infiltrate, you think the word STOP in your head. You then replace the negative thought with a positive one. The idea is to plan, in advance, a series of opposite, positive self-statements. If you preplan and memorize your positive thoughts, they will be easier to recall when needed.

So, you could be ready with self-talk such as, "I can beat that hill," or "I know I can get far down field with the ball," or "I know I can make that shot." By focusing on the positive thoughts you eliminate distractions that hinder performance. Once a negative thought has been displaced, the athlete can develop a narrow, undistractible type of concentration. This is what we've seen with sport performers operating at the highest levels.

As we have shown, in high-performance situations both entertainers and athletes must deal with high pressure. While everyone has their own way of dealing with stressful situations, we've provided some examples that both research and personal experience have found to be effective in building hardiness and enhancing performance. Not every technique works for everyone. You should experiment and try the ones that you feel comfortable with. You can build your hardiness-challenge by trying out new approaches for managing your high-pressure situations.

Chapter 11

The Role of Hardiness in First Responders

Police and Firefighters

"Police officers, firefighters, EMTs, they are all out there every single day literally just a phone call away for anyone who needs them."
—Doreen Croni (American author of children's picture books)

Some occupational groups are often cited for their high levels of stress and subsequent burnout. As a result, many studies have focused on burnout levels and protective factors for people in these careers. A number of those jobs fall into the category of first responders—police, firefighters, paramedics, and emergency workers. In this chapter we'll explore some of the challenges experienced by professionals in high-risk public safety positions. Specifically, we'll look at police officers and firefighters. By understanding more about how people in these high-risk groups navigate the stress and trauma in their lives, we can learn more about managing our own challenges.

Hardiness and Policing

Much of the research looking at police officer stress has focused on the nature of frontline policing, such as patrolling, arrests, callouts, and organizational stressors. Officers on the front line, patrolling neighborhoods, often face immediate, objective threats. It's not hard to imagine some of the threats they face in their day-to-day work.

Interestingly, one study of police officers showed that police demonstrated no greater negative effects from stress, such as burnout, when compared with other occupational groups such as journalists, construction managers, and air traffic controllers (Richardsen & Martinussen, 2005). Another study, looking at 3,000 police officers, found that police officers did have higher levels of health complaints than physicians (Berg, Hem, & Ekeberg, 2006). There have been studies showing that hardiness, especially hardiness-commitment, is associated with less depression and psychological distress among police officers (Andrew et al., 2008).

When it comes to the different types of jobs that police officers do, less attention has been paid to police investigators. The stresses experienced by investigators have been described as secondhand, subjective threats. Investigators have to deal firsthand with victims of serious crimes and their next of kin, graphic depictions of crime scenes, media attention in high profile cases, and court preparation and deadlines. When looking at the various challenges they confront, it was found that dealing with victims of traumatization was one of the worst stressors these investigators faced.

The types of traumas police investigators must deal with vary. For example, investigating financially oriented crimes such as theft may expose investigators to victims who are under psychological and emotional distress. Assault investigators are exposed to victims who are traumatized by vicious physical attacks. Assault crimes tend to be motivated by aggression, and the trauma is often physically graphic as well as psychological and emotional. You would expect that investigating physical crimes would lead to greater stress and burnout of investigators than investigating economic crimes.

One Norwegian police study looked at the differences in coping with stress between police investigators who work on non-violent crimes, as compared to those working on violent crimes. This included investigators of sexual and physical assaults on one hand, and investigators of less offensive crimes, such as financial or environmental offenses on the other (Fyhn, Fjell, & Johnsen, 2016). The researchers suspected that the assault investigators would be hardier, primarily because hardier people would be more likely to select jobs that are more stressful. They also believed that hardier police officers, in general, would be less susceptible to burnout and other physical symptoms. The study included 156 Norwegian police officers.

The results supported the researchers' hypotheses. Hardiness was, in fact, a powerful predictor of resistance to burnout in these police officers. High-hardy investigative officers were less likely to experience stress-related burnout. Also, investigators of assault crimes had higher hardiness scores than investigators of nonviolent crimes. Assault crime investigators likewise reported higher levels of social support, meaningfulness (in their work), and personal health complaints.

The interesting thing about the hardiness measure in this study was that of the three hardiness factors, commitment was the biggest predictor of burnout for this group. It was the main buffer against burnout as well as the best differentiator between the two types of police officers. The assault investigators were significantly higher in hardiness-commitment than the other officers.

It's quite likely that the high level of hardiness-commitment among the violent crime investigators enables them to reframe challenging situations as growth opportunities, increasing their commitment to solve cases, and seeing their job as restoring justice to victims. They are also able to assign meaning to what may seem to others as senseless cases.

The amount of burnout and sickness absence did not differ between the two investigator groups. The assault crime investigators, however, had significantly more health complaints than the other group. They reported more musculoskeletal pain, which often accounts for high levels of absenteeism at work. However, this group also showed less absenteeism than the average for people with these complaints. It seems that a possible negative side effect of the high hardiness-commitment in this group is that these officers continue to work even when they're in pain.

Hardy individuals, based on this research, may sometimes be overconfident in their ability to handle challenges. This, in turn, can lead to neglecting signals of work strain, which can result in both subjective and eventually more objective health concerns.

One Way That Firefighters Cope with Stress

Firefighters are another group in the public safety sphere who deal with traumatic situations routinely. Firefighters have also been identified as a group that suffers from a high level of mental health problems. Studies have found that they are at high risk for substance abuse (Wagner, Heinrichs, & Ehlert, 1998), depression (Bacharach & Bamberger, 2007), cardiovascular disease and death (Kales, Soteriades, Christophi, & Christiani, 2007), post-traumatic stress disorder (Del Ben, Scotti, Chen, & Fortson, 2006), increased work-related stress (Schaubroeck, Ganster, & Fox, 1992), injury (Scheelar, 2002), and low work satisfaction (North et al., 2002).

Firefighters, like police officers, cope with many difficult situations and circumstances. While there have been dozens of studies evaluating traditional approaches of coping with stress in these groups, including meditation, mindfulness, and relaxation, there have been few studies looking at nontraditional stress reduction methods. Many approaches tend to promote distracting the participant from thinking about or dealing with the traumatic event, or avoiding the stressful situation altogether. Avoidance is generally not a coping style used by high-hardy people. One of the ways that veteran first responders often deal with traumatic events is by facing them head on.

An interesting look at how firefighters deal with stress involves the study of what's referred to as "gallows humor" (Alvarado, Scott, Scott, & Bledsoe, 2011). This type of humor has been defined by researchers, when applied to firefighters, as "dark humor or crass joking. It is humor that treats serious, frightening, or painful subject matter in a light or satirical way, and is used in response to incidents that elicit an emotional response from firefighters or from your average bystander" (Alvarado et al., 2011, p. 2; Haslam & Mallon, 2003).

While this type of humor may seem inappropriate or even disgusting to many average citizens, there are theories that try to explain its use. For example, by engaging in gallows humor along with playful rivalry among peers, many firefighters (and perhaps police officers too) are able to partially offset the stress that comes with their jobs. As well, it boosts the positive relationships and cohesion with their coworkers. Humor increases the closeness of the group, adds to feelings of support, and potentially acts as a safety valve for releasing accumulated stress.

Researchers have reported that this type of humor, which can involve at least one other person, fits well within the ways that firefighters relate to each other. Gallows humor is described as a way in which firefighters can distance themselves from the actual trauma while still being engaged in the incident.

A group of researchers in Los Angeles carried out an interesting study looking at the relationships among gallows humor, other coping mechanisms, stress, and hardiness. They used an earlier version of the Hardiness Resilience Gauge as part of their battery. Questionnaires were sent out to over 3,600 active firefighters, and they received back about 1,000 completed responses. This was a great sample because it covered a variety of terrains within a large metropolitan area: suburban, city, beach, and mountain landscapes. It also included a variety of positions within the fire department.

The investigators reported numerous findings, but some were extremely relevant to hardiness. The most common coping strategy used in the face of trauma was described as prosocial. This involves the camaraderie among peers and other forms of social support. Among the top three self-disclosed mechanisms of coping was gallows humor. The use of gallows humor was highly correlated with hardiness. In other words, firefighters who were high in the hardiness mindset were more likely to use this type of humor as part of their ability to cope with stressful or traumatic situations. The researchers went on to point out that gallows humor has been documented as commonly used among other first responders, including police officers, paramedics, doctors, emergency room personnel, military personnel, and social workers (Alvarado et al., 2011).

There is some additional research showing links between hardiness, humor, and health. One interesting study looked at hardiness, humor, and coping in a group of severely wounded military personnel from the Iraq and Afghanistan conflicts. Findings here showed that wounded soldiers who were high in hardiness used more humor, and this was in part a way of putting a stop to unpleasant thoughts and emotions (Bartone et al., 2019).

In another example, a study of freshman cadets at West Point found that male cadets high in hardiness made more use of humor in coping with stress and also reported fewer health problems and hospitalizations (Priest & Bartone, 2001). So, when first responders use gallows humor, it may be in part a way of maintaining their focus on the job without dwelling too much on the depressing and horrifying things they've seen.

Hardiness and Homicide Police Investigator Mark Mendelson

Mark Mendelson was the lead homicide investigator responsible for the investigation and court prosecution of over 100 homicides for the second largest police force in Canada, the Metropolitan Toronto Police (the largest is the RCMP, Royal Canadian Mounted Police). When you meet him, you might mistake him for the perfect TV cop. In fact, he spends some of his time now on TV commenting on the big crimes of the day. He still does investigations and goes to court, but he now does it through his own investigative agency.

Mark is tall, but not imposing. He's extremely friendly, affable, and positive, yet somewhat low key. I'm sure that many of the people he's investigated have mistakenly believed, on first impression, that they could easily outsmart him. Fortunately, many of them are now spending the better part of their lives in a prison cell.

One of the questions we asked Mark was about how stressful policing really was for him. He said that the most stressful aspects of homicide work are the long hours required at the outset of an investigation. It is not uncommon to go for 72 hours without sleep in the initial stages of an investigation, especially when there is a known outstanding suspect.

In addition, there is much pressure placed on the investigator from the family of the deceased, and dealing with their anxiety and anger. The mere fact that they have never experienced a situation like a murder means they don't appreciate the time it takes to do an investigation correctly and legally. They have preconceived notions from TV shows that these matters are solved in less than 60 minutes.

Lastly, the pressure from the media in a high-profile murder can be overwhelming if you haven't trained the media properly and gained their respect. And as always, there are the constant inquiries from senior officers, such as the chief, who likes to be updated in high-profile matters, as the media will try to swoop in on them as well.

NAVIGATING A LONG AND STRESSFUL INVESTIGATION

Just to get a feel for what it can be like dealing with these horrible situations, we asked Mark about what one of his "big wins" was like for him. He described his biggest win as being his investigation of a double murder that occurred in 1995. Two sisters, ages 16 and 19, were murdered in their basement by a jilted ex-boyfriend and his pathological cousin. The girls were Marsha and Tammy Ottey, and the two accused were Rohan Ranger and Adrian Kinkead.

The investigation took him six months before there was an arrest. There were two trials and an appeal, which took years to complete. Kinkead, following these murders, had also murdered a public transit subway ticket collector and brutally raped nine women (the detailed facts can be Googled).

Mark caught Kinkead in Miami and Ranger in Kingston, Jamaica. In the end, they are both serving life sentences, and Kinkead will be deported back to Jamaica, if and when he ever gets out of prison. It was satisfying because they were cold, calculating killers. The girls were angels, and Mark reported that the parents were the most supportive parents he had ever encountered in any homicide.

MEASURING MARK'S HARDINESS AND EMOTIONAL INTELLIGENCE

We asked Mark to take our Hardiness Resilience Gauge and the EQ-i 2.0 (emotional intelligence assessment). His hardiness results can be seen in Figure 11.1.

Mark Mendelson
May 24, 2019

TOTAL HARDINESS

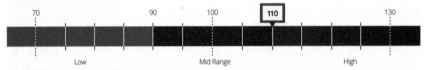

What your score means

• Your result indicates that your total level of hardiness falls in the **High** range.

• You are likely very capable of tackling stressful and unexpected situations that come your way. Your high level of hardiness often protects you from the negative effects of stress and you are able to respond to surprising and stressful situations in a healthy and adaptive manner.

• You likely have the coping skills necessary to help you deal with stressful circumstances. For example, rather than trying to ignore or avoid the stressful situation, you likely try to fix it and work on eliminating the source of your stress.

HARDINESS SUBSCALES

CHALLENGE

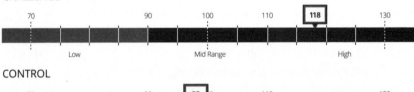

CONTROL

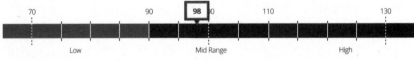

COMMITMENT

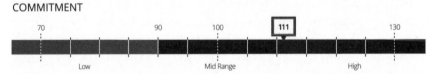

On the pages that follow, you will find more information on your Challenge, Control, and Commitment scores. As you move through the report, think about how you might see these hardiness qualities emerge in your day-to-day life. If you choose to implement the recommended developmental strategies highlighted for you, you can ensure that you are setting yourself up for success when faced with stressful and changing situations.

MHS © Copyright of MHS 2019. All rights reserved.   3

1.1.1

FIGURE **11.1**   Mark Mendelson's Hardiness Profile

(Used with permission from Multi-Health Systems, 2019.)

Mark's highest score is his challenge subscale. As an investigator, it's all about searching for clues and solving mysteries. Being able to keep going, even when you hit roadblocks, or lose time going down the wrong road, requires hardiness-challenge. Also, a big part of success in this area is being able to change direction once you discover you've gone down the wrong path. Whereas having high grit might give you the drive to just keep going, hardiness-challenge incorporates the ability to know when something isn't working and the flexibility to shift to a different approach.

Another big part of hardiness-challenge is the ability to reframe a stressful event or situation into a more manageable way of thinking about it. If we just focus on how stressful or horrible something is, we don't advance our coping with it. If we change the way we think about it, we can move forward and try solving the situation or moving on. One way of changing our frame of mind, as pointed out in the previous section, is through humor. In the case of first responders we find gallows humor used in this way. As well as restructured thinking, the importance of social support cannot be overemphasized—including from peer groups. We can see how this plays out in a quote Mark gave us:

> I found the single most effective way to deal with the stress was to ALWAYS maintain a sense of humor during the course of an investigation. It often manifests itself in rather "dark humor," but it is vital to decompressing. In addition, to take time away from the investigation, even for an hour or so and hide away, have a meal, have a glass of wine with your partner, and talk about something completely irrelevant. Your colleagues are the best escape, as they've been there, seen it and done it. Did I mention wine??

Mark's second highest score is in hardiness-commitment. Working in this type of first responder career is something you do because you believe in the mission. You certainly don't become a police officer, firefighter, or paramedic to become rich. It's not about the money. Doing this kind of job, where you risk your life, carries with it a sense of mission or purpose. Mark certainly embodies that in his work. As cautious as he is, in the dangerous environments they work in, police officers never know when they might take a bullet.

Hardiness-control is in the midrange for Mark. Once again, we see the situation of someone who works within a certain set of parameters. Police officers today are highly regulated. If you don't follow certain procedures when making an arrest, for example, you can put yourself, the case, and the police force at risk. Also, as previously mentioned, when investigating a high-profile crime, you are under pressure from the family of the victim, the media, and the police chief. It's not really a scenario where you can be freewheeling with your choices.

On the emotional intelligence side, Mark scored very high, as we expected. His highest score is in flexibility. This may seem paradoxical for someone who operates in a very rule-bound environment. Making mistakes in collecting evidence or questioning a suspect without the proper procedures can cost you a case. But Mark's flexibility comes out in his ability to look at a case in multiple ways. If you come to conclusions too quickly with the limited number of facts you have at the beginning of a case, you could close your mind to other possibilities. Far too often police investigators, perhaps due to pressure, close in too quickly on a suspect. They then focus on evidence that leads to a conviction of that suspect. They can sometimes disregard important evidence that may exonerate their initial suspect or lead in another direction. Mark's success rate in solving these crimes can be attributed in some degree to his flexibility.

His second highest emotional intelligence score is in emotional self-awareness. This refers to being aware of his emotions and what they mean for him. We see this in Mark's ability to know when to take a break from the investigation and clear his head. Some investigators, especially those with high grit, may just keep going even when it may not be productive. Taking time out and using humor are ways of regulating emotions during times of stress. This can be very healthy.

MARK'S WORDS OF WISDOM

We wanted to ask Mark what lessons he could pass on to people early in their careers as police investigators. While his advice is geared towards criminal investigators, we believe some of what he says can apply to anyone:

> I trained a large number of new detectives in the homicide squad and always passed on a few pearls of wisdom. Always "think court." In other words, think about how you will answer questions and be tested on your investigative techniques two years down the road, in trial.
>
> Delegate as much of the less urgent tasks to others, when possible. Homicide detectives just by their nature are control freaks, and you have to learn to trust your subordinates and let them carry some of the tasks.
>
> Again, never stop trying to laugh. If you're exhausted and simply not thinking clearly, walk away, take a walk or grab a nap, and come back in a fresher frame of mind. Always remember that it is your investigation, but don't be afraid to ask other more senior members for their thoughts and ideas. You never stop learning.
>
> Enjoy the hunt, don't try to rationalize how someone could do something that horrific to another person, or a baby, but try to understand the psyche and learn from it.
>
> One practice I always taught was to have the new guys sign the "glory waiver." In other words, you've made it to the big office, you're great at what you do, but to remember we are a team and don't let your ego get in the way. When a case is solved... we've all solved it...not just you. To get into homicide, you automatically have a big ego, but just don't let it get to your head!"

Can Hardiness Help in the Selection of Police Officers?

It seems pretty clear that hardiness is an important factor for police officers. So, the question is, would it make sense to use hardiness as part of the selection process for police? Well, the good news is that someone has already asked that question, and the answer is interesting. A study was carried out in the United States federal tactical law enforcement assessment and selection (A&S) program (Soccorso, Picano, Moncata, & Miller, 2019).

For this program 71 experienced male law enforcement personnel took part in a weeklong physically and psychologically rigorous assessment and selection course for an elite tactical law enforcement unit with a specialized national security mission. Before starting the course, they were all administered an earlier version of the Hardiness Resilience Gauge.

Throughout the course the candidates were tested on a number of attributes. They were evaluated on their motivation, physical fitness and stamina, perseverance, stress tolerance, leadership ability, law enforcement skills (e.g., marksmanship), and small-unit tactical and field skills. These tests were all conducted under high-demand conditions. The candidates were sleep deprived and had to undergo austere living conditions.

Of the 71 officers who started the assessment and selection course, only 43 or 60% of them completed and were selected. Of those who failed, the largest number (35%) were eliminated for not meeting the performance standards of the course. Other reasons candidates failed included poor motivation or attitude (20%), illness or injury (20%), voluntary withdrawal (15%), and failure to meet marksmanship standards (10%). There were no differences on any of the hardiness scales related to the reasons for their elimination. Candidates who left the course for medical reasons were not included in further analysis.

The candidates who successfully completed the course showed significantly higher scores in total hardiness than the nonselected candidates. Thus, hardiness was a predictor of success in the assessment and selection course for these officers. The researchers calculated that for every one-point increase in the hardiness scale, the odds of selection increased by 13%.

Of the three facets of hardiness, hardiness-commitment was the best predictor of success for these candidates. The hardiness predictions were especially strong for younger officers and older officers who scored high in cognitive ability (IQ type) tests. It's hard to explain this finding, but it may have to do with the size of the sample. Perhaps future studies, with larger samples, can help shed more light on these differences.

Some Things We Can Learn from First Responders

Police investigators who work on violent crimes tend to be high in hardiness-commitment. This factor enables them to be somewhat protected from the stresses they encounter. They can reframe situations in such a way that makes them seem less stressful. For example, they turn challenging situations into opportunities. How would you do this with some of the stresses you experience in your own life?

Well, you can start by thinking of the last time you were stressed out by something. Imagine that stressful situation. Run it through your mind. How did it make you feel? If you became emotional thinking about it, then think about it again, although try to just think of the events, without any emotion. Do a play-by-play in your mind of the stressful event.

Once you are able to imagine the event with minimal or no emotion, then you can start to ask yourself questions about the event. What about the situation made it so stressful? How did you handle the situation? How might you have handled it differently? What would the result have been if you had handled it differently? What have you learned, about yourself or others, as a result of the situation? How might you apply this knowledge in the future?

Commitment also relates to mission and meaning. Do you have a mission? What does your work mean to you? We can see that police officers have purpose in trying solve cases, helping bring justice to the community, and protecting victims. But even more than that, they learn to assign meaning to what may seem to be meaningless cases. How would you go about taking some of your more boring tasks at work and making them more meaningful?

We also learned that it could be helpful to walk away from the stressful situation for a brief time to clear your head when you feel overstressed. Social support was also found to be extremely important in coping with tough times. Draw on the people around you to share your thoughts with at work. Having a supportive family can also be very helpful. Finally, don't be afraid to laugh.

You may not need gallows humor, but humor nevertheless can help you get through tough situations.

In the following chapters we'll look at more examples of how the hardiness mindset has helped people get through tough times and succeed better in their lives.

Chapter 12

The Hardy Leader

"No matter what your current condition, how or where you grew up, or what education or training you feel you lack, you can be successful in your chosen endeavor. It is spirit, fortitude, and hardiness that matter more than where you start."
—Jack Ma (Chinese business magnate, one of China's richest men)

Can hardiness help you be a better leader? Based on a growing body of evidence, the answer appears to be yes. Leaders today operate in a world where things are changing faster than ever before. What looks like a good strategy today can be a total disaster when the environment shifts, which is happening more and more often. Harvard professor Ron Heifetz argues that in order to succeed in this rapidly changing environment, leaders need more than ever to be adaptive. In his book *Leadership Without Easy Answers*, Heifetz makes the case that truly adaptive leaders are curious and willing to try new approaches, courageous enough to endure the discomforts of change, and committed enough to follow through on their ideas. They also recognize that they can't control or manage such complex challenges alone; the adaptive leader works on building an organization and workforce that share these qualities (Heifetz, 1994). And while adaptive leadership can be learned, it is rooted in personal attitudes, behaviors, and habits.

The hardiness mindset can have a major influence on a person's capacity to adapt. As we have seen, considerable research shows that people who stay healthy and continue to perform well under highly stressful conditions possess the three interrelated qualities of commitment, control, and challenge, the three Cs of hardiness (Bartone, 1999; Kobasa, 1979).

To recap, commitment reflects a strong interest and engagement with the world, and an abiding sense that life is meaningful and worthwhile. Control is the belief that through effort and action you can influence important outcomes. Challenge is an attitude of curiosity, being receptive to the variety of changes in life. When faced with new or changing conditions, high-hardy persons tend to perceive these as challenging opportunities to learn and grow. They also prefer proactive problem-solving coping strategies for dealing with change. Hardiness is clearly linked to several of Heifetz's principles of adaptive work for leaders. Most importantly, hardiness-challenge sets an attitude in which change is expected and even welcomed. The high-hardy leader is thus better equipped to address Heifetz's second principle, "identify the adaptive challenge." As a high-hardy leader, you perceive important changes in the environment more quickly, and are thus better able to identify how the organization needs to change in order to cope with the new reality (Bartone, 2017).

Hardiness likewise enhances your capacity as a leader to "get on the balcony" and see what is going on across multiple levels in your organization. This is mainly a function of hardiness-commitment, which extends to three important spheres of life: the social world, the physical world, and the world of self, what existentialists called *Mitwelt, Umwelt,* and *Eigenwelt* (Binswanger, 1963).

Those high in commitment routinely pay more attention to all three spheres, and so are better able to take a broad view of the organization as well as the external environment. This also ties in with emotional intelligence, as the high-hardy person is both more socially aware and also more attuned to his or her own emotions and reactions. With greater awareness of how people are reacting to the stressors of change, as a leader you are able to take the right steps to "regulate distress" across the workforce, another important function of the adaptive leader (Heifetz & Laurie, 2001)

The control dimension of hardiness also facilitates adaptive leadership work, particularly in regard to what Heifetz calls "giving the work back to the people." This relates closely to hardiness-control. High-hardy leaders understand the importance of having a sense of control and believing that your actions matter. So they are motivated to look for ways to involve workers at all levels in decision-making, while also making sure to maintain good two-way communications.

World's 50 Greatest Leaders

In their April 2019 edition, *Fortune Magazine* announced their selection of the world's 50 greatest leaders. Among them were many leaders you would expect to see—Bill Gates (philanthropist, founder of Microsoft), Satya Nadella (CEO of Microsoft), Tim Cook (CEO of Apple), and others (Fry & Heimer, 2019)

There were also some unexpected picks—Anna Nimiriano, editor-in-chief of the *Juba Monitor* newspaper in South Sudan; Antonio Horta-Osorio, CEO of Lloyds Banking Group who openly struggles with mental health issues; and Jacinda Ardern, prime minister of New Zealand and new mother.

But most exciting for us was the headline of the article, "This Is the Emotional Quality That the World's Greatest Leaders All Share." That quality, and we had nothing to do with this article, was hardiness. The writers state:

> Research points to a personality style called "hardiness," identified among business executives by psychologist Suzanne C. Kobasa decades ago and validated many times among the broader population since then. Hardy individuals don't see the world as threatening or see themselves as powerless against large events; on the contrary, they think change is normal, the world is fascinating, they can influence events, and it's all an opportunity for personal growth. In studies of fourth-year West Point cadets, Col. Paul T. Bartone of National Defense University found that hardiness was by far the best predictor of which cadets, male and female, would earn the highest leadership ratings.

Of course, we were pleased to see this work cited in the article.

The article went on to say (and we can't help ourselves from quoting this):

> Decades of research show that hardy individuals just don't feel stress the way most people do. So when CEO Satya Nadella makes an epic gamble like staking Microsoft's future on cloud computing, or Los Angeles Rams coach Sean McVay bets his career on a new style of offense, they're able to do it in part because they're simply less afraid. It gets better: Research also suggests that these leaders, through their priorities, advice, and personal example, can impart their way of seeing the world to those they lead.

And that brings us to our next section.

Coaching Hardiness

There are a number of things that leaders can do to build up hardiness attitudes and behaviors in themselves and their organizations, making them more adaptive. The focus should be on the three Cs of psychological hardiness: commitment, control, and challenge.

Hardiness-commitment is all about being engaged in the surrounding world and in the self. Leaders can grow hardiness-commitment throughout the organization in large part by communicating a strong and clear vision. Multiple methods and repetition inculcate the vision in ways that foster engagement by the workers in significant ways. Seeking their input and ideas is the next step.

Leaders also should strive to role model commitment, by being available, visible, and curious about all aspects of the work within the organization. Perhaps most important, leaders should take the time and trouble to communicate and explain to workers what they are doing and why. The more workers understand the overall purpose and meaning behind what they are doing, the greater will be their sense of commitment.

Hardiness-control is the belief that one's actions can influence events within one's own life as well as having the ability to influence the world. Leaders can increase this sense of control by ensuring that the tasks and duties assigned to workers are within their capabilities and skill levels. Tasks that are too easy can lead to boredom, while those that greatly exceed worker abilities can be overwhelming and anxiety-producing. Whether in training programs or production activities, it is best to stick with a gradual schedule in which small, manageable tasks are presented first, followed by more demanding ones as skill and confidence improve. In this way, the leader creates what Heifetz and Laurie (2001) call a "holding environment" in which workers feel safe, while at the same time pushing them somewhat beyond their familiar comfort zones.

The third C of hardiness, challenge, involves adopting a positive outlook on change, being actively interested in new things and situations, and being curious about options and avenues for making advancements. The challenge aspect of hardiness can be encouraged across the organization by a number of leader actions and workplace policies. Probably most important, and one of the easiest to implement, is the role-modeling established by leaders.

The high-challenge person enjoys variety and sees change as a chance to learn and grow, rather than something to be feared and avoided. Leaders should demonstrate this approach in their own daily lives, especially where they are most visible to employees— at work. When confronted with surprising events, the high-hardy leader shows a calm demeanor and an interest in learning more and solving the problem. He or she accepts responsibility for failures, and is careful not to blame others when things go wrong. Also, the high-hardy leader is willing to shift and change approaches in the face of changing conditions, and to experiment with new ideas.

In addition to modeling these qualities, the adaptive, high-hardy leader creates a work environment that rewards and reinforces the hardiness mindset across the workforce. This can be done, for example, through policies that permit flexible routines and schedule changes. Below are some more specific coaching strategies for building up hardiness-commitment, control, and challenge in leaders and organizations.

Coaching Techniques to Build Hardiness

Techniques for coaching focus on the three primary hardiness facets of commitment, control, and challenge.

HARDINESS-COMMITMENT

To build commitment, leaders should be encouraged to:

- Take some time each day to think about what's important and interesting to you; reflect on your personal goals and values.
- Work on increasing skills and competencies in some area you care about. Take pride in your past successes and achievements.
- Pay attention to what's going on around you and in the bigger world: read, observe, and listen!
- Allow your workers to have input into organizational policies and activities; seek their input and ideas.
- Perform team- and cohesion-building activities that also enhance commitment to the group and to the shared values of the organization.
- Be fair, and don't take special privileges for yourself or show favoritism. When difficulties arise, such as pay cuts or long hours to meet production deadlines, share the hardships evenly, and do not exempt yourself!
- Interact visibly with employees on a regular basis. Get around and be seen!
- Take the time to talk with workers and explain policies and decisions. The more workers understand the purpose and meaning behind their activities, the greater will be their sense of commitment.

HARDINESS-CONTROL

To build hardiness-control, leaders should be encouraged to:

- Focus your time and energy on things you can control or influence. Don't waste time (and build frustration) on things that are outside of your capabilities to fix.
- Give work assignments that match or slightly exceed worker abilities, allowing them to fully engage and realize success; this enhances their sense of control and mastery.

- For difficult jobs, break them up into manageable pieces so progress can be seen.
- Provide your employees with the needed resources to accomplish assigned tasks.

HARDINESS-CHALLENGE

The third C of hardiness, challenge, involves taking a positive outlook on change and being actively interested in new things and situations. To build hardiness-challenge, leaders should be encouraged to do the following:

- Don't follow a rigid schedule. Allow for variation and surprises. Consider rotating employees into different jobs to give them some variety, while also building their knowledge of the overall organization (this also builds commitment).
- When failure occurs, first ask: what can I learn from this? Employees who fail at a task should be counseled and encouraged to view the experience as a learning opportunity and chance to improve and do things better next time.
- Try out new things and take reasonable risks. While we all need some stability and routine in our lives, having the courage and willingness to experiment is also important. This fosters a climate of innovation and challenge.

Together, these approaches can lead to increased attitudes of personal hardiness in you as a leader, as well as in the people you lead, which in turn will create a more adaptive organization. In the next chapter we'll look more closely at hardiness and leader development at one of the world's premier leadership training grounds: the US Military Academy at West Point.

Chapter 13

Hardiness at the US Military Academy—West Point

"75% of the time I feel like I'm in a meat grinder,
and 25% of the time I feel like a rock star."
—New cadet describing his first summer at West Point

Have you ever wondered what makes a good leader? Ever had a job where you were dependent on other people to do their part in order to complete a project? Would you like to be a better leader yourself? In this chapter, we'll pay a visit to one of the foremost leadership training institutions in the country, the US Military Academy at West Point, New York. We'll take a look at how hardiness impacts on the cadets' performance in this high-stress environment and in particular on their performance as developing leaders. We'll also look at how hardiness helps cadets to survive in this crucible of stress and stick with it to graduation. As it turns out, we'll also see how hardiness can help *you* to persist through difficulties and become a better leader.

While serving as a US Army psychologist, one of us (Paul) had the opportunity to live and work at West Point for a six-year tour of duty. Founded in 1802, West Point is the nation's oldest military academy. It is nestled in the hills along the beautiful Hudson River valley, just about an hour's drive north of New York City.

As a faculty member assigned to the Department of Behavioral Sciences and Leadership, I had daily contact with cadets as students, advisees, and research participants. It was a unique opportunity to learn firsthand about the life, challenges, and stress of being a military academy cadet.

Welcome to West Point

The cadet experience begins in late June on R-Day, or Reception Day, when the new cadets are issued uniforms and equipment, and are marched to the barber shop for haircuts. Next comes a grueling seven weeks of summer field training known colloquially as "Beast Barracks," a reference to the beastly conditions the new cadets face there. Days are long and strictly regimented, with intensive physical and military skills training. About 2–3% of cadets drop out sometime during this period. For those who survive, the training ends with a 12-mile road march with full backpacks.

For the next four years, cadets must balance their time carefully to meet the daily challenges in three main areas: academic, military, and physical. With each passing year, they are given more leadership responsibilities. The pressure to perform is often intense, with little room for failure or time off. It's not a surprise then that by the time of graduation four years later, most West Point classes have lost about 20% of their original members.

I arrived at West Point with my family in July of 1997, right in the middle of summer training for the newest class that would graduate in 2001. We watched as these young men and women would run by our quarters, hot and sweaty and bending under the weight of full combat gear. Often, an upper-class cadet would be running alongside, yelling encouragement mixed with taunts.

Later, we sat near the finish line outside the superintendent's quarters by the main parade field, as the new cadets completed their final 12-mile road march. This is one of the few times they are allowed to see their families for a brief period. Many family members came out to welcome and cheer on their sons and daughters. Thinking about those who didn't make it, I felt there was an important research question here. What separates those who make it from those who drop away? Based on my earlier research with hardiness and performance under stress, I suspected hardiness might be part of the answer.

Becoming Leaders

One of my first duties at West Point was to help manage a long-term research project that was tracking a single West Point class over time, from entry to graduation and beyond. The central question was: what accounts for the development of good leadership skills and performance in these young men and women? While good leadership is recognized as important for success in many walks of life including the military, it has proven devilishly difficult to predict who will make a good leader and who will not. An advantage at West Point is that there are several well-developed methods for measuring effective leadership, based mainly on supervisor and peer ratings (U.S. Corps of Cadets, 1995).

In trying to predict good leadership outcomes, West Point has historically relied mostly on cognitive measures like SAT scores and high school GPAs, as well as sports and leader activities in high school. Of these traditional measures, only college entrance exam scores (SATs and ACTs) have shown much power to predict either leadership performance at the academy or who makes it to graduation. This led us into several studies seeking to find other factors, including personality ones, that might explain who will survive and thrive in the demanding environment of West Point.

In one such study, I tested several cognitive and noncognitive (personality) measures to see which, if any, might predict leadership performance while at the academy (Bartone, 1999). Cognitive measures included logical reasoning, problem-solving, a spatial intelligence mental rotation task, and also entrance exam scores that cover both verbal and math abilities. The personality measures included an earlier version of the Hardiness Resilience Gauge, social judgment (the ability to size up and react appropriately in social situations), a measure of values orientation, and several scales to measure what are known as "Big Five" personality factors (emotional stability, extraversion, agreeableness, openness, and conscientiousness).

Leadership was carefully measured using military performance grades received over the entire four years at the academy. These grades are based on supervisor ratings that are heavily weighted towards leadership skills. Leadership ratings are made on the following performance areas: influencing others, consideration for others, planning and organizing, supervising, delegating, decision-making, developing subordinates, teamwork, and communication skills.

Results showed that college entrance exams and hardiness were the strongest predictors of leader performance, followed by social judgment, traditional values, and the Big Five factors of extraversion (dominance), emotional stability, and conscientiousness (work orientation). Here was compelling evidence that cadets who are high in hardiness are able to thrive and develop as good leaders in the tough West Point environment.

Additional studies with cadets further confirmed the importance of hardiness in leader development and performance. For example, when following up on a class of cadets about four years after graduation, their hardiness scores as cadets predicted adaptability and performance as young Army officers, as rated by their bosses (Bartone, Kelly, & Matthews, 2013). This was a quite rigorous study, in that hardiness was measured shortly after the cadets arrived at West Point, while leader performance was assessed about seven years later when they were junior Army officers. So, hardiness was found to be a positive factor that helped cadets develop into more effective and adaptable leaders.

In another long-term follow-up study, a survey was mailed in 2002 to all graduates of the class of 1998, about four years after graduation. This survey also included an earlier form of the Hardiness Resilience Gauge, as well as measures of transformational leadership, general health, and career intentions. Results showed that hardiness was the strongest predictor of current health, as well as intentions to stay in the Army for a career (Psotka, Bartone, & Legree, 2005).

It turns out that hardiness is also correlated with transformational leadership, a style of leadership marked by consistency, persistence, concern for individuals, and the ability to inspire and motivate others (Bass, 1985). In addition, hardiness-commitment was strongly related to intentions to stay in the Army. Thus, cadets high in hardiness are more likely to continue a career as Army officers, and are developing into more effective leaders at the same time.

In yet another follow-up study on a larger group of cadets, we applied multiple regression statistical techniques that let you evaluate several variables simultaneously to see which if any are having the greatest impact on performance grades. Here, military leadership grades for the entire four years served as the outcome variable, and men (N=989) and women (N=152) from an entire West Point class were looked at separately.

Of all the variables entered into the analysis, hardiness turned out to be the strongest predictor of leader performance for men, and even stronger for women. Other predictors were transformational leadership style for both sexes, extraversion for men, and agreeableness for women (Bartone & Snook, 2000). This study provides further hard evidence that being high in hardiness is an advantage at West Point, especially for female cadets. These findings spurred us to wonder how hardiness might be working for the women cadets in particular at West Point.

Women at West Point

As a result of congressional action, West Point started to admit women for the first time in 1976. That first class included 119 women. Of those, only 62 (52%) made it to graduation four years later. These young women had a tough time and faced frequent resistance and harassment from male cadets, and even some faculty who disagreed with the new policy. Since then, the percentage of women at West Point has risen to about 20%, or around 240 per class.

While women are more accepted today in the Corps of Cadets, they still face many hurdles. They are required to meet all of the same requirements as the men in academic, military, and physical performance (physical standards are aligned with those of the Army, which maintains somewhat different standards for women). And women cadets are still a minority in a population of mostly men.

Considering the extra stress that West Point women face, it made sense to explore the role of hardiness for them in particular. So, we ran several studies looking at how hardiness might be operating as a stress resilience factor for the female cadets. The first interesting finding to emerge was that as a group, female cadets are higher in overall hardiness than their male counterparts (Bartone & Priest, 2001). This is not a huge surprise and is most likely the result of a self-selection factor. That is, only women who are higher in hardiness decide to apply to West Point in the first place, knowing that it is going to be a challenging and difficult experience.

Despite their higher levels of hardiness, women cadets still report higher levels of stress and more health symptoms than men. The higher stress levels most likely reflect the additional challenges of having to survive and perform in what is still a strongly male-dominated environment. Interestingly, however, stress was correlated with symptoms only in female cadets who were relatively low in hardiness. In other words, being high in hardiness protects female cadets from stress related health problems. Also, the high-hardy female cadets received better leader performance grades, despite their higher stress levels. It seems clear then that for women operating in the stressful environment of West Point, being high in hardiness gives an advantage, helping them to stay healthy and perform better as leaders.

Who Drops Out? Hardiness and the Ability to Persist

One of the leadership qualities that is valued at West Point is the ability to persist, to stay with a task and see it through to a successful finish. And as mentioned earlier, about 20% of each entering class drops out somewhere along the way. Given the links between hardiness, leadership performance, and health in cadets, we wondered if hardiness might have a positive influence on a cadet's ability to stick with the program through all four years. Well, in a series of studies conducted at West Point, hardiness did prove to be a robust predictor of who stays through to graduation and who drops out.

In one of the first looks at this question, colleagues at West Point and I tracked the class that entered in 2004, through their cadet basic training and first semester of classes. Over this early stressful six-month period, about 9% of cadets dropped out, or 108 out of 1,223 (Kelly, Matthews, & Bartone, 2005). Results showed that being low in hardiness-commitment was a significant predictor of attrition in this group. In contrast, tests used routinely in the admissions process, such as college entrance exams and high school class rank, did not predict who dropped out.

After this intriguing finding, we wanted to see if it was a fluke, or if it would hold true for other cadet groups as well. So, we looked at all the cadets who entered West Point over a five year period, from 2001 to 2005. The results were even stronger this time and consistent across all five classes (Kelly & Bartone, 2006).

As you can see in Figure 13.1, cadets who dropped out during the first summer of basic training were significantly lower in overall hardiness levels and in the three hardiness facets of challenge, control, and commitment.

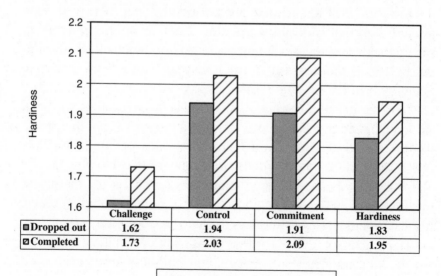

	Challenge	Control	Commitment	Hardiness
□ Dropped out	1.62	1.94	1.91	1.83
▨ Completed	1.73	2.03	2.09	1.95

□ Dropped out ▨ Completed

FIGURE **13.1** Hardiness Scores of West Point Cadets Who Dropped Out (N=319) Versus Those Who Completed N=4,902) Cadet Basic Training

Of the cadets who survive the first summer of basic training, not all of them make it to graduation four years later. All told, only around 80% of those who begin West Point as freshmen complete all four years. This isn't too surprising, considering everything that cadets have to do. The academic program is one of the country's most demanding. Failing just two courses usually leads to dismissal. In addition to academics, cadets also spend part of each day in physical and military training activities. Every cadet is required to play a sport and maintain high standards of physical fitness.

But perhaps the most difficult part of West Point involves the military training. From the very first day, cadets must dress precisely in military uniform and abide by an extensive set of military regulations. They learn to march, fire weapons, and survive in the field. Summers are spent in more advanced military training, including attending Army parachuting (Airborne) and helicopter (Air Assault) schools. As they become upperclassmen, cadets are given increased leadership duties and are responsible for training and mentoring juniors cadets. The daily schedule is tightly regimented, with long days often running from 6:30 a.m. to midnight.

On top of all this, cadets are frequently sleep deprived. One study found that cadets were getting less than six hours of sleep per night during the academic cycle (Miller, Shattuck, & Matsangas, 2010). Without question, the four-year West Point experience is a very challenging one for the cadets.

In order to see if hardiness also predicts which cadets will stick through the program all the way to graduation, we did another study, this time looking at four West Point classes that graduated in 2005, 2006, 2007, and 2008 (Kelly & Bartone, 2005). By combining classes like this, we obtained a larger number of subjects for the study, in this case 4,895 cadets. With more subjects and multiple classes, results are more reliable and less likely to be affected by chance.

Here again, hardiness turned out as a highly significant discriminator, with graduates showing higher hardiness levels compared to the dropouts. So, the answer is yes, cadets entering West Point who are high in hardiness are more likely to survive the program all the way through to graduation four years later. And they also perform better while there. Our research found that across these four class cohorts, hardiness was a strong predictor of military performance grades over the entire time at West Point. So, hardiness is a valuable resource for cadets in managing the stressors of life at West Point, helping them to stay healthy and grow into more effective and adaptable leaders. So what does the hardy cadet look like?

Portrait of a Hardy Cadet

During my years at West Point, my family participated in the cadet sponsorship program, which matches up cadets with local families that they can visit on weekends. Our "adopted" cadets would come over to our quarters on Sundays, eat a home-cooked meal, watch TV, and more often than not catch up on some sleep. Through this program, and also as a faculty member, I got to know many cadets quite well. Many of our conversations revolved around the difficulties and challenges they were facing at West Point, as well as in their own families.

Cadet Vincent Martinez was a Plebe (freshman) when we first met through the sponsorship program. His parents lived in Texas, where they'd moved from Puerto Rico before he was born. A somewhat shy, short kid with a winning smile, Vince was a regular at our house on Sundays. He was endlessly curious to know about our own travels and Army assignments and seemed to soak up information like a sponge.

Despite this, he struggled a bit academically, while excelling in his military and physical training courses. He quickly found himself in leadership roles in his cadet company, where he discovered he enjoyed helping younger cadets to master the various tasks and requirements of military training at West Point, whether that be packing a rucksack or rappelling down a cliff.

As I got to know him better over the coming years, Vince impressed me as being quite high in hardiness. He enjoyed new experiences and challenges, which was one of his main reasons for enrolling in West Point. He described this as a good way to know himself better and what he was capable of. And when he failed at something (plenty of this as a cadet!), he would try to break it down and see what he could change to do better the next time. This shows hardiness-challenge. He also wanted to be a role model and leader for younger cadets, by showing them how to deal with failures in a constructive way.

Vince also had a strong sense of hardiness-control. Despite the regimented lifestyle and daily schedule, he always believed that his ultimate success or failure would be the result of his own decisions and not a matter of luck or "bad breaks" or some higher authority. When he saw that he was in danger of failing his Systems Engineering course, he sought out extra help from a cadet tutor in his company. In his junior year he suffered a knee injury on the obstacle course, which prevented him from running. So, he took up cycling with the cadet bicycle team to maintain his physical fitness. He was in charge of his own destiny.

Finally, Vince was clearly high in hardiness-commitment. He was always interested and curious about the world around him, at West Point and beyond. Even seemingly trivial tasks like packing a ruck or learning to recite "cadet knowledge" (e.g., how many gallons of water are there in Lusk Reservoir?) were seen as meaningful, because they were part of a larger, important enterprise. He was curious about himself, wanting to understand and improve himself as a person and an officer.

Vince wanted to build his skills and competencies and was confident in his ability to grow. And he likewise was committed and engaged with his social world, his fellow cadets, friends, and family. His peers rated him as the most effective leader in his company, the one they turned to for advice. Vince graduated in the top 10% of his class and went on to serve with distinction as an Army infantry officer, and later in the Medical Service Corps.

Beyond West Point

Of course, West Point is not the only college that has a problem with students dropping out before graduation. In fact, according to the National Center for Education Statistics, up to 40% of students who begin a four-year college program in the US never finish. And this dropout rate is even worse for black and minority students (National Center for Education Statistics, 2019). If hardiness is related to retention and success at a college like West Point, might it predict success at civilian colleges as well?

The answer appears to be yes. For example, in a multicollege cooperative study, students higher in hardiness were more likely to persist to graduation at Ithaca College, East Carolina University, Mississippi State University, Elon University, Pacific Lutheran University, and Texas A&M University (Lifton et al., 2006). According to the study's main author, the colleges planned to use these results in order to provide low-hardiness students with special training and support to help them build their hardiness attitudes and make it to graduation.

Making Yourself a Hardy Leader

The West Point research confirms that hardiness—commitment, control, and challenge—facilitates healthy coping and also helps in growing effective leaders. So, what can you do to improve yourself as a hardy leader? Many of the points in the previous chapter on hardiness coaching techniques can also be applied to yourself. Now take a moment, and ask yourself a few questions about your own leadership approach:

Commitment

- ◆ Am I doing a good job communicating our mission, what we're doing, and why it's important? What are some other things I might do to reinforce this message?
- ◆ Do I show a personal interest in those I'm leading? Do *they* have a sense that I'm interested in their welfare and advancement?
- ◆ Am I fair in allocating rewards and responsibilities?

Control

- ◆ Am I open to feedback from employees, subordinates, and team members? Do I let them know that their input is valued?

- In setting tasks and responsibilities, do I allow employees, subordinates, or team members some level of control and autonomy over the details on how to get the job done?
- Have I done enough to assure the team has the resources needed to do the mission?

Challenge

- Am I setting a good example when it comes to changes? Do I show my subordinates that I'm willing to take some chances and try new approaches?
- How do I react to mistakes and failures? Do I berate and punish those responsible, or try to turn it into a learning experience?
- Am I willing to allow my subordinates, employees, and team members some variety in work assignments, routines, and schedules?

While every situation is different, if you find that any of these points apply to you, then you've got some pathways to focus on that will improve your effectiveness as a hardy leader. In the next chapter we'll zoom in on some of the ways that stress can make people sick, and how hardiness can help to keep you healthy.

Chapter 14

Hardiness and Your Health

*"A wise man should consider that health is the greatest
of human blessings and learn how by his own thought to
derive benefit from his illnesses."*
—Hippocrates (Greek philosopher and physician,
father of modern medicine)

It is now well known that stress can make you sick. At the same
time, stress is a necessary part of life, unavoidable for us mere
humans. So, the real question is not how to avoid stress, but how
to live with it and stay healthy while coping with the stressors of
life. In this chapter we discuss some of the research showing that
hardiness, and the coping strategies that high-hardy people use in
dealing with stress, is a big part of the answer.

In his fascinating book *Why Zebras Don't Get Ulcers,* Robert
Sapolsky outlines the many ways that stress can make us sick
(Sapolsky, 2004). As we discussed in Chapter 8, the body's stress
response is healthy and adaptive when we are facing a true crisis
or challenge. But it gets us into trouble when it's not appropriate
for the situation, when it goes on for too long, or when it's trig-
gered too often by events that don't really call for a crisis response.

For example, if your blood pressure shoots up and you find
yourself getting angry every time you're in the slow checkout line
at the grocery store, you're probably having a stress response
that is out of proportion to the situation. If this happens often
enough, you're probably putting yourself at risk for developing

some stress-related health problem, which includes cardiovascular disease, high blood pressure, stroke, and diabetes. Stress, or how you handle stress, can also damage other parts of your body, such as the immune system, and increase your vulnerability to colds and flu as well as more serious diseases like arthritis and cancer.

Hardiness and Heart Disease

Heart disease and stroke are the number one causes of death around the world, killing around 18 million people a year. And stress is a major contributor (Castelli et al., 1986). One of the earliest studies looking at hardiness and heart disease was done by Howard and colleagues in 1986 (Howard, Cunningham, & Rechnitzer, 1986). They found that highly stressed managers who were low in hardiness developed high blood pressure and triglycerides over time, two markers for heart disease. But the managers who were high in hardiness did not develop these problems, despite their high stress levels. A similar study found that hardiness was a buffer against blood pressure rises in people exposed to a stressful laboratory task (Contrada, 1989).

Another study looked at adult students at the National Defense University in Washington, DC. These were mid-career professionals, both military and civilian, enrolled in a one-year intensive master's degree program. All students received free health checks including cholesterol and blood glucose screenings. For this study, students also completed the Dispositional Resilience Scale, an earlier version of the Hardiness Resilience Gauge.

The study results showed that students who were high in hardiness had more of the good cholesterol (high density lipoprotein—HDL) and less of the bad (low density lipoprotein—LDL) in their bloodstreams (Bartone, Valdes, & Sandvik, 2016). Once again, this points to hardiness as a protective factor against heart disease and its precursors.

Another interesting study was done in Iran, comparing a group of coronary heart disease patients with a group of normal, healthy people (Hamid, 2007). Here, the healthy group showed significantly higher hardiness levels, and were also higher in social support, while also reporting lower levels of stress. So once again we see that hardiness appears as a protective factor, and that social support from family and friends can also act as a buffer against the ill effects of stress. This underscores an issue that we discussed more in Chapter 8, that people high in hardiness tend to appraise situations as less stressful to begin with, and so don't experience the same kinds of stress reactions as low-hardy people do.

Stroke is also a serious consequence of heart disease. An interesting study on hardiness and stroke was done by Irene Hartigan for her doctoral dissertation research in Cork, Ireland. She studied 100 stroke survivors and wanted to see what factors distinguished those who adapted and were coping well after the stroke from those who were not. Hartigan measured hardiness with an earlier version of the Hardiness Resilience Gauge and also looked at physical functioning, living arrangements, and length of hospital stay as predictors.

What she found was that hardiness and physical functioning were the best predictors of positive adjustment in the post-stroke recovery period (Hartigan, 2015). So not only is hardiness a protective factor, but if you do end up with some kind of heart problem, being high in hardiness can help you recover and adjust better in the aftermath.

Hardiness and Diabetes

Diabetes is a serious illness that is on the rise, currently affecting over 135 million people worldwide, including many children (Moore, Zgibor, & Dasanayake, 2003). While many factors, including family background, can contribute to diabetes, stress is a major cause and can make diabetes worse for those who have it (Sapolsky, 2004). While there have not yet been studies of hardiness as a potential protective factor against diabetes, there are several studies on hardiness in diabetic patients.

It turns out that if you already have diabetes, and if your hardiness levels are high then you're more likely to stick with the treatment regimen and manage the disease better over the long term (Ross, 1991). This means you can expect a better outcome. Along these same lines, insulin-dependent diabetes patients (also called type 1 diabetes) who are higher in hardiness show better physiological adaptation to the illness, better regulation of their blood sugar levels, and fewer eye and kidney problems (Pollack, 1989a).

Of course, it's best not to get diabetes in the first place. Sticking to a healthy diet and exercising regularly can certainly help. But if you do end up with some form of diabetes, your hardiness mindset can help you deal with it in a more constructive and healthy way.

Hardiness and the Immune System

The immune system provides the body's defenses against infection and disease. Ever since the 1960s, it's been recognized that stress can damage the immune system and so increase our vulnerability to disease. Some of the earliest studies in this area found that when mice are stressed by exposing them to electric shock or loud noises, they are more susceptible to infection by viruses such as herpes simplex and poliomyelitis (Rasmussen, 1969).

Humans also show stress-related declines in immune system functioning. For example, studies have found that exposure to a variety of life stressors such as caring for the chronically ill or the death of a spouse is associated with impaired immune system responses (Kiecolt-Glaser & Glaser, 1991; Bartrop, Lazarus, Luckherst, & Kiloh, 1977). It's even been shown that stress can increase your susceptibility to the common cold and flu (Cohen, Tyrell, & Smith, 1991).

Once again, not everyone reacts the same way to the stressors of life, and that's true for the immune system too. It turns out that if you're high in hardiness, your immune system seems to be not so bothered by stress. Researchers at the University of Texas-Austin were among the first to report on this, finding that blood samples from high-hardy individuals showed more robust immune responses when exposed to a variety of infectious agents (Dolbier et al., 2001).

A similar study drew blood samples from high-hardy and low-hardy students under examination stress and analyzed them for several markers of immune system functioning. Results showed that the high-hardy group had stronger and more balanced immune system responses (Ghafourian, Shiravi, Hamid, Hemmati, & Kooti, 2013). And a study in Norway found that navy cadets who were high in all three hardiness facets—challenge, control, and commitment—had healthier immune systems than those who were low in at least one of these elements (Sandvik et al., 2013).

So, what's the bottom line? While there is more yet to learn about how hardiness may influence your immune system, the evidence to date points to a clear link between hardiness and better immune system functioning under stress. By cultivating a hardiness mindset of challenge, control, and commitment, you are likely keeping your immune system strong at the same time.

Hardiness and Cancer

As with heart disease and diabetes, stress is one of the factors that can increase your risk of getting some kind of cancer, although the evidence here is somewhat mixed. For example, a recent review of studies on stress and breast cancer found 26 studies that did identify a link. However, 18 studies in the review did not find any connection between stress and getting cancer (Chiriac, Baban, & Dumitrascu, 2018).

On the other hand, stress has definitely been found to be a factor in how fast cancer progresses. Multiple studies show that psychological stress contributes to cancer proliferation and tumor growth (Moreno-Smith, Lutgendorf, & Sood, 2010). And as with several other diseases, a major culprit seems to be an impaired immune system. For most people, the immune system just doesn't work as well when they're under a great deal of stress. When this happens, it's easier for cancer to hide from the protective cells in your immune system, and then spread to other parts of your body (Calcagni & Elenkov, 2006).

Can hardiness play a role here? While there are not many studies bearing directly on this question, we know that hardiness contributes to a healthier immune system under stress. So, we can infer that hardiness may provide some protection against aspects of cancer that are stress related.

Other studies have been done that do show hardiness makes a positive difference for people who have been diagnosed with cancer, contributing to better adaptation, coping, and well-being (Seiler & Jenewein, 2019). For example, one study of Iranian women with breast cancer found that hardiness, as well as marital satisfaction, helped these women adjust positively to their condition, and even derive benefits from the experience (Aflakseir, Nowroozi, Mollazadeh, & Goodarzi, 2016).

Another study of breast cancer patients reported similar results, with women high in hardiness showing greater life satisfaction, despite the cancer (Taheri, Ahadi, Kashani, & Kermani, 2014). For Israeli survivors of malignant melanoma cancer, hardiness was positively related to well-being and level of functioning, and negatively related to distress (Hamama-Raz, 2012). Thus, the high-hardy survivors adjusted more positively to the cancer.

So, what does this mean for you? Hardiness is certainly no magic bullet. It won't prevent you from getting cancer. However, if you should get cancer, being high in hardiness will help you to adjust and cope in a positive, healthy way.

Hardiness and Arthritis

Arthritis is a crippling disease that involves a breakdown of cartilage in the joints, leading to swelling, stiffness, and pain. Rheumatoid arthritis is a special type that is brought about by a disorder of the immune system. It's known as an autoimmune disease, since the immune system is attacking its own bodily tissues. Of the various factors that can influence the severity and intensity of arthritis, psychological stress is a well recognized one (Walker, Littlejohn, McMurray, & Cutolo, 1999). Can hardiness provide any protection against this disease?

There are a few studies that have looked into this question. Researchers at the Arizona State University studied 33 women with rheumatoid arthritis, measuring hardiness and several indicators of health and immune system functioning (Okun, Zautra, & Robinson, 1988). They found that hardiness, and especially hardiness-control, was related to better perceived health and also a healthier immune system (circulating T cells). So, the women higher in hardiness control were adjusting better and maintaining better health than those low in hardiness control.

A similar study examined another, larger group of women (*N* = 122) with rheumatoid arthritis, looking at their hardiness, illness severity, and psychological well-being (Lambert, Lambert, Klipple, & Mewshaw, 1989). The results showed hardiness was a significant predictor of well-being in these patients, no matter the severity of the disease. So, in the case of rheumatoid arthritis, a hardiness mindset can not only help you cope with the disease, but appears to also influence how fast the disease progresses. This makes sense, since we know that hardiness is linked to a healthier immune system.

Health, Hardiness, and Social Support

In their study of arthritis patients, Vickie Lambert and her colleagues (1989) at Case Western Reserve University and Walter Reed Army Medical Center also found that social support was an important predictor of well-being for these patients. And patients who were high in hardiness were also high in social support. This suggests that arthritis patients high in hardiness may be better at developing and making use of support from friends and family in confronting stressful situations such as serious illness.

Of course, it's also possible that social support, at least the right kinds of support, can help to increase your hardiness attitudes. When the social support you are getting encourages you to take steps to deal with problems, that is just the kind of coping that hardy people engage in. It's known as "transformational coping" because it involves viewing the stressful situation as something you can manage by taking action and making use of the resources available (Kobasa & Puccetti, 1983). In so doing, you transform the event from a potentially damaging stressor into an opportunity to demonstrate and build up your capabilities.

Social support can also work in a negative way, if it encourages you to avoid dealing with your problems. For example, if you're having a conflict with your boss at work, and your spouse offers sympathy while encouraging you to just not think about it and have another drink, that is avoidance coping. It's not likely to solve anything, and the same problems will be there when you go to work the next day. It's much better to think about ways to resolve the problem, perhaps by talking with your boss, or even changing jobs if necessary. This is the kind of active, problem-solving coping that people high in hardiness tend to use when dealing with stressful situations.

Hardiness and Sleep

Sleep is one of the most important things we can do to maintain our health, and one of the simplest. And most of us don't get enough of it. According to the National Sleep Foundation, adults 26 to 64 years old need a minimum of seven hours of sleep a night in order to maintain good health (Hirshkowitz et al., 2015). And yet on average, over half of Americans (53%) report less sleep than that during the work week (National Sleep Foundation, 2013). Young people and teenagers need even more sleep, with a recommended 8–10 hours per night. However, most are getting only 7 to 7.5 hours on weeknights (Hansen, Janssen, Schiff, Zee, & Dubocovich, 2005). Lack of sleep can definitely make you sick, as well as degrade your well-being and performance.

For example, a study of high school students in Rhode Island found that those who were getting less sleep reported more illnesses including cold and flu, sore throat, muscle pain, fatigue, stomach problems, and (for women) menstrual pain (Orzech, Acebo, Seifer, Barker, & Carskadon, 2014). Many other studies have documented that poor quality sleep, or not enough sleep, increases your risk for a variety of illnesses including heart disease, obesity, and diabetes (Alvarez & Ayas, 2004). Sleep deprivation even makes you more vulnerable to the common cold (Cohen, Doyle, Alper, Janicki-Deverts, & Turner, 2009).

Can hardiness provide any protection against the ill effects of sleep loss? There is at least indirect evidence that it can, to some degree. We know from other studies that people high in hardiness tend to have stronger, more robust immune systems. Sleep deprivation disrupts the immune system, leaving us more susceptible to all the health problems mentioned above and more (Bryant, Trinder, & Curtis, 2004). So, to the extent hardiness contributes to a healthy, balanced immune system, the high-hardy person will be more tolerant of sleep loss.

There is some research support for this idea, and it comes from the world of shift workers. Shift workers, such as nurses, typically experience frequent sleep loss due to irregular hours and the disruption of their normal day/night circadian body clocks. You experience this yourself as jet lag whenever you have to travel across time zones. For example, in one study of shift work nurses in Norway, nurses who were high in hardiness showed greater tolerance and less fatigue, depression, and anxiety on the job than those low in hardiness (Natvik et al., 2011).

Similar findings come from another study of Norwegian nurses, this time looking at effects of shift work over a longer two-year period. Again, nurses high in hardiness showed less fatigue, anxiety, and depression over time. This study also looked at the three facets of hardiness and found that commitment and challenge had the strongest protective effects (Saksvik-Lehouillier, Bjorvatn, Magerøy, & Pallesen, 2016).

Are you a morning person or a night person? Some people are naturally more alert and active in the mornings. We call these early chronotypes, or larks. Others are more active later in the day and at night. These people are called late chronotypes, or owls. A growing body of research shows that compared to owls, larks are more resistant to the ill effects of shift work and sleep deprivation (Juda, Vetter, & Roenneberg, 2013; van de Ven et al., 2016).

A recent study looked at hardiness and chronotype in over 1,000 West Point military academy cadets. Life at West Point, which was discussed in Chapter 13, can be quite stressful for cadets, and sleep deprivation is common. In this study, cadets who were high in hardiness (especially control and commitment) tended to be larks, and they also performed better in their physical and military leadership programs (Kelly, Matthews, & Kelly, 2019). So, here is more evidence that being high in hardiness contributes to better sleep and provides some protection against the damaging effects of sleep deprivation.

Hardiness and Health Habits

One of the ways that hardiness can help to keep you healthy is by encouraging you to take up healthy practices, such as exercising, eating healthier foods, and even sleeping more. Being high in hardiness-commitment means in part being more plugged-in and engaged with the world around you. High hardy people are likely to be more aware of the value of exercise and other practices for maintaining their health. Being high in commitment also means you are more attuned to and interested in yourself, your own body and mind.

Being high in commitment means you are more aware of how different things in your environment, and your own choices and behaviors, can impact you. So, the person high in hardiness may choose to do things, like exercise, that help him or her stay healthy. And they may be more inclined to avoid the things, like smoking or eating high-sugar foods, that can make them sick. Likewise, being high in hardiness-control means you believe you can influence outcomes, so are more willing to make the choices and do the things that lead to good health, like exercising and not smoking.

An early study with Chicago executives found that both hardiness and exercise were valuable resources in buffering the ill effects of stress, as was social support from friends and family (Kobasa, Maddi, Puccetti, & Zola, 1985). In this study, hardiness and exercise were largely unrelated. This shows that you could be low in hardiness and still be a big exerciser or be high in hardiness and not much of an exerciser.

Still, there is plenty of evidence that hardiness is linked more directly to exercise and other healthy habits. For example, researchers at the University of Alabama tested out hardiness and a variety of health practices as possible buffers in the relation between stress and illness for undergraduates. In this study, health practices included exercise, diet, personal hygiene, and substance abuse (Wiebe & McCallum, 1986). The results showed that hardiness had a direct effect on health and also an indirect effect through health practices. In other words, students high in hardiness were engaging in more healthy practices (and fewer unhealthy ones), which in turn was leading them to better health outcomes (less illness). A more recent study in Japan looked at 468 college students and found that those who exercised regularly were also higher in hardiness (Monri, Tajima, & Matsueda, 2014). Interestingly, students who engaged in group exercise (as opposed to solo activities) were the highest of all in hardiness. This may relate to that aspect of commitment that involves engagement and interest in other people—the social world.

Other research shows that hardiness is related to healthy habits. For example, among adult patients suffering from a chronic illness, those who were high in hardiness were more involved with a variety of health promotion activities (Pollack, 1989b). Along the same lines, a study of older adults found that hardiness was linked with more exercise, healthy nutrition, relaxation practices, and general health promotion (Nicholas, 1993). Looked at another way, a study found that college students who were low in hardiness were more likely to engage in unhealthy habits, including smoking, doing drugs, poor diet, and lack of exercise (Nagy & Nix, 1989).

So, the evidence is pretty clear that if you're high in hardiness, one of the ways you stay healthy under stress is by maintaining good health habits. Hardy people are more aware of how what they do can affect their health. And they are willing to make lifestyle choices that lead to better health. If you are high in hardiness, most likely you are paying attention to your diet, exercising, and looking for other ways to keep up your health.

Using the Three Cs of Hardiness to Stay Healthy

In this chapter we've covered some of the major health problems and areas where having a hardiness mindset can make a difference in keeping you healthy despite stressful life experiences.

To be sure, many factors besides stress contribute to poor health or illness, including family history and exposure to infection and toxins in the environment. But being high in hardiness can help you deal with stress in ways that raise your resistance to illness and help you ward off many health problems. And if you should be unlucky enough to develop a major illness, a hardy outlook can help you adjust and cope more positively with the situation.

Sometimes, no matter what you do to stay healthy, illness knocks on your door. A few years ago, one of us (Paul) was diagnosed with late-stage throat cancer. Of course, this kind of news comes as a shock, and so I spent some time wondering if the doctors maybe had it wrong. But once I accepted the reality, I began to think about what I could do about it. My wife and I spent a lot of time researching different treatment options and went to several medical centers getting second and third opinions before settling on a treatment plan and hospital. As best we could, we took control of my medical care.

I also made choices throughout the treatment that I thought would lead to a better outcome. For example, the doctors recommended that I reduce my coffee intake, since caffeine can interfere with the effectiveness of treatment. Although I'd been a heavy coffee drinker for years, I quit drinking coffee completely at that point. I trusted the doctors' advice and was fully committed to giving the treatment my best effort, regardless of the final result. Curiously enough, I came to see the cancer as an interesting challenge. It was certainly a new experience for me and provided an unusual and dramatic learning opportunity. Although like most of us I'd cared for family members with cancer, this was my first chance to experience it for myself on the patient side. It really gave me a new understanding and appreciation for what cancer patients go through. When you have cancer, no matter how good the treatment, you never know if you'll live to tell the tale. It brings you face to face with your own death.

Sitting in the radiation oncology waiting room, or in the chemotherapy infusion center, I had a chance to observe and talk with other cancer patients, many of them worse off than I was. On an almost daily basis, I was amazed and humbled by the courage and dignity I saw in people of all ages who were struggling with some type of cancer. I also learned a lot about myself in going through it. While I wouldn't wish it on anyone, I'm truly glad that I had this life experience.

So, what steps can you take to improve your odds of staying healthy? Your sense of hardiness-commitment involves an interest in yourself, as well as family, friends, and work. Use that commitment to yourself to examine your lifestyle and see if there are areas where you can shift your habits in a more healthy direction. This could involve exercise, diet, sleep, or something else. You're worth it!

Your sense of hardiness-challenge also comes into play, reminding you that change is good, a chance to learn and get better. In this case, challenge yourself into some healthier habits. Maybe you need to exercise more or eat less or differently. Where can you make a change? Take the stairs instead of the elevator. Eat a more balanced diet. Have a salad now and then instead of that burger or pizza. Drink more water instead of sugary drinks. Go to bed earlier. You can try different things until you find the ones that fit in with your lifestyle and that you can keep up.

In making these changes, you're also applying your sense of hardiness-control. You have the power to choose how you are going to live, how you spend your time, what you eat and drink. Control is never absolute, of course. We all have to accommodate to various demands and requirements of the society we live in. However, most of us have more control than we realize. Look around you and find something in your life that may be affecting your health in a bad way. Then think about what you can do to fix it!

Chapter 15

Moving From Life Stress to Life Success

The Role of Hardiness in Turning Around Your World

"Note to self: every time you were convinced you couldn't go on, you did."
—Unknown

We're sure you've heard about people who have gone through terrible life experiences, yet, somehow, they have essentially turned their lives around for the better. Many people "get through" bad experiences or bad times. But not everyone makes a life-changing decision to change their circumstances significantly towards what we'll refer to as thriving.

The term resilience often comes to mind in this regard. However, resilience, as defined by the dictionary refers to "the capacity to recover quickly from difficulties; toughness." Resilience is about returning back to where you were before the crisis. What about people who excel above and beyond where they were before the crisis? Some people get through difficult times by becoming more engaged, more challenged, and more in control of their lives. We call it hardiness.

We wanted to conclude this book by providing you with some real examples of how hardiness has played a role in people's transitions through serious life challenges. In this chapter we focus on how individuals high in hardiness overcame stressful experiences, and used them as a springboard to a better, more fulfilling life. We'll present some examples of people who experienced life-changing events, yet managed to emerge, not just where they were prior to the event, but in a new place with added meaning to their lives.

From Tragic Loss to Uplifting the Lives of Others

Bonnie Carroll served 30 years in the US Air Force (USAF), retiring from there as a Major. She held the position of Chief of Casualty Operations, Headquarters United States Air Force and worked on the Headquarters USAF National Security and Emergency Preparedness staff in the Pentagon. She has also worked in Washington, DC, holding political appointments in both the Reagan and Bush administrations, including a stint in the White House as Executive Assistant for Cabinet Affairs.

Bonnie was extremely accomplished and successful in her career. She was leading a fulfilling and happy life both at work and with her family. But her world changed tragically on November 12, 1992, when her husband, Brigadier General Tom Carroll, was killed in an Army C-12 plane crash. As most of us know, the death of a family member can be devastating, especially when unexpected. It's a fear that many military families live with every day.

When Bonnie's husband died, she sought some kind of emotional support. She assumed that for military families there was someplace you could go, even if only to meet with other families who have already been through such a tragic experience. She went from place to place within the military, the government, and elsewhere. She was shocked to discover the lack of support—either governmental or private.

Bonnie then did what seemed only natural to her. She started an organization to help these families. She founded and is the current president and CEO of the Tragedy Assistance Program for Survivors (TAPS). TAPS is the leading national military service organization providing compassionate care, casework assistance, and 24/7/365 emotional support for those impacted by the death of a military loved one. For her pioneering work she was awarded the 2015 Presidential Medal of Freedom from President Obama.

We interviewed Bonnie to learn more about what it takes to go from one's own personal tragedy to developing a sense of purpose and helping thousands of other families deal with grief and loss. She helped us by agreeing to take the Hardiness Resilience Gauge and the Emotional Quotient Inventory 2.0. Her hardiness scores can be seen in Figure 15.1.

We certainly weren't surprised that Bonnie had a high hardiness score. It's among the highest scores that we've seen. Her hardiness-commitment score is especially high. It should be obvious by now that she is driven by a higher purpose. In her words, "I saw creating this organization as the only way to move forward." She pointed out that it was not her first choice to create an organization, but she reached a point where she felt she had to. This type of purpose or mission in one's life can be a driving force.

Her challenge score was her next highest. She explained this as part of her need to take action in situations. When something needs to be done, she finds challenge in leading the way. She mentioned that when she went through basic training upon joining the Air Force, it was grueling and difficult. Most of the other recruits complained and didn't like it. She, however, found it challenging and fun. People high in challenge are able to take difficult situations and see them in a different light. It's that restructuring of our thoughts and attitudes that helps us get through the difficult situations.

Bonnie's hardiness-control score was also quite high. As she put it, "Control is a choice. It is moving your energy towards opportunity." She believes we are hardwired at a young age to behave the way we do. Bonnie's mother died when she was young, and she had to take on the role of looking after her father. Taking charge seems to be natural for her. Her hardiness mindset has positioned her for a leadership role.

Bonnie's emotional intelligence score was also extremely high. Her highest score is in flexibility. It may seem counterintuitive for

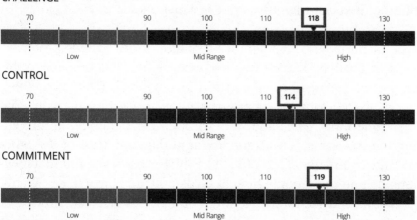

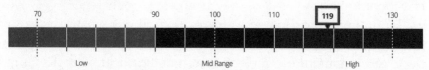

© Copyright of MHS 2019. All rights reserved.

FIGURE 15.1 Bonnie Carroll's Hardiness Profile

(Used with permission from Multi-Health Systems, 2019.)

someone who has been so long in the military, with all its rules and regulations, to be high in flexibility. But that's another reason why Bonnie stands out. Being flexible means you find what leeway there is within the rules, and do your best to adapt and get things done.

Her second highest score is in self-actualization. Self-actualized people have found their niche and are doing what they love to do in life. Similar to hardiness-commitment, it demonstrates a strong sense of purpose. In addition, highly actualized people contribute to helping others grow and to bettering the world. When you speak with Bonnie you know how passionate she is about what she is doing.

One of the things we can learn from Bonnie is to find our purpose. Out of tragedy we can find new meaning in life. When bad things happen in our lives we can choose to sit back and suffer, or move forward with a cause. We may not be able to change the world alone, but if we rally others to our cause we can certainly make a dent. That dent might just make a difference in the world, and improve our own lives along the way.

Transcending One's Circumstances

One of us (Steven) was giving a presentation at the annual meeting of an international group of networked executive search firms. Following the presentation there was a cocktail party at the offices of the firm hosting the event. It was a beautiful environment. The firm occupied the main floor of a historic old bank with high ceilings right in the heart of downtown Montreal. Following cocktails, we went to dinner at a nearby restaurant.

I was seated near the host, Karen Groom, president of Groom & Associates, one of Canada's leading recruitment and staffing agencies with offices across the country. I was interested in Karen's story and how she built such a successful firm, especially as a woman entrepreneur with two of her daughters working at the agency. My impression was that Karen was very personable, attractive, youthful, and gracious as a host. I assumed she must have come from a wealthy family, gone to prestigious schools, and basically used family connections to build her impressive business. So, I decided to engage Karen and learn about her rise to success.

I hate to admit it, as a psychologist, but I don't think I could have been more wrong about my impressions. Only after some prodding and gentle nudging was Karen willing to divulge her story. It was not a pretty one. She grew up in Verdun, one of the poorest areas of Montreal at the time, as the oldest of seven children. Her family was very poor. Her father occasionally worked as a truck driver, but there was not much money earned. There was also physical abuse in their household. It was not a pleasant situation for her.

Karen was seven years old when she heard the news. She doesn't really know much about the details to this day, but her father was killed in a gang-related murder. You can imagine how difficult that could be for a seven-year-old girl to process. Her emotions were quite mixed, as the loss of a father is tragic, but the abuse she grew up with would likely end.

I wondered what Karen's hardiness profile would be like. How could someone recover from such a difficult upbringing? Karen's hardiness profile is shown in Figure 15.2.

As you can see, Karen has a very high overall hardiness score. She is also very high in hardiness-challenge. She embraces change. She longed to get out of her neighborhood in Verdun ever since she could remember. She also loved school. She enjoyed learning new things and always believed in change.

When asked about the people around her while growing up she said, "The environment was one in which negativity thrived and little emphasis was placed on work or career." Karen never bought into that mindset. Gratitude was always important for her. When her father was murdered and the story hit the newspapers, people started sending gifts to her family. She was grateful for every opportunity she was given.

Karen also scored very high in hardiness-commitment. She grew up with a strong sense of purpose. Ever since she can remember she was motivated to get out of her neighborhood. Her two main driving forces were to provide for her family and

Karen Groom
June 11, 2019

TOTAL HARDINESS

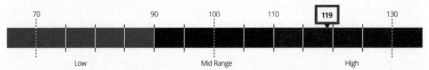

| 70 | | 90 | 100 | 110 | **119** | 130 |

Low   Mid Range   High

What your score means

- Your result indicates that your total level of hardiness falls in the **High** range.

- You are likely very capable of tackling stressful and unexpected situations that come your way. Your high level of hardiness often protects you from the negative effects of stress and you are able to respond to surprising and stressful situations in a healthy and adaptive manner.

- You likely have the coping skills necessary to help you deal with stressful circumstances. For example, rather than trying to ignore or avoid the stressful situation, you likely try to fix it and work on eliminating the source of your stress.

HARDINESS SUBSCALES

CHALLENGE

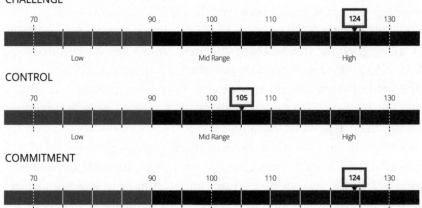

| 70 | | 90 | 100 | 110 | **124** | 130 |

Low   Mid Range   High

CONTROL

| 70 | | 90 | 100 | **105** | 110 | 130 |

Low   Mid Range   High

COMMITMENT

| 70 | | 90 | 100 | 110 | **124** | 130 |

Low   Mid Range   High

On the pages that follow, you will find more information on your Challenge, Control, and Commitment scores. As you move through the report, think about how you might see these hardiness qualities emerge in your day-to-day life. If you choose to implement the recommended developmental strategies highlighted for you, you can ensure that you are setting yourself up for success when faced with stressful and changing situations.

MHS © Copyright of MHS 2019. All rights reserved.   3
1.1.1

FIGURE 15.2   Karen Groom's Hardiness Profile

(Used with permission from Multi-Health Systems, 2019.)

to build a legacy for her children. She wanted them to have the opportunities she never had—Karen never graduated from college. Her drive and commitment enabled both of those dreams to come true.

Karen makes no secret of the fact that her goal has been to be financially secure and live a comfortable lifestyle. For those of us who grew up comfortable, and perhaps take it for granted, it may be hard to understand why this can be so important. If you had to spend time living in a deprived environment for any significant amount of time, then you would really understand what this means.

Growing up in poverty, Karen also longed to have a close and supportive group—family and friends that she could trust. She wanted to be grounded and happy, just lead a normal life. But she also wanted to be self-reliant and able to provide a secure lifestyle. After all, really, who wouldn't?

Hardiness-control is in the midrange for Karen. Her score is at a level where she believes she determines her own outcomes. When asked, she reported that she always believed she could control her own world. At the same time, she knew about things she couldn't fix, such as child abuse. This would be a bit of a confusing message, even today.

What about Karen's emotional intelligence score? Well, no real surprise here either. Karen scores very high in emotional intelligence. Her highest score is in flexibility, similar to Bonnie's score. Karen had to adapt her life from dire circumstances and be in survival mode from early on in life. From this she learned not to sweat the small stuff. She has no trouble being flexible in situations when needing to move forward.

Her next highest areas were in optimism and independence. She makes it clear that she looks at the positive side in life: "I will always look for the good in situations. I believe there is a solution for every problem."

As for independence, ever since her father was killed, she took on a leadership role in her family—starting at age seven. She learned at a young age to reach for the stars and to do things her way. She readily admits she was never a follower. She was the high school homecoming queen and considered herself a free spirit, even in high school.

A big part of Karen's success is likely due to her high intelligence. She loved school and did well in her classes. Her personal circumstances didn't allow her to complete college. She told us her initial dream was to be a TV journalist, like Barbara Walters. She felt if she worked hard enough, she could get there.

It was this drive that led her to develop her own very successful company in the human resource field. In many ways Karen is a model to women who strive for independence, entrepreneurship, and financial success. And, as I found out, she can accomplish all this and still be a nice person.

From Tragedy to the World Stage

Dr. Izzeldin Abuelaish was already well known where he was raised, in the Gaza strip. It was not an easy place to grow up in, with a long history of conflict. He trained as an obstetrician/gynecologist who specializes in infertility treatment. He lived in Gaza and worked in Israel for much of his life. He's also a Harvard-trained public health expert. He crossed the line between Israelis and Palestinians for most of his life, as a physician who treats patients on both sides.

Tragedy struck his life on January 16, 2009, during the Israeli-Gaza conflict at that time. While Izzeldin, his eight children, brothers, sisters-in-law, and their families were seemingly safe and protected in their family home, an Israeli tank shell exploded in the girls' bedroom where his daughters Shatha, Mayar, Bessan, Aya, and his niece Noor were reading or doing homework. Mayar, Bessan, Aya, and Noor were killed in the explosion, and Shatha was severely injured. The loss was devastating for Izzeldin. Who can imagine the pain of losing not just one but three daughters and a niece?

Most people, along with their grief, would no doubt experience a great deal of anger, desire for revenge, and hate. But Dr. Abuelaish is not most people. While the tragic experience changed him, the change was in a totally unexpected direction.

He began a crusade, but not a crusade of rage. It was a crusade against hatred and revenge. His story is summarized in a book he wrote, *I Shall Not Hate: A Gaza Doctor's Journey* (Abuelaish, 2017). He has appeared in many forums including radio, TV, and newspapers, and has been praised by world leaders for his work on an international scale.

One of the authors (Steven) is working with Dr. Abuelaish on developing a hate scale that would allow us to identify the components of hate and lead to specific interventions. Dr. Abuelaish, a medical doctor, sees hate as contagious, something that needs to be treated just like we treat other contagious diseases. Our research has taken us to measure hate in populations in North America as well as in the Middle East.

I asked Dr. Abuelaish to take our hardiness and emotional intelligence assessments because he is so unique in his life experience and in his response to extremely stressful situations. His profile can be seen in Figure 15.3.

Dr. Abuelaish has the highest profile we have ever seen on the Hardiness Resilience Gauge. His highest score is in hardiness-challenge. He approaches many of life's stresses as challenges to be overcome. He is a creative thinker and seems to always look for solutions, not dwell on problems. No problem seems too large for him. Taking on the challenge of eradicating hate, which to him is like eliminating polio or smallpox, is an achievable goal in his eyes.

Control is something he has always been strong in. Growing up in difficult circumstances in Gaza, he was able to complete his education in medicine and practice in different countries. When he needed more experience for his training, he was not afraid to approach an Israeli hospital and arrange to work there. For Izzeldin, there is always a way to get something done if you really want to. He has many, many friends, both on the Israeli side and in the Palestinian and greater Arab world.

It is easy to see Izzeldin's high level of commitment to his cause. We have spent significant time together, working on this

ID#567
June 28, 2019

TOTAL HARDINESS

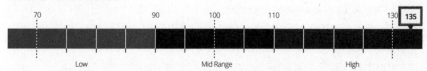

What your score means

- Your result indicates that your total level of hardiness falls in the **High** range.

- You are likely very capable of tackling stressful and unexpected situations that come your way. Your high level of hardiness often protects you from the negative effects of stress and you are able to respond to surprising and stressful situations in a healthy and adaptive manner.

- You likely have the coping skills necessary to help you deal with stressful circumstances. For example, rather than trying to ignore or avoid the stressful situation, you likely try to fix it and work on eliminating the source of your stress.

HARDINESS SUBSCALES

CHALLENGE

CONTROL

CbMMITMENT

On the pages that follow, you will find more information on your Challenge, Control, and Commitment scores. As you move through the report, think about how you might see these hardiness qualities emerge in your day-to-day life. If you choose to implement the recommended developmental strategies highlighted for you, you can ensure that you are setting yourself up for success when faced with stressful and changing situations.

MHS © Copyright of MHS 2019. All rights reserved.   3
1.1.2

FIGURE 15.3   Dr. Izzeldin Abuelaish's Hardiness Profile

(Used with permission from Multi-Health Systems, 2019.)

incredibly complex project, with no outside funding to date. In addition to his commitment to fighting hate, he runs a nonprofit organization in memory of his daughters called Daughters For Life Foundation. Their mission is to create educational opportunities for young women from the Middle East and help them become strong, well-informed women who are able to speak up and change their communities and the face of the world.

As expected, Izzeldin's emotional intelligence score is extremely high. His highest score was in social responsibility. This is no surprise considering the amount of his time that he spends on causes to make the world a better place. He carries his message to leaders around the world and has transformed his career from a physician treating one person at a time to a catalyst influencing thousands of people.

His next highest scales are assertiveness and self-actualization. His high self-actualization relates to his mission and his desire to make the world a better place. He loves what he does and is fully immersed in his work. His assertiveness enables him to get things done. He is a person of action who does not have a lot of patience for endless chatter. His commitment has helped him navigate through many difficult obstacles. It can be hard to imagine someone starting in such difficult circumstances rising to the level he is today.

Once again, we learn that tragedies in our lives can be very painful, but we must learn to move on. Blaming others is not a productive solution. Hate, blame, and revenge do not make things better. In fact, these emotions have negative physiological consequences. Turning grief into constructive energy not only helps you work through it, but can also provide a way to memorialize the loved one(s) you've lost.

■ ■ ■

There are lessons here for all of us. The ability to rise above tragedies and move forward, looking for greater solutions, takes a great deal of hardiness across all three facets. While few people ever display this level of hardiness, we can see what can happen and the potential we can reach if we continue to develop this mindset.

New Life in a New Country: Struggles and Achievements

One of the authors (Steven) contributes, with the donation of assessments and evaluation assistance, to an innovative and unique program for homeless women called Up With Women. The program is run by a dynamic, formerly homeless woman named Lia Grimanis, who was featured in Steven's previous book, *The EQ Leader* (Stein, 2017).

As part of our involvement with this program we have the opportunity to review test protocols of dozens of homeless women going through this program as part of their individual development (through coaching) and program evaluation. One day, a member of my team noticed an unusual profile from a participant in this group. Her hardiness-resilience score was unusually high compared to other women from this program. The comparison can be seen in Figure 15.4. We decided to explore further, with permission from the group and the individual herself.

The woman's name is Leni Rose Bereber, and she emigrated to Canada from the Philippines. She had a very difficult childhood, growing up in poverty in her birth country. From her earliest years, she lived in adversity. Her father was an alcoholic, and her mother suffered from severe depression. She got married young and had two children. She earned money to help support her family through various part-time jobs that included giving

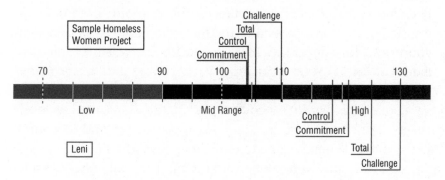

FiGURE **15.4** Comparison of Leni Rose Bereber's Hardiness Scores with Sample of Homeless Women

(Used with permission from Multi-Health Systems, 2019.)

massages and using the healing powers that she gained from her grandmother.

Leni Rose was poor and desperate and dreamed of getting her family out of the Philippines for a better life. She earned enough money to come to Canada on her own at 28 years of age as part of a program that allowed for the sponsoring of live-in caregivers. After two years working as a caregiver in Canada, she applied to sponsor her husband and two sons to join her. It took five years for the approval to come through. Shortly after her family's arrival, one of her sons developed cancer. At age 14 he succumbed to his illness and passed away.

The strain in her unhappy marriage became unbearable at this point, and she left her husband after 29 years of marriage. Escaping from her situation when she did left her homeless. Without a home, she lived in shelters for about nine months. Leni Rose's Hardiness Resilience Gauge profile can be seen in Figure 15.5.

Leni Rose's hardiness score is very high. When you speak with her, she is amazingly upbeat about her situation. Leni has experienced many traumas throughout her life yet manages to maintain a positive attitude. She embraced the coaching program offered by Up With Women and continues developing herself. She has taken a number of workshops that were offered through the program as well as individual coaching.

Her hardiness-challenge score is also very high. She seems to learn from each of her bad experiences and manages to bounce back from difficult life circumstances. When asked about her coping strategies, she reports that she feels she has control over situations and for support, "I like to read books, watch Oprah. I've read *Pulling Your Own Strings* (Wayne Dyer) and *Seven Habits* (Stephen Covey)."

Leni's high hardiness-control and hardiness-challenge levels can be seen in her constant striving to be better, and to control her own life. When it came to emigrating from the Philippines she stressed how she went alone to the Canadian embassy in Manila

TOTAL HARDINESS

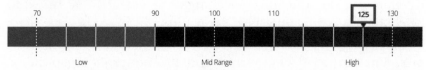

What your score means

- Your result indicates that your total level of hardiness falls in the **High** range.

- You are likely very capable of tackling stressful and unexpected situations that come your way. Your high level of hardiness often protects you from the negative effects of stress and you are able to respond to surprising and stressful situations in a healthy and adaptive manner.

- You likely have the coping skills necessary to help you deal with stressful circumstances. For example, rather than trying to ignore or avoid the stressful situation, you likely try to fix it and work on eliminating the source of your stress.

HARDINESS SUBSCALES
CHALLENGE

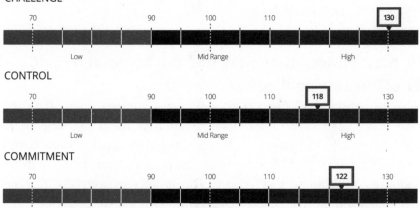

CONTROL

COMMITMENT

On the pages that follow, you will find more information on your Challenge, Control, and Commitment scores. As you move through the report, think about how you might see these hardiness qualities emerge in your day-to-day life. If you choose to implement the recommended developmental strategies highlighted for you, you can ensure that you are setting yourself up for success when faced with stressful and changing situations.

MHS © Copyright of MHS 2019. All rights reserved.   3
1.1.1

FIGURE **15.5**   Leni Rose Bereber's Hardiness Profile

(Used with permission from Multi-Health Systems, 2019.)

to make her application. She is a take-charge person who does not sit back and just let things happen.

Her commitment and control scores reflect her purpose to develop and do something meaningful in her life. She wants to help other women who have been through what she has. She's been working as a coach for other women in the Up With Women program. She found a home and work in a nonprofit organization. She has also taken courses that would qualify her as an immigration consultant and is currently working to set up her own immigration consultation business. We have seen many examples of people with a hardy mindset, even coming from traumatic conditions, rise above their life challenges.

Once again, we can learn from Leni's experiences. After overcoming one obstacle, we can keep going and learn to overcome the next one. Each win can provide the motivation—or the oxygen— to face the next challenge.

Physical Fitness, Hardiness, and the Stress of a Child's Life-Threatening Illness

Rosalie Brown has been a fitness instructor for over 30 years. She was voted one of the top personal trainers in Canada by *IMPACT,* a leading national fitness magazine, and is considered one of Canada's Top 25 Influential Personal Trainers by CanFitPro, Canada's leading fitness training program. Rosalie has worked with celebrities and professional athletes including Chuck Norris, Lori Greiner, Paula Abdul, Lennox Lewis, Christie Brinkley, Bobby Hull, and Suzanne Somers. Over one million fitness DVDs featuring her have been sold. Her YouTube workout channel has logged over 10 million views. Rosalie is bubbly, passionate, and, if you watch one of her videos, makes exercising contagious.

It would be hard to tell from watching Rosalie, but she's had her share of life's tragedies. Shortly after a family vacation in the Dominican Republic, her daughter, Kirsten, seemed to have a cold. The cold quickly got worse, and when she was taken to a physician, they were told she had bronchitis. When Kirsten kept deteriorating, they were then told it was pneumonia and she was sent for x-rays. Rosalie then noticed her daughter's skin was turning grey. The x-ray identified a hole in her lung. She was immediately airlifted to a hospital where she was intubated and put in intensive care. Rosalie and her husband, Rob, were told that the doctors had to explore the damage to her lungs.

Six hours later the surgeon told Rosalie and Rob that their child wouldn't make it through the night. They were in total shock. Rosalie and her husband stayed positive and decided to spend the night with their daughter. Kirsten was pumped full of water to keep her blood pressure readings within normal range while living on respirators. Rosalie never gave up hope. She and her husband moved beside the hospital (to a Ronald McDonald House) to stay with their daughter. Rosalie managed to keep up a basic exercise routine as she felt she needed to be strong for her daughter. Fortunately, Kirsten fully recovered and now leads a normal and satisfying life.

Rosalie is a very strong and determined person. She's spent years defying what others have told her she couldn't or shouldn't do, things that went against her positive hardiness mindset. We wanted to get a look at her hardiness profile. She agreed to take the Hardiness Resilience Gauge (HRG) and the Emotional Quotient Inventory 2.0 (EQ-i 2.0). Her hardiness profile is in Figure 15.6.

Rosalie's total hardiness score is in the high range. This is reflective of her can-do attitude. She shared several stories of her hardiness-challenge and hardiness-commitment coming into play. She sees stress-producing roadblocks as a challenge, and her strong purpose in life is her driving force. Just a few examples will make this clear.

In high school Rosalie won athlete of the year, even though she describes herself at that time as "a very curvy pasta loving Italian girl." However, it wasn't her natural athletic abilities that propelled her into health and fitness. It was a mean comment she overhead one of her classmates make, "Why would he want to date that fat Italian girl?" that brought out the "I'll show you" in Rosalie.

Her alcoholic father threatened her not to waste her time going to university. In fact, he said if she went, she wouldn't

Rosalie Brown
July 6, 2019

TOTAL HARDINESS

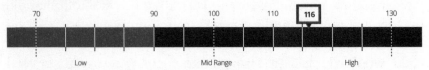

What your score means

- Your result indicates that your total level of hardiness falls in the **High** range.

- You are likely very capable of tackling stressful and unexpected situations that come your way. Your high level of hardiness often protects you from the negative effects of stress and you are able to respond to surprising and stressful situations in a healthy and adaptive manner.

- You likely have the coping skills necessary to help you deal with stressful circumstances. For example, rather than trying to ignore or avoid the stressful situation, you likely try to fix it and work on eliminating the source of your stress.

HARDINESS SUBSCALES
CHALLENGE

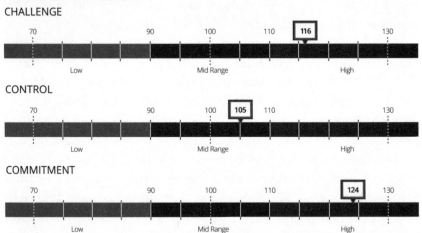

CONTROL

COMMITMENT

On the pages that follow, you will find more information on your Challenge, Control, and Commitment scores. As you move through the report, think about how you might see these hardiness qualities emerge in your day-to-day life. If you choose to implement the recommended developmental strategies highlighted for you, you can ensure that you are setting yourself up for success when faced with stressful and changing situations.

≋MHS © Copyright of MHS 2019. All rights reserved.   3
1.1.2

FIGURE 15.6 Rosalie Brown's Hardiness Profile

(Used with permission from Multi-Health Systems, 2019.)

be welcome back home. Once again, Rosalie's "I'll show you" attitude came out as she went to a highly regarded university and graduated.

When she was 42 years old, she needed a hip replacement. The first surgeon she went to told her, "It's time to change careers. You won't be teaching fitness classes again, so you should look for another career." She gave another "I'll show you" and looked for a new surgeon. Well, it turned out he must have been an excellent doctor and surgeon because if you watch Rosalie on YouTube, you'll see her still doing her nonstop and contagious exercise routines.

Rosalie actually uses "Oh ya?? I'll show you" as a motivator to keep herself going. Her hardiness-commitment score is extremely high, and her life purpose is a big part of this drive. She believes the research that suggests we control 70% of our health and aging with the decisions we make every day. Only 30% of how we age is controlled by genetics.

Her highest scores in her emotional intelligence assessment were in self-actualization and optimism. Rosalie is very high in self-actualizing as she has found what she loves to do in life. Not only does she love what she does, but she helps other people get into and stay in shape. Her optimism is also extremely high. It carries her forward in her ability to overcome obstacles and remain passionate about what she is doing and where she is going. Her positivity is infectious. She has touched the lives of many people and made them better for it—physically and mentally. It's no wonder she gets millions of views on her YouTube channel.

We can learn to adopt Rosalie's "I'll show you" attitude when we're told "no" or "you can't." It takes a certain amount of self-confidence and drive, but once we get started, we can build on our successes and learn from our mistakes.

■ ■ ■

In this chapter we have provided a number of real-life examples of how hardiness plays out in different people's lives. The various components of hardiness—commitment, control, and challenge—can be valuable tools for getting you through life's bumps in the road. Your mindset is a powerful ally. The hardiness concept is a way to help you frame situations, as we have shown, to move you forward in your life and achieve your goals.

Conclusion

Our goal in this book has been to give you a new way of looking at the stress you encounter in your life and perhaps even help those around you. We've presented the role that hardiness can play for you. By being aware of and learning to develop the three Cs of hardiness you have new tools that can help you every day.

We have outlined how increasing your hardiness can make a difference for you in your health, work, athletics, performance, and leadership. We anticipate that this book will stimulate many researchers and others to look at additional avenues where increasing hardiness can make a difference. We'd be thrilled to hear from you about how increasing your hardiness has had an effect on your life.

We hope that this book has given you the knowledge, tools, and inspiring examples to help you lead a hardier life. We have seen the power of the hardiness mindset in many cases, as we have outlined in this book. By adjusting your mindset and seeing obstacles through the lens of hardiness commitment, control and challenge, we believe you can lead a more fulfilling, healthy and longer life.

References

Introduction

The American Institute of Stress (2006). AIS Workplace stress survey. Retrieved from https://www.stress.org/workplace-stress

National Institute for Occupational Safety and Health (1999). *Stress ... at work.* DHHS (NIOSH) Publication No. 99-101. Retrieved from https://www.cdc.gov/niosh/docs/99-101/default.html

Chapter 1

Aiken, M. (2016). *The cyber effect: A pioneering cyberpsychologist explains how human behavior changes online.* New York, NY: Spiegel & Grau.

Averill, J. R. (1973). Personal control over aversive stimuli and its relationship to stress. *Psychological Bulletin, 80,* 286–303.

Bartone, P. T. (1989). Predictors of stress-related illness in city bus drivers. *Journal of Occupational Medicine, 31,* 657–663.

Bartone, P. T. (1999). Hardiness protects against war-related stress in Army Reserve forces. *Consulting Psychology Journal, 51,* 72–82.

Bartone, P. T., Roland, R. R., Picano, J. J., & Williams, T. J. (2008). Personality hardiness predicts success in U.S. Army Special Forces candidates. *International Journal of Selection and Assessment, 16,* 78–81.

Cannon, W. B. (1915). *Bodily changes in pain, hunger, fear and rage: An account of recent researches into the function of emotional excitement.* New York, NY: D. Appleton and Company.

Fischer, A., Ziogas, A., & Anton-Culver, H. (2018). Perception matters: Stressful life events increase breast cancer risk. *Journal of Psychosomatic Research, 110,* 46–53.

Fiske, D. W., & Maddi, S. R. (Eds.). (1961). *Functions of varied experience.* Homewood, IL: Dorsey Press.

Frankl, V. (1960). *The doctor and the soul.* New York, NY: Knopf.

Holmes, T. H., & Rahe, R. H. (1967). The Social Readjustment Rating Scale. *Journal of Psychosomatic Research, 11,* 213–218.

Keller, A., Litzelman, L., Wisk, L. E., Maddox, T., Cheng, E.R., Creswell, P. D., & Witt, W. P. (2012). Does the perception that stress affects health matter? The association with health and mortality. *Health Psychology, 31*(5), 677–684.

Kobasa, S. C. (1979). Stressful life events, personality and health: An inquiry into hardiness. *Journal of Personality and Social Psychology, 42,* 168–177.

Layne, C. M., Warren, J. S., Watson, P. J., & Shalev, A. Y. (2007). Risk, vulnerability, resistance and resilience: Toward an integrative conceptualization of posttraumatic adaptation. In M. J. Friedman, T. M. Keane, & P. A. Resick, *Handbook of PTSD: Science and practice* (pp. 497–520). New York, NY: Guilford.

Maddi, S. R. (1967). The existential neurosis. *Journal of Abnormal Psychology, 72,* 311–325.

Maddi, S. R. (1989). *Personality theories: A comparative analysis.* Chicago, IL: Dorsey.

Maddi, S. R., & Kobasa, S. C. (1984). *The hardy executive.* Homewood, IL: Dow Jones-Irwin.

McEwen, B. S. (2008). Central effects of stress hormones in health and disease: Understanding the protective and damaging effects of stress and stress mediators. *European Journal of Pharmacology, 583*(2-3), 174–185.

Seligman, M. E. (1975). *Helplessness: On depression, development and death.* San Francisco, CA: Freeman.

Selye, H. (1978). *The stress of life.* New York, NY: McGraw-Hill. (Original work published 1956)

Thack, L., & Woodman, R. W. (1994). Organizational change and information technology: Managing on the edge of cyberspace. *Organizational Dynamics, 23*(1), 30–46.

White, R. W. (1959). Motivation reconsidered: The concept of competence. *Psychological Review, 66,* 297–233.

Chapter 2

Abuelaish, I., & Arya, N. (2017). Hatred: A public health issue. *Medicine, Conflict and Survival, 33*(2), 125–130.

Abuelaish, I., Stein, S., Stermac, J., & Mann, S. (2019). Development of the Abuelaish Hatred Scale Questionnaire (AHSQ). Working Paper, MHS Assessments, Toronto, Canada.

Binswanger, L. (1963). *Being in the world: Selected papers.* New York, NY: Basic Books.

Frankl, V. (2007). *Man's search for meaning: An introduction to logotherapy.* Boston, MA: Beacon Press. (Original work published 1959)

Herman, J. (1992). *Trauma and recovery: The aftermath of violence from domestic abuse to political terror.* New York, NY: Basic Books.

Jobs, S. (2005). *You've got to find what you love.* Stanford University commencement address. Palo Alto, California. Retrieved from http://news.stanford.edu/news/2005/june15/jobs-061505.html

Langer, L. (1982). *Versions of survival: The Holocaust and the human spirit.* Albany: State University of New York Press.

McCain, J. S. (2008, January 28). John McCain, Prisoner of War: A First-Person Account. Retrieved from https://www.usnews.com/news/articles/2008/01/28/john-mccain-prisoner-of-war-a-first-person-account

Riza, S. D., & Heller, D. (2015). Follow your heart or your head? A longitudinal study of the facilitating role of calling and ability in the pursuit of a challenging career. *Journal of Applied Psychology, 100*(3), 695–712.

Szasz, T. (2003, July). The secular cure of souls: "Analysis" or dialogue? *Existential Analysis*, 14, 203–212.

Winfrey, O. (1997, February 17). *What Oprah learned from Jim Carrey – Oprah's Lifeclass*. Retrieved from http:// www.oprah.com/oprahs-lifeclass/what-oprah-learned-from-jim-carrey-video.

Zerach, G., Karstoft, K.-I., & Solomon, Z. (2017). Hardiness and sensation seeking as potential predictors of former prisoners of wars' posttraumatic stress symptoms trajectories over a 17-year period. *Journal of Affective Disorders*, 218, 176–181.

Chapter 3

Boukes, M., & Vliegenthart, R. (2017). News consumption and its unpleasant side effect. *Journal of Media Psychology*, 29(3), 137–147. doi:10.1027/1864–1105/a000224

Burgdorfa, J., & Panksepp, J. (2006). The neurobiology of positive emotions. *Neuroscience and Biobehavioral Reviews*, 30, 173–187.

Kendler, K. S., Liu, X. Q., Gardner, C. O., McCullough, M. E., Larson, D., & Prescott, C. A. (2003). Dimensions of religiosity and their relationship to lifetime psychiatric and substance use disorders. *American Journal of Psychiatry*, 160, 496–503.

Soderstrom, M., Dolbier, C., Leiferman, J., & Steinhardt, M. (2000). The relationship of hardiness, coping strategies, and perceived stress to symptoms of illness. *Journal of Behavioral Medicine*, 23(3), 311–328.

Uchino, B. N., Cacioppo, J. T., & Kiecolt-Glaser, J. K. (1996). The relationship between social support and physiological processes: A review with emphasis on underlying mechanisms and implications for health. *Psychological Bulletin*, 119, 488–531.

Chapter 4

Aronson, J., Fried, C. B., & Good, C. (2002). Reducing the effects of stereotype threat on African American college students by shaping theories of intelligence. *Journal of Experimental Social Psychology*, 38, 113–125.

Bronson, F. (2002). *The Billboard book of number 1 hits*. New York, NY: Billboard Books.

Chiu, C., Hong, Y., & Dweck, C. S. (1997). Lay dispositionism and implicit theories of personality. *Journal of Personality and Social Psychology*, 73, 19–30.

Crum, A. S. (2013). Rethinking stress: The role of mindsets in determining stress response. *Journal of Personality and Social Psychology*, 4, 716–733.

Dweck, C. (2008). Can personality be changed? The role of beliefs in personality and change. *Current Directions in Psychological Science*, 17, 391–394. doi:10.1111/j.1467-8721.2008.00612.x

Dweck, C. S. (2016). *Mindset: The new psychology of success*. New York, NY: Ballantine Books.

Girodo, M., & Stein, S. J. (1978). Self-talk and the work of worrying in confronting a stressor. *Cognitive Therapy and Research*, 2(3), 305–307.

Grant, R. M. (2005). *Contemporary strategy analysis.* Hoboken, NJ: Wiley-Blackwell.

Jamieson, J. P., Nock, M. K., & Mendes, W. B. (2012, August). Mind over matter: Reappraising arousal improves cardiovascular and cognitive responses to stress. *Journal of Experimental Psychology General,* 141(3), 417–422. doi:10.1037/a0025719

Meichenbaum, D. (1975). Self-instructional methods. In F. H. Kanfer & A. P. Goldstein (Eds.), *Helping people change* (pp. 357-391). New York, NY: Pergamon Press.

O'Brien, L. (2007). *Madonna: Like an icon.* San Francisco, CA: HarperCollins.

Pietrolungo, S. (September 2, 2009). Madonna closes tour in Tel Aviv: Second highest grossing trek of all time. *Billboard.* Retrieved from https://www.billboard.com/articles/photos/live/267516/madonna-closes-tour-in-tel-aviv-2nd-highest-grossing-trek-of-all-time

Somerfield, M. R., & McCrae, R. R. (2000). Stress and coping research: Methodological challenges, theoretical advances, and clinical applications. *American Psychologist,* 55, 620–625.

Stein, S. (1976). *A comparison of three cognitive strategies in the experimental reduction of stress* (MA thesis). Ottawa, ON: University of Ottawa.

Chapter 5

Allen, P. (2011, April 24). My favorite mistake: Paul Allen. *Newsweek.* Retrieved from https://www.newsweek.com/my-favorite-mistake-paul-allen-66489

Bartone, P. T., Krueger, G. P., Roland, R. R., Sciarretta, A. A., Bartone, J. V., & Johnsen, B. H. (2017). *Individual differences in adaptability for long duration space exploration missions.* Houston, TX: Johnson Space Center, National Aeronautics and Space Administration. Retrieved from https://www.academia.edu/36043109/Individual_Differences_in_Adaptability_for_Long_Duration_Space_Exploration_Missions

BBC. (2016, December 5). Lady Gaga says she has PTSD after being raped at 19. *BBC News.* Retrieved from https://www.bbc.com/news/world-us-canada-38218247

Bollinger, L., & O'Neill, C. (2008). *Women in media careers: Success despite the odds.* Lanham, MD: University Press of America.

Daum, K. (2016). *37 quotes from Thomas Edison that will inspire success.* Retrieved from https://www.inc.com/kevin-daum/37-quotes-from-thomas-edison-that-will-bring-out-your-best.html

Fischer, D. (2000). *Science fiction film directors, 1895–1998.* Jefferson, NC: McFarland & Co.

Forbes. (2014, August 22). Oprah Winfrey. *Forbes.*

Gates, B. (1999). *Business @ the speed of thought: Succeeding in the digital economy.* New York, NY: Warner Books.

Goldman, A. S., & Goldman, D. A. (2017). *Prisoners of time: The misdiagnosis of FDR's 1921 illness.* Bellevue, WA: EHDP Press.

Hayhurst, J., Hunter, J. A., Kafka, S., & Boyes, M. (2015). Enhancing resilience in youth through a 10-day developmental voyage. *Journal of Adventure Education & Outdoor Learning,* 15(1), 40–52. doi:10.1080/14729679.2013.843143

Hirschberg, L. (2011, July 1). From the vaults: The fall and rise of Christina Aguilera. *W Magazine*. Retrieved from https://www.wmagazine.com/story/christina-aguilera-cover-story

King, T. (1991). Introduction to *Carrie*. In S. King, *Carrie (Collector's Edition)*. New York, NY: Plume.

Lee, Y.-R., & Enright, R. D. (2019). A meta-analysis of the association between forgiveness of others and physical health. *Psychology & Health*, 1–18. doi:10.1080/08870446.2018.1554185

McQuillan, M. (1989). *Van Gogh*. London: Thames and Hudson.

Morgan, H. (1986, March 4). Troubled girl's evolution into an Oscar nominee. *The New York Times*, p. C17.

Mowbray, N. (2003, March 2). Oprah's path to power. *The Guardian*.

Munezane, Y. (2015). Enhancing willingness to communicate: Relative effects of visualization and goal setting. *The Modern Language Journal, 99*(1), 175–191.

Tracy, K. A. (2013). *Superstars of the 21st century: Pop favorites of America's teens*. ABC-CLIO. ISBN 978-0-313-37737-2

Verdi, B. (2009, August 24). What I learned from Turnberry: Lessons you can take from my miss at the 2009 British Open. *Golf Digest*.

Ward, G. C., & Burns, K. (2014). *The Roosevelts: An intimate history*. New York, NY: Knopf Doubleday.

Weinraub, B. (1993, December 12). Steven Spielberg faces the Holocaust. *The New York Times*.

Chapter 6

Baldwin, C. L., Finley, A. J., Garrison, K. E., Crowell, A. L., & Schmeichel, B. J. (2018). Higher trait self-control is associated with less intense visceral states. *Self and Identity, 18*(5), 576–588. doi:10.1080/15298868.2018.1495666

Brockes, E.. (2009, April 11). It's the gift that keeps on taking. *The Guardian*. Retrieved from https://www.theguardian.com/lifeandstyle/2009/apr/11/michael-j-fox-parkinsons

Cox, S. P. (2000). *Leader character: A model of personality and moral development* (Doctoral dissertation). Oklahoma: University of Tulsa.

DeWall, C. N., Finkel, E. J., & Denson, T. F. (2011). Self-control inhibits aggression. *Social and Personality Psychology Compass, 5*, 458–472.

Duckworth, A. (2016). *Grit: The power of passion and perseverance*. New York, NY: Simon & Schuster.

Larson, E. B., & Yao, X. (2005). Clinical empathy as emotional labor in the patient-physician relationship. *JAMA, 293*(9), 1100–1106.

Marchese, D. (2019, March 1). Michael J. Fox on Parkinson's, taking the wrong roles and staying positive. *The New York Times Magazine*. Retrieved from https://www.nytimes.com/interactive/2019/03/01/magazine/michael-j-fox-parkinsons-acting.html

Maruish, M. E. (2004). Symptom Assessment-45 Questionnaire (SA-45). In M. E. Maruish (Ed.), *The use of psychological testing for treatment planning and outcomes assessment: Instruments for adults* (pp. 43–78). Mahwah, NJ: Erlbaum.

Mischel, W., Shoda, Y., & Rodriguez, M. L. (1989). Delay of gratification in children. *Science,* 244(4907), 933–938.

Packer, G., Best, D., Day, E., & Wood, K. (2009). Criminal thinking and self-control among drug users in court mandated treatment. *Criminology & Criminal Justice: An International Journal,* 9, 93–110.

Schmeichel, B. J., Vohs, K. D., & Baumeister, R. F. (2003). Intellectual performance and ego depletion: Role of the self in logical reasoning and other information processing. *Journal of Personality and Social Psychology,* 85(1), 33–46.

Shoda, Y., Mischel, W., & Peake, P. K. (1990). Predicting adolescent cognitive and self-regulatory competencies from preschool delay of gratification: Identifying diagnostic conditions. *Developmental Psychology,* 26(6), 978–986.

Tangney, J. P., Baumeister, R. F., & Boone, A. L. (2004). High self-control predicts good adjustment, less pathology, better grades, and interpersonal success. *Journal of Personality,* 72, 271–324.

Yam, K. C., Lian, H., Ferris, D. L., & Brown, D. (2017). Leadership takes self-control. Here's what we know about it. *Harvard Business Review.*

Chapter 7

Csíkszentmihályi, M. (1990). *Flow: The psychology of optimal experience.* New York, NY: Harper & Row.

Pozen, R. C., & Downey, K. (2019, March 28). What makes some people more productive than others. *Harvard Business Review.* Retrieved from https://hbr.org/2019/03/what-makes-some-people-more-productive-than-others

Zainal, N. H., & Newman, M. G. (2019). Relation between cognitive and behavioral strategies and future change in common mental health problems across 18 years. *Journal of Abnormal Psychology,* 128(4), 295–304.

Chapter 8

Bartone, P., Roland, R., Picano, J., & Williams, T. (2008). Personality hardiness predicts success in U.S. Army Special Forces candidates. *International Journal of Selection and Assessment,* 16, 78–81.

Bartone, P., Snook, S. A., & Tremble, T. R. (2002). Cognitive and personality predictors of leader performance in West Point cadets. *Military Psychology,* 14, 321–338.

Bartone, P., Valdes, J., & Sandvik, A. (2016). Psychological hardiness predicts cardiovascular health. *Psychology, Health and Medicine,* 21, 743–749. doi:10.1080/13548506.2015.1120323

Castelli, W., Garrison, R., Wilson, P., Abbott, R., Kalousdian, S., & Kannel, B. (1986). Incidence of coronary heart disease and lipoprotein cholesterol levels: The Framingham Study. *JAMA,* 256, 2835–2838.

Contrada, R. (1989). Type A behavior, personality hardiness, and cardiovascular responses to stress. *Journal of Personality and Social Psychology,* 57, 895–903.

Dolbier, C., Cocke, R., Leiferman, J., Steinhardt, M., Schapiro, S., Nehete, P., ... Sastry, J. (2001). Differences in immune responses of high vs. low hardy healthy individuals. *Journal of Behavioral Medicine*, 24, 219–229.

Fisher, J., Young, C., & Fadel, P. (2010). Central sympathetic overactivity: Maladies and mechanisms. *Autonomic Neuroscience*, 148, 5–15.

Friedman, M., & Rosenman, R. (1974). *Type A behavior and your heart*. New York, NY: Knopf.

Gerritson, R., & Band, G. (2018). Breath of life: The respiratory vagal stimulation model of contemplative activity. *Frontiers in Human Neuroscience*, 12. Retrieved from https://doi.org/10.3389/fnhum.2018.00397

Hanton, S., Evans, L., & Neil, R. (2013). Hardiness and the competitive anxiety response. *Anxiety, Stress and Coping*, 16, 167–184.

Haufler, A. J., Lewis, G. F., Davila, M. I., Westhelle, F., Gavrilis, J., Bryce, C. I., ... McDaniel, W. (2018). Biobehavioral insights into adaptive behavior in complex and dynamic operational settings: Lessons learned from the Soldier Performance and Effective, Adaptable Response Task. *Frontiers in Medicine*, 4, 217. doi: 10.3389/fmed.2017.00217

Houston, B., & Snyder, C. (1988). *Type A behavior pattern: Research, theory and practice*. New York, NY: Wiley.

Howard, J., Cunningham, D., & Rechnitzer, P. (1986). Personality (hardiness) as a moderator of job stress and coronary risk in Type A individuals: A longitudinal study. *Journal of Behavioral Medicine*, 9, 229–244.

Kobasa, S. (1979). Stressful life events, personality and health: An inquiry into hardiness. *Journal of Social and Personality Psychology*, 37, 1–11.

Kobasa, S., Maddi, S., & Kahn, S. (1982). Hardiness and health: A prospective study. *Journal of Personality and Social Psychology*, 42, 168–177.

Lazarus, R., & Folkman, S. (1984). *Stress, appraisal, and coping*. New York, NY: Springer.

Maddi, S., & Hess, M. J. (1992). Personality hardiness and success in basketball. *International Journal of Sport Psychology*, 23, 360–368.

Manenschijn, L., Schaap, L., van Schoor, N., van der Pas, S., Peeters, G., Lips, P., ... van Rossum, E. (2013). High long-term cortisol levels, measured in scalp hair, are associated with a history of cardiovascular disease. *Journal of Clinical Endocrinology and Metabolism*, 98, 2078–2083. doi:10.1210/jc.2012–3663

Mason, H., Vandoni, M., Debarbieri, G., Cordrons, E., Ugargol, V., & Bernardi, L. (2013). Cardiovascular and respiratory effect of yogic slow breathing in the yoga beginner: What is the best approach? *Evidence Based Complementary and Alternative Medicine*, [753504].Retrieved from http://dx.doi.org/10.1155/2013/743504

Pandey, D., & Shrivastava, P. (2017). Mediation effect of social support on the association between hardiness and immune response. *Asian Journal of Psychiatry*, 26, 52–55.

Perez-Tilve, D., Hofmann, S., Basford, J., Nogueiras, R., Pfuger, P., Patterson, J., ... Arnold, M. (2010). Melanocortin signaling in the CNS directly regulates circulating cholesterol. *Nature Neuroscience*, 13, 877–882.

Sandvik, A., Bartone, P., Hystad, S., Phillips, T., Thayer, J., & Johnsen, B. (2013). Psychological hardiness predicts neuroimmunological responses to stress. *Psychology, Health and Medicine,* 18, 705–713. Retrieved from http://dx.doi.org/10.1080/13548506.2013.772304

Sandvik, A., Gjevestad, E., Aabrekk, E., Øhman, P., Kjendlie, P., Hystad, S., ... Johnsen, B. (2019). Physical fitness and psychological hardiness as predictors of parasympathetic control in response to stress: A Norwegian police simulator training study. *Journal of Police and Criminal Psychology,* 1–14. Retrieved from https://doi.org/10.1007/s11896–019–09323–8

Segerstrom, S., & Miller, G. (2004). Psychological stress and the human immune system: A meta-analytic study of 30 years of inquiry. *Psychological Bulletin,* 130, 601–630. doi: 10.1037/0033–2909.130.4.601

Thayer, J., & Lane, R. (2007). The role of vagal function in the risk for cardiovascular disease and mortality. *Biological Psychology,* 74, 224–242.

World Health Organization. (2017). *Cardiovascular diseases (CVDs) fact sheet.* New York, NY: World Health Organization. Retrieved May 30, 2019, from https://www.who.int/en/news-room/fact-sheets/detail/cardiovascular-diseases-(cvds)

Zorrilla, E., DeRubeis, R., & Redei, E. (1995). High self-esteem, hardiness and affective stability are associated with higher basal pituitary-adrenal hormone levels. *Psychoneuroendocrinology,* 20, 591–601.

Chapter 9

Allan, R. B. (1997). Alcoholism, drug abuse and lawyers: Are we ready to address the denial? *Creighton Law Review,* 31, 265–277.

Bartone, P. (1989). Predictors of stress-related illness in city bus drivers. *Journal of Occupational Medicine,* 31(8), 657–663. doi:10.1097/00043764–198908000–00008

Beck, C. J., Sales, B. D., & Benjamin, G. A. (1995–96). Lawyer distress: Alcohol-related problems and other psychological concerns among a sample of practicing lawyers. *Journal of Law & Health,* 10 (1), 1–60. Retrieved from https://pdfs.semanticscholar.org/a53c/caac05214a0eb7a93da70f25fedbbf4a0de0.pdf

Boyer, R., & Brunet, A. (1996, Jan 1). Prevalence of post-traumatic stress disorder in bus drivers. *Santé Mentale au Québec,* 21(1), 189–208.

Chtibi, H., Ahami, A., Azzaoui, F., Khadmaoui, A., Mammad, K., & Elmassioui, F. (2018). Study of psychological resilience among health care professionals in Ibn Sina Hospital/Rabat/Morocco. *Open Journal of Medical Psychology,* 7, 47–57.

Cooper, C. L. & Sutherland, V. J. (1987). Job stress, mental health, and accidents among offshore workers in the oil and gas extraction industries. *Journal of Occupational Medicine,* 29, 119–126.

DelVecchio, R. (2019, January 1). Think your job is stressful? Try plowing 20 tons of glass and metal through snarled traffic, bike messengers, and jaywalkers. *HealthDay.* Retrieved from https://consumer.healthday.com/encyclopedia/heart-health-22/misc-stroke-related-heart-news-360/bus-drivers-646402.html

Evans, G., & Johansson, G. (1998). Urban bus driving: An international arena for the study of occupational health psychology. *Journal of Occupational Health Psychology, 3*(2), 99–108.

Kim, M., & Beehr, T. A. (2019). Thriving on demand: Challenging work results in employee flourishing through appraisals and resources. *International Journal of Stress Management*, 1–15. Retrieved from http://dx.doi.org/10.1037/str0000135

Kobasa, S. (1982). Commitment and coping in stress resistance among lawyers. *Journal of Personality and Social Psychology, 42*, 707–717.

Kobasa, S., & Puccetti, M. (1983). Personality and social resources in stress resistance. *Journal of Personality and Social Psychology, 45*, 839–850.

Lyon, A. (2015). *Lawyer's Guide to Wellbeing and Managing Stress*. London: Ark Group.

Oliver, C. M. (2010). *Hardiness, well-being, and health: A meta-analytic summary of three decades of research* (Doctoral dissertation). Retrieved from *Dissertation Abstracts International*, Section B: The Sciences and Engineering.

Pierson, P. B., Hamilton, A., Pepper, M., & Root, M. (2018). Stress, hardiness and lawyers. *Journal of the Legal Profession, 42*, 1–92. University of Alabama Legal Studies Research Paper No. 3120491. Retrieved from https://papers.ssrn.com/sol3/papers.cfm?abstract_id=3120491

Shellenbarger, S. (2007, Dec 13). Even lawyers get the blues: Opening up about depression. *Wall Street Journal*.

Chapter 10

Csíkszentmihályi, M. (1990). *Flow: The psychology of optimal experience* (1st ed.). New York, NY: Harper & Row.

Golby, J., & Sheard, M. (2004). Mental toughness and hardiness at different levels of rugby league. *Personality and Individual Differences, 37*(5), 933–942.

Hacker, C. M. (2013). *The competitive cauldron: The sport/performance perspective*. Paper presented at the American Psychological Association Convention, Honolulu, Hawaii.

Hanton, S., Neil, R., & Evans, L. (2013). Hardiness and anxiety interpretation: An investigation into coping usage and effectiveness. *European Journal of Sport Science, 13*(1), 96–104. doi:10.1080/17461391.2011.635810

Kegelaers, J., & Wylleman, P. (2019). Exploring the coach's role in fostering resilience in elite athletes. *Sport, Exercise, and Performance Psychology, 8*(3), 239–254. https://doi-org.library.smu.ca/10.1037/spy0000151.supp

Mackenzie, N. G. (2018, October 2). Five secrets of mentally tough athletes. espnW.com.

Masters, K. S., & Ogles, B. M. (1998). Associative and dissociative cognitive strategies in exercise and running: 20 years later, what do we know? *The Sport Psychologist, 12*, 253–270.

Sheard, M., & Golby, J. (2006). Effect of a psychological skills training program on swimming performance and positive psychological development. *International*

Journal of Sport and Exercise Psychology, 4(2), 49–169. doi:10.1080/ 1612197X.2006.9671790

Sheard, M., & Golby, J. (2010). Personality hardiness differentiates elite-level sport performers. *International Journal of Sport and Exercise Psychology,* 8(2), 160–169.

Vealey, R. S., & Perritt, N. (2015). Hardiness and optimism as predictors of the frequency of flow in college athletes. *Journal of Sport Behavior,* 38(3), 321–338.

Chapter 11

Alvarado, G. E., Scott, R., Scott, S. T., & Bledsoe, S. (2011). *Coping and firefighters: An analysis of the use of gallows humor and other coping mechanisms as they relate to facets of hardiness and resiliency.* Paper presented at the American Psychological Association Convention, Washington, DC..

Andrew, M., McCanlies, E., Burchfiel, C., Charles, L., Hartley, T., Fekedulegn, D., & Violanti, J. (2008). Hardiness and psychological distress in a cohort of police officers. *International Journal of Emergency Mental Health,* 10(2), 137–147.

Bacharach, S. B., & Bamberger, P. A. (2007, August). 9/11 and New York City firefighters' post hoc unit support and control climates: A context theory of the consequences of involvement in traumatic work-related events. *Academy of Management Journal,* 50(4), 849–868.

Bartone, P., Ellis, K., Lampton, N., Colford, M., Dickinson, I., & Bowles, S. (2019). *Hardiness predicts post traumatic growth in severely wounded servicemen and their spouses.* Paper presented at the National Academy of Practice Annual Convention, Washington, DC. Retrieved from http://www.hardiness-resilience.com/ docs/NAP2019%20poster.pdf

Berg, A., Hem, E., Lau, B., & Ekeberg, O. (2006). An exploration of job stress and health in the Norwegian police service: A cross sectional study. *Journal of Occupational Medicine and Toxicology,* 1(1), 26.

Del Ben, K. S., Scotti, J. R., Chen, Y.-C., & Fortson, B. L. (2006, Jan.-Mar.). Prevalence of posttraumatic stress disorder symptoms in firefighters. *Work & Stress,* 20(1), 37–48.

Fyhn, T., Fjell, K. K., & Johnsen, B. H. (2016). Resilience factors among police investigators: Hardiness-commitment a unique contributor. *Journal of Police Criminal Psychology,* 31, 261–269.

Haslam, C., & Mallon, K. (2003, Jul.-Sep.). A preliminary investigation of posttraumatic stress symptoms among firefighters. *Work & Stress,* 17(3), 277–285.

Kales, S. N., Soteriades, E. S., Christophi, C. A., & Christiani, D. C. (2007, Mar). Emergency duties and deaths from heart disease among firefighters in the United States. *New England Journal of Medicine,* 356(12), 1207–1215.

North, C. S., Tivis, L., McMillen, J. C., Pfefferbaum, B., Cox, J., Spitznagel, E. L., ... Smith, E. M. (2002, July). Coping, functioning, and adjustment of rescue workers after the Oklahoma City bombing. *Journal of Traumatic Stress,* 15(3), 171–175.

Priest, R., & Bartone, P. (2001). Humor, hardiness and health. *International Society for Humor Studies.* College Park, Maryland. Retrieved July 17, 2019, from http:// www.hardiness-resilience.com/docs/hardhumorhealth.pdf

Richardsen, A., & Martinussen, M. (2005). Factorial validity and consistency of the MBI-GS across occupational groups in Norway. *International Journal of Stress Management, 12*(3), 289–297.

Schaubroeck, J., Ganster, D. C., & Fox, M. L. (1992, Jun). Dispositional affect and work-related stress. *Journal of Applied Psychology, 77*(3), 322–335.

Scheelar, J. F. (2002). A return to the worker role after injury: Firefighters seriously injured on the job and the decision to return to high-risk work. *Work: Journal of Prevention, Assessment & Rehabilitation, 19*(2), 181–184.

Soccorso, C. N., Picano, J. J., Moncata, S. J., & Miller, C. D. (2019). Psychological hardiness predicts successful selection in a law enforcement special operations assessment and selection course. *International Journal of Selection and Assessment, 27*(3), 291-295.

Wagner, D., Heinrichs, M., & Ehlert, U. (1998, December). Prevalence of symptoms of posttraumatic stress disorder in German professional firefighters. *The American Journal of Psychiatry, 155*(12), 1727–1732.

Chapter 12

Bartone, P. T. (1999). Hardiness protects against war-related stress in Army reserve forces. *Consulting Psychology Journal, 51*, 72–82.

Bartone, P. T. (2017). Leader influences on resilience and adaptability in organizations. In U. Kumar (Ed.), *The Routledge international handbook of psychosocial resilience* (pp. 355–368). New York, NY: Routledge.

Binswanger, L. (1963). *Being in the world: Selected papers of Ludwig Binswanger.* New York, NY: Basic Books.

Fry, E., & Heimer, M. (2019, May). This is the emotional quality that the world's greatest leaders all share. *Fortune*, p. 54.

Heifetz, R. A. (1994). *Leadership without easy answers.* Cambridge, MA: Harvard University Press.

Heifetz, R. A., & Laurie, D. L. (2001, December). The work of leadership. *The Best of Harvard Business Review* 1–14.

Kobasa, S. C. (1979). Stressful life events, personality and health: An inquiry into hardiness. *Journal of Personality and Social Psychology, 42*, 168–177.

Chapter 13

Bartone, P. (1999). Personality hardiness as a predictor of officer cadet leadership performance. *International Military Testing Association—NATO Officer Selection Workshop* (pp. 7.1–7.5). Monterey, CA: International Military Testing Association. Retrieved from https://ia801304.us.archive.org/29/items/DTIC_ADP010353/DTIC_ADP010353.pdf

Bartone, P., Kelly, D., & Matthews, M. (2013). Psychological hardiness predicts adaptability in military leaders: A prospective study. *International Journal of Selection and Assessment, 21*(2), 200–210.

Bartone, P., & Priest, R. (2001). Sex differences in hardiness and health among West Point cadets. Paper presented at the American Psychological Society Convention, Toronto, Canada. Retrieved from http://www.hardiness-resilience.com/docs/aps01totc.pdf

Bartone, P., & Snook, S. (2000). Gender differences in predictors of leader performance over time. Paper presented at the American Psychological Society Convention, Miami Beach, Florida. Retrieved from http://www.hardiness-resilience.com/docs/Bartone%20Snook%20aps2000b.pdf

Bass, B. M. (1985). *Leadership and performance beyond expectations*. New York, NY: Free Press.

Kelly, D., & Bartone, P. (2005). *Personality hardiness, attrition and leader performance at West Point*. Paper presented at the American Psychological Association, Washington, DC. Retrieved from http://www.hardiness-resilience.com/docs/Kelly&Bartone-APA05b.pdf

Kelly, D., & Bartone, P. (2006). *Who drops out? Attrition at West Point is related to hardiness*. International Applied Military Psychology Seminar, Berlin, Germany. Retrieved from http://www.hardiness-resilience.com/docs/Kelly&Bartone-IAMPS%202006.pdf

Kelly, D., Matthews, M., & Bartone, P. (2005). *Hardiness predicts adaptation to a challenging military training environment*. International Applied Military Psychology Seminar, Washington, DC.

Lifton, D., Seay, S., McCarly, N., Olive-Taylor, R., Seeger, R., & Bigbee, D. (2006). Correlating hardiness with graduation persistence. *Academic Exchange Quarterly, Fall*, 277–282.

Miller, N., Shattuck, L., & Matsangas, P. (2010). Longitudinal study of sleep patterns of United States Military Academy cadets. *Sleep, 33*, 1623–1631.

National Center for Education Statistics. (2019, February). *Indicator 23: Postsecondary Graduation Rates*. Retrieved June 25, 2019, from Status and Trends in the Education of Racial and Ethnic Groups: https://nces.ed.gov/programs/raceindicators/indicator_RED.asp

Psotka, J., Bartone, P., Legree, P., Sherwood, T., Milan, L., & Robinson, D.R. (2005). *Traditional versus consensus based assessment (CBA) of leadership to predict U.S. Military Academy—West Point graduates' career intent*. International Applied Military Psychology Symposium, Washington, DC. Retrieved from http://www.hardiness-resilience.com/docs/Psotka%20etal%20IAMPS%202005.pdf

US Corps of Cadets. (1995). *Leadership evaluation and development ratings (USCC Regulation 623–1)*. West Point, NY: US Military Academy.

Chapter 14

Aflakseir, A., Nowroozi, S., Mollazadeh, J., & Goodarzi, M. (2016). The role of psychological hardiness and marital satisfaction in predicting posttraumatic growth in a sample of women with breast cancer in Isfahan. *Iranian Journal of Cancer Prevention, 9*, e4080. doi: 10.17795/ijcp-4080

Alvarez, G., & Ayas, N. (2004). The impact of daily sleep duration on health: A review of the literature. *Progress in Cardiovascular Nursing, 19,* 56–59.

Bartone, P., Valdes, J., & Sandvik, A. (2016). Psychological hardiness predicts cardiovascular health. *Psychology, Health and Medicine, 21,* 743–749. doi:10.1080/13548506.2015.1120323

Bartrop, R., Lazarus, L., Luckherst, E., & Kiloh, L. (1977). Depressed lymphocyte function after bereavement. *Lancet, 1,* 834–836.

Bryant, P., Trinder, J., & Curtis, N. (2004). Sick and tired: Does sleep have a vital role in the immune system? *Nature Reviews: Immunology, 4,* 457–467.

Calcagni, E., & Elenkov, I. (2006). Stress system activity, innate and T helper cytokines, and susceptibility to immune-related diseases. *Annals of the New York Academy of Science, 1069,* 62–76.

Castelli, W., Garrison, R., Wilson, P., Abbott, R., Kalousdian, S., & Kannel, B. (1986). Incidence of coronary heart disease and lipoprotein cholesterol levels: The Framingham Study. *JAMA, 256,* 2835–2838.

Chiriac, V., Baban, A., & Dumitrascu, D. (2018). Psychological stress and breast cancer incidence: A systematic review. *CLUJUL Medical, 91,* 18–26.

Cohen, S., Doyle, W., Alper, C., Janicki-Deverts, D., & Turner, R. (2009). Sleep habits and susceptibility to the common cold. *Archives of Internal Medicine, 169,* 62–67.

Cohen, S., Tyrell, A., & Smith, A. (1991). Psychological stress and susceptibility to the common cold. *New England Journal of Medicine, 325,* 606–612.

Contrada, R. (1989). Type A behavior, personality hardiness, and cardiovascular responses to stress. *Journal of Personality and Social Psychology, 57,* 895–903.

Dolbier, C., Cocke, R., Leiferman, J., Steinhardt, M., Schapiro, S., Nehete, P., … Sastry, J. (2001). Differences in immune responses of high vs. low hardy healthy individuals. *Journal of Behavioral Medicine, 24,* 219–229.

Ghafourian, M., Shiravi, Z., Hamid, N., Hemmati, A., & Kooti, W. (2013). The relationship of hardiness and immune system cells. *Journal of Isfahan Medical School, 31,* 260.

Hamama-Raz, Y. (2012). Does psychological adjustment of melanoma survivors differ between genders? *Psycho-Oncology, 21,* 255–263.

Hamid, N. (2007). The relationship between hardiness, social support and stress with coronary heart disease. *International Journal of Cardiology, 122*(Supplement 1), S111. Retrieved from https://www.internationaljournalofcardiology.com/article/S0167–5273(08)70713–7/abstract

Hansen, M., Janssen, I., Schiff, A., Zee, P., & Dubocovich, M. (2005). The impact of school daily schedule on adolescent sleep. *Pediatrics, 115,* 1555–1561.

Hartigan, I. (2015). *Physical function, psychosocial adaptation, and hardiness post stroke.* (Doctoral dissertation). Cork, Ireland: University College Cork. Retrieved from https://cora.ucc.ie/handle/10468/1950

Hirshkowitz, M., Whiton, K., Albert, S., Alessi, C., Bruni, O., DonCarlos, L., … Catesby Ware, J. (2015). National Sleep Foundation's updated sleep duration recommendations. *Sleep Health, 1,* 233–243. Retrieved from http://dx.doi.org/10.1016/j.sleh.2015.10.004.

Howard, J., Cunningham, D., & Rechnitzer, P. (1986). Personality (hardiness) as a moderator of job stress and coronary risk in Type A individuals: A longitudinal study. *Journal of Behavioral Medicine, 9*, 229–244.

Juda, M., Vetter, C., & Roenneberg, T. (2013). Chronotype modulates sleep duration, sleep quality, and social jet lag in shift workers. *Journal of Biological Rhythms, 28*, 141–151.

Kelly, D., Matthews, M., & Kelly, C. (2019). Lark or owl, affect, hardiness and performance of West Point cadets. Paper presented at the Association for Psychological Science, Washington, DC. Retrieved from http://www.hardiness-resilience.com/docs/Kelly-Matthews-Kelly%20aps2019.pdf

Kiecolt-Glaser, J., & Glaser, R. (1991). Stress and immune function in humans. In R. Ader, D. Felton, & N. Cohen, *Psychoneuroimmunology* (2nd ed.). San Diego, CA: Academic Press.

Kobasa, S., & Puccetti, M. (1983). Personality and social resources in stress resistance. *Journal of Personality and Social Psychology, 45*, 839–850.

Kobasa, S., Maddi, S., Puccetti, M., & Zola, M. (1985). Effectiveness of hardiness, exercise and social support as resources against illness. *Journal of Psychosomatic Research, 29*, 525–533.

Lambert, V., Lambert, C., Klipple, G., & Mewshaw, E. (1989). Social support, hardiness and psychological well-being in women with arthritis. *IMAGE: Journal of Nursing Scholarship, 21*, 128–131.

Monri, T., Tajima, M. M., & Matsueda, S. (2014). Relationship between hardiness and exercise habits in Japanese undergraduates. *Kawasaki Journal of Medical Welfare, 19*, 38–44. Retrieved from https://core.ac.uk/download/pdf/51478800.pdf

Moore, P., Zgibor, J., & Dasanayake, A. (2003). Diabetes: A growing epidemic of all ages. *Journal of the American Dental Association, 134*, 1–15.

Moreno-Smith, M., Lutgendorf, S., & Sood, A. (2010). Impact of stress on cancer metastasis. *Future Oncology, 6*, 1863–1881.

Nagy, S., & Nix, C. (1989). Relations between preventive health behavior and hardiness. *Psychological Reports, 65*, 339–345.

National Sleep Foundation. (2013). *2013 international bedroom poll*. Retrieved from https://sleepfoundation.org/sites/default/files/RPT495a.pdf

Natvik, S., Bjorvatn, B., Moen, B. E., Mageroy, N., Sivertsen, B., & Pallesen, S. (2011). Personality factors related to shift work tolerance in two- and three shift workers. *Applied Ergonomics, 42*, 719–724.

Nicholas, P. (1993). Hardiness, self-care practices and perceived health status in older adults. *Journal of Advanced Nursing, 18*, 1085–1094.

Okun, M., Zautra, A., & Robinson, S. (1988). Hardiness and health among women with rheumatoid arthritis. *Personality and Individual Differences, 9*, 101–107.

Orzech, K., Acebo, C., Seifer, R., Barker, D., & Carskadon, M. (2014). Sleep patterns are associated with common illness in adolescents. *Journal of Sleep Research, 23*, 133–142.

Pollack, S. (1989a). Adaptive responses to diabetes mellitus. *Western Journal of Nursing Research, 11*, 265–280.

Pollack, S. (1989b). The hardiness characteristic: A motivating factor in adaptation. *Advances in Nursing Science,* 11, 53–62.

Rasmussen, A. J. (1969). Emotions and immunity. *Annals of the New York Academy of Science,* 164, 458–461.

Ross, M. (1991). Hardiness and compliance in elderly patients with diabetes. *The Diabetes Educator,* 17, 372–375.

Saksvik-Lehouillier, I., Bjorvatn, B., Magerøy, N., & Pallesen, S. (2016). Hardiness, psychosocial factors and shift work tolerance among nurses: A 2-year follow-up study. *Journal of Advanced Nursing,* 72, 1800–1812.

Sandvik, A., Bartone, P., Hystad, S., Phillips, T., Thayer, J., & Johnsen, B. (2013). Psychological hardiness predicts neuroimmunological responses to stress. *Psychology, Health and Medicine,* 18, 705–713. Retrieved from http://dx.doi.org/10.1080/13548506.2013.772304

Sapolsky, R. (2004). *Why zebras don't get ulcers.* New York, NY: St. Martin's Griffin.

Seiler, A., & Jenewein, J. (2019). Resilience in cancer patients. *Frontiers in Psychiatry,* 10, 208. Retrieved from https://doi.org/10.3389/fpsyt.2019.00208

Taheri, A., Ahadi, H., Kashani, F., & Kermani, R. (2014). Mental hardiness and social support in life satisfaction of breast cancer patients. *Procedia: Social and Behavioral Sciences,* 159, 406–409.

van de Ven, H., van der Klink, J., Vetter, C., Roenneberg, T., Gordijn, M., Koolhaas, W., … Bültmann, U. (2016). Sleep and need for recovery in shift workers: Do chronotype and age matter? *Ergonomics,* 59, 310–324.

Walker, J., Littlejohn, G., McMurray, N., & Cutolo, M. (1999). Stress system response and rheumatoid arthritis: A multilevel approach. *Rheumatology,* 38, 1050–1057.

Wiebe, D., & McCallum, D. (1986). Health practices and hardiness as mediators in the stress-illness relationship. *Health Psychology,* 5, 425–438.

Chapter 15

Abuelaish, I. (2017). *I shall not hate: A Gaza doctor's journey.* Toronto: Vintage Canada.

Stein, S. J. (2017). *The EQ leader: Instilling passion, creating shared goals, and building meaningful organizations through emotional intelligence.* Hoboken, NJ: Wiley.

Acknowledgments

We would like to thank all those who supported us in putting together this book. We'd like to thank the team at Wiley, especially our editors Vicki Adang and Catherine Mallon, Shannon Vargo, Sally Baker, and Peter Knox; the team at MHS including Sydney Mann who was so helpful in pulling together data, retrieving references, along with Donna Penticost, Kelly McDonald, Lindsay Ayearst, Jon Stermac, and the marketing and R&D team; and all those people who agreed to take the Hardiness Resilience Gauge (HRG) and allow their stories to be part of our book. Finally, we'd like to thank our wives, Rodeen and Jocelyn, who endured the process of our writing this book.

About the Authors

STEVEN J. STEIN, PhD, is a clinical psychologist and the founder and executive chair of Multi-Health Systems (MHS), a leading assessment and behavior analytics company. He is a former chair of the Psychology Foundation of Canada, former president of the Ontario Psychological Association, former assistant professor in the Department of Psychiatry at the University of Toronto, and former adjunct course director in the Psychology Department at York University. He teaches at the Directors College of Canada, a university-accredited corporate director education program. He is a fellow of the Canadian Psychological Association. His work has been featured in numerous newspapers, TV shows, radio programs, podcasts, webinars, and magazines. He shares information on emotional intelligence and hardiness with audiences around the world.

COL (RET) PAUL T. BARTONE is currently a Visiting Research Fellow at the Institute for National Security Policy, National Defense University. Over his 25-year career in the US Army, Bartone served as commander of the US Army Medical Research Unit-Europe, and later taught leadership and psychology at the Industrial College of the Armed Forces and at the US Military Academy, West Point, where he also was director of the Leader Development Research Center. As the Army's senior research psychologist, he served as research psychology consultant to the surgeon general, and as assistant corps chief for Medical Allied Sciences. A Fulbright scholar, Bartone is past-president of the American Psychological Association's Society for Military Psychology, a charter member of the Association for Psychological Science, and a life member and fellow of the American Psychological Association. He holds an MA and PhD in psychology and human development from the University of Chicago.

Index